THE LAW OF FAILURE

If a broker-dealer liquidates in federal bankruptcy court, why does an insurance company liquidate in state court, and a bank outside of court altogether? Why do some businesses reorganize under state law "assignments" rather than under the better-known chapter 11 of the Bankruptcy Code? Why do some laws use the language of bankruptcy but without advancing the policy goals of the Bankruptcy Code? In this illuminating work, Stephen J. Lubben tackles these questions and many others related to the collective law of business insolvency in the United States. In the first book of its kind, Lubben notes the broad similarities between the many insolvency systems in the United States, while describing the fundamental differences lurking therein. By considering the whole sweep of these laws – running the gamut from chapter 11 to obscure receivership provisions of the National Bank Act – readers will acquire a fundamental understanding of the "law of failure."

Stephen J. Lubben holds the Harvey Washington Wiley Chair in Corporate Governance and Business Ethics at Seton Hall Law School. From 2010 to 2017 he was the "In Debt" columnist for the *New York Times*'s DealBook page. He has been widely quoted by courts and the media on chapter 11 cases, and has been retained as an expert in insolvency cases around the world. He previously practised law with the New York and Los Angeles offices of Skadden, Arps, Slate, Meagher & Flom as a member of the corporate restructuring department.

The Law of Failure

A TOUR THROUGH THE WILDS OF AMERICAN BUSINESS INSOLVENCY LAW

Stephen J. Lubben

Seton Hall University School of Law

CAMBRIDGE
UNIVERSITY PRESS

CAMBRIDGE
UNIVERSITY PRESS

University Printing House, Cambridge CB2 8BS, United Kingdom
One Liberty Plaza, 20th Floor, New York, NY 10006, USA
477 Williamstown Road, Port Melbourne, VIC 3207, Australia
314–321, 3rd Floor, Plot 3, Splendor Forum, Jasola District Centre, New Delhi – 110025, India
79 Anson Road, #06-04/06, Singapore 079906

Cambridge University Press is part of the University of Cambridge.
It furthers the University's mission by disseminating knowledge in the pursuit of education,
learning, and research at the highest international levels of excellence.

www.cambridge.org
Information on this title: www.cambridge.org/9781107190290
DOI: 10.1017/9781108100069

First published 2018

Printed in the United States of America by Sheridan Books, Inc.

A catalogue record for this publication is available from the British Library.

Library of Congress Cataloging-in-Publication Data

Names: Lubben, Stephen J., 1971- author.
Title: The law of failure : a tour through the wilds of American business
   insolvency law / Stephen J. Lubben, Harvey Washington Wiley Chair in
   Corporate Governance & Business Ethics, Seton Hall University School
   of Law.
Description: Cambridge, United Kingdom; New York, NY, USA: Cambridge
   University Press, 2018. | Includes bibliographical references and index.
Identifiers: LCCN 2018012848| ISBN 9781107190290 (hardback) | ISBN
   9781316640418 (paperback)
Subjects: LCSH: Business failures—Law and legislation—United States. |
   BISAC: LAW / Banking.
Classification: LCC KF1539 .L93 2018 | DDC 346.7307/8—dc23 LC record
available at https://lccn.loc.gov/2018012848

ISBN 978-1-107-19029-0 Hardback
ISBN 978-1-316-64041-8 Paperback

To the memory of
Monty (1921–2016)
of Calvin Street, the *SS Craftsman*,
and Benecia Avenue

CONTENTS

INTRODUCTION

This book is something of a travel story. It recounts my journey through the whole of American business insolvency law. From Nevada's special provisions for insolvent campgrounds to the grand, and perhaps now endangered, provisions of the Dodd-Frank Act, signed into federal law by President Barack Obama on July 21, 2010, that created an Orderly Liquidation Authority (OLA) to address future Lehman Brothers.[1] It has been an eventful trip.

In the United States, most people equate insolvency with bankruptcy and the Bankruptcy Code. Business insolvency thus brings to mind comparatively familiar terms like "chapter 7" and "chapter 11," even if most nonbankruptcy lawyers only have the vaguest of notion of what those laws entail. The same lawyers will usually mumble something about the Bankruptcy *Act*, even though it has been the Bankruptcy *Code* since the days of a single *Star Wars* film and the Sex Pistols performing live in concert.

A commercial lawyer, especially if she does not practise at a place where billing rates exceed $1,000 per hour, might have some general familiarity with things like "assignments for the benefit of creditors," and even state court receiverships. Lawyers at law firms where the billing rates do reach such stratospheric levels might view these devices as unseemly relics of an earlier age.

Another group of lawyers will have experience with specialized insolvency regimes for specific types of businesses. The most obvious are

---

[1] Although the new president, Donald Trump, has launched several verbal attacks on Dodd-Frank, as this book goes to print (mid-2018), the law remains in place.

those that proliferate among what we might broadly term the financial industry. Insurance companies, banks, credit unions, broker-dealers, and the like all have their own special rules for going bust. There could be more – the creation of specialized insolvency regimes for other businesses is only limited by the interests of legislators and the persistence of lobbyists. In the United States, there is also a theoretical limit on state insolvency laws that arises from the United States Constitution, but as we will see, that does not always hinder the creation of state insolvency laws, even if it renders them of dubious utility.

Before writing this book, I attempted to read the whole of American insolvency law. I believe I have largely succeeded. What follows is my attempt to make sense of all of it. It's not easy. Campground receiverships?

Of course, my ability to comprehend this great mass of law is limited by the abilities of an academic, sitting in a library in Manhattan, to understand the need for a special insolvency regime for grain silos, to again take but one example. But when such questions arose, I attempted to ask people who might know the answers, even if they did not necessarily know me. In many cases these people did respond, and I am grateful for their help.

This project has three principal goals. My first goal is to identify the points of commonality between the various insolvency statutes. Examining this common core is unheard of in a world where bankruptcy attorneys are regarded as quite distinct from banking or securities attorneys, despite the reality that each of them may be involved in an insolvency proceeding of a major American firm.

Second, I want to inspect the differences between these insolvency systems and to address any justification for the separation. If a broker-dealer liquidates in a proceeding before a federal bankruptcy judge, why does an insurance company liquidate in a state court, and a bank outside of court altogether? If we accept that banks are different, for example, and fail in different ways than "real economy" firms, does that justify keeping banks out of the traditional bankruptcy system?

My ultimate goal, as I discuss in the last chapter, is to begin a conversation about what our business insolvency law should look like. I view the insolvency system as a crucial, and often overlooked, part of the larger American entrepreneurial structure and consider that future laws might be better designed if we had a complete understanding of our law of failure. For example, Dodd-Frank might have provided for a clean break between OLA[2] and the Bankruptcy Code, instead of leaving large financial institutions sometimes subject to OLA, and sometimes subject to the Code. Lengthy, costly exercises like having financial institutions prepare "living wills" under the Bankruptcy Code are largely pointless if the big banks never liquidate under the Code.[3] Such a feature might have been omitted had Congress had access to a considered body of research on the goals and structure of our insolvency laws.

I end up concluding that there are two broad types of laws lurking within the general heading of "business insolvency law." First is the kind familiar to bankruptcy attorneys: laws that promote equal treatment of creditors, after sorting the creditors among classes. Exactly what that treatment will be is left to either a trustee applying a set of rules (in chapter 7 type mechanisms) or creditor bargaining (in chapter 11 like mechanisms). Most receiverships, assignments, and other general insolvency laws fit within this category, along with the Bankruptcy Code.

The other broad type of law gives one or more groups priority treatment over all others. We often see these laws in the financial institution context, but they exist elsewhere and they could, in theory, spread much further. Essentially, the legislature – federal or state – has decided that some groups of creditors should be spared the effects of a business's failure. These sorts of laws invoke the same basic language as the first type of insolvency laws, but their aims are different, as I note in the final two chapters.

Before we begin, I should also note that there are two clear approaches to a project such as this. One is to provide an encyclopedic account of all of American insolvency law. This would require dozens of volumes – the third and final edition of Ralph Clark's treatise on receiverships alone had four volumes, and he often neglected much of

---

[2] Orderly Liquidation Authority, in Dodd-Frank's Title II. I discuss this in more detail in Chapter 4.

[3] But not entirely pointless, if they lead to rationalization of the corporate structure, and perhaps a better understanding of how to head off financial distress.

the fine detail. In case you had any doubt – perhaps, like the TARDIS, this little tome is bigger on the inside? – this is not the approach I have taken. Nobody would read such an endeavor, and no modern publisher would support it.

Instead, I try to distill the key points of the insolvency regimes I examine and present a broad overview of the terrain in an easily readable form. The goal is to explain the key differences and why each of the insolvency systems currently in place in American law does or does not make sense. This book will not make you an expert in any of the specific examples I discuss, because my aim is to alert readers to the variety of approaches that exist, rather than dwell on the minutiae.

So we begin.

But first, I would be remiss if I did not acknowledge the helpful comments I received along the way from Abbye Atkinson, Peter Clapp, Oscar Couwenberg, Melissa Jacoby, John Pottow, Richard Levin, Adam Levitin, Mike Simkovic, David Skeel, Joseph Sommer, and Jay Westbrook. As with everything I do, I owe special thanks to my wife, Jennifer Hoyden. Everything is better with her.

1 WHY BUSINESS INSOLVENCY LAW?

Let's begin by asking *why* business insolvency law? That is, why do we need any special laws dealing with business insolvency when we already have laws that allow creditors to collect on their unpaid debts?

When America became an independent nation, business bankruptcy and bankruptcy in general were one and the same. The 1800 Bankruptcy Act followed English traditions and made bankruptcy a process that only applied to "merchants" – individuals engaged in business.[1]

Early English laws were mostly aimed at ensuring equal collection by creditors. The fear was that debtors would play favorites or hide assets. Bankruptcy was a means to bring the debtor-merchant and his or her finances out into the open.

That gives us some insight into why we need business insolvency laws in addition to general creditor collection laws. Collection laws act as an adjunct to general contract law and are typically focused on a single creditor collecting debt from a single debtor.[2] In this country, some states prohibit favoring one creditor over another but many other states affirmatively permit it. In the second sort of jurisdiction, the same problems that motivated Elizabethan parliaments to enact bankruptcy laws clearly remain. Debt collection law in general is focused on providing a remedy to a creditor, rather than to creditors writ large.

---

[1] H. H. Shelton, Bankruptcy Law, Its History and Purpose, 44 *Am. L. Rev.* 394, 399–400 (1910). See generally Bruce H. Mann, *Republic of Debtors: Bankruptcy in the Age of American Independence* (Cambridge: Harvard University Press, 2002). Cf. Emily Kadens, The Pitkin Affair: A Study of Fraud in Early English Bankruptcy, 84 *Am. Bankr. L.J.* 483 (2010).

[2] E.g., *Faith Properties, LLC* v. *First Commercial Bank*, 988 So. 2d 485, 491 (Ala. 2008).

But the widespread embrace of limited liability business entities – starting with New York's adoption of the French limited partnership concept in 1822,[3] and accelerating full speed with the 1990s invention of myriad unincorporated limited liability entities – necessarily split business and personal insolvency law. Once we moved beyond sole proprietorships and general partnerships, the failure of a business no longer meant the principals would be locked up in debtors' prison or their families hounded into the poorhouse. And thus business insolvency law truly begins as a distinct topic at this point.

Today there are innumerable business entities. There is an enormous variety of types of corporation alone – traditional business corporations, professional corporations, charitable corporations, mutual benefit corporations, religious corporations, cooperative corporations, corporations sole,[4] and even Native American tribal corporations.[5] Then there are the partnerships: limited partnerships, limited liability partnerships, limited liability limited partnerships, joint ventures, and of course, venerable old general partnerships. The latter can be formed intentionally, or by accident or inattention – more likely the latter these days. Limited liability companies, and their cousins, series limited liability companies (each "series" within these is almost, but not quite, a separate entity), round off the field.[6]

The equity and transparency concerns remain, but the commonly touted "fresh start" considerations fall by the wayside once the business

---

[3] *Ames* v. *Downing*, 1 Bradfr. 321, 329–32 (N.Y. Surr. 1850). See David C. King, Regulation of Foreign Limited Partnerships, 52 *B.U.L. Rev.* 64 (1972).

[4] Cal. Corp. Code § 10002.

[5] That is, corporations formed under tribal law. Many tribes also provide for limited liability companies. See also 25 U.S.C. § 5124 (section 17 of the 1934 Indian Reorganization Act) ("The Secretary of the Interior may, upon petition by any tribe, issue a charter of incorporation to such tribe ..."); Evan Way, *Raising Capital in Indian Country*, 41 *Am. Indian L. Rev.* 167, 175 (2016). ("A section 17 corporation must be wholly owned by the tribe, which precludes any capital investment into the corporation from potential non-tribal investors.")

[6] Del. Code Ann. tit. 6, § 18–215. Illinois, Iowa, Nevada, Oklahoma, Tennessee, Texas, Utah, and Puerto Rico have also enacted series or cell LLC statutes. The California Franchise Tax Board has taken the position that each series in a series LLC is a separate entity and therefore must file its own tax return and pay its own LLC annual tax and fee, if it is registered to do business in California, which places a pretty significant damper on their use for any interstate businesses. Protected cells in insurance companies are somewhat similar.

is legally distinct from the founders.[7] In the 1980s this led a host of bankruptcy scholars – along with a few well-intentioned interlopers – to propose ways in which chapter 11 of the Bankruptcy Code, enacted in 1978, might be trashed in favor of more "contractual" solutions.

No doubt these efforts were at least in part consistent with the larger deregulatory agenda of the early, "unreconstructed" law-and-economics movement, and its real-world allies in the Reagan Administration, the idea being that no statute or other regulatory scheme could be justified if the "same thing" could be achieved by "private ordering." There is no indication that practicing lawyers or legislators ever took these academic schemes too seriously.

But hundreds of pounds (or kilograms) of law review articles did reveal a general consensus that "common pool" problems might justify business bankruptcy or insolvency laws.[8] Namely, just like a bank run, the rush of individual creditors to collect from a distressed debtor might ultimately destroy value for everyone.[9]

In reality, the much-ballyhooed common pool problem was simply a fancy new name for a long-recognized issue. In the early 1930s, Learned Hand pithily observed that in the absence of a railroad receivership process that addressed all creditors at once, those creditors would levy against the debtor-railroad "until the road was stripped to the bone."[10] Judge Hand crucially did not state that federal bankruptcy law must solve this problem, but rather that some sort of collective insolvency process was needed to supersede routine debt collection law.[11]

The law-and-economics scholars of the Reagan era focused a bit too narrowly on this specific issue, neglecting other benefits like the efficiency of gathering litigation in a single forum, and applying a

---

[7] Charles Seligson, Major Problems for Consideration by the Commission on the Bankruptcy Laws of the United States, 45 *Am. Bankr. L.J.* 73, 106 (1971).

[8] Largely beginning with Thomas H. Jackson, The Logic and Limits of Bankruptcy Law (1986), and his earlier law review articles that provide the basis for the book. Jackson's picture of bankruptcy law is bottomed on a belief that bankruptcy should be a transparent procedure that mirrors non-bankruptcy law, and his strange conception of debtor passivity or indifference, in the face of the debtor and its owner's realization that the unsecured creditors are the "true" owners of the debtor.

[9] Vern Countryman, The Concept of a Voidable Preference in Bankruptcy, 38 *Vand. L. Rev.* 713, 728 n. 100 (1985).

[10] Ex parte Relmar Holding Co., 61 F.2d 941, 942 (2d Cir. 1932).

[11] David Gray Carlson, Philosophy in Bankruptcy, 85 *Mich. L. Rev.* 1341, 1346 (1987).

single set of rules to a company's collapse, regardless of whether its assets might be located in Irvine or Nashua. There is also some benefit in triggering every creditor's right to collect simultaneously, once a sufficient number have begun to collect.

The simultaneous treatment of all creditors not only addresses the "common pool" problem, but also advances governmental policies like protection of employees or other creditors with less bargaining power than banks or bondholders.[12] Creditors with defaults that are triggered easily or early could well walk off with all of the debtor's assets, while other creditors face a debtor with doubtful ability to pay, but who has not done enough to default just yet.

As summarized by the Canadian Supreme Court:

> The single proceeding model avoids the inefficiency and chaos that would attend insolvency if each creditor initiated proceedings to recover its debt. Grouping all possible actions against the debtor into a single proceeding controlled in a single forum facilitates negotiation with creditors because it places them all on an equal footing, rather than exposing them to the risk that a more aggressive creditor will realize its claims against the debtor's limited assets while the other creditors attempt a compromise.[13]

In short, once the press of creditors against a business has moved beyond a few raindrops, and appears heading toward a deluge, there are clear benefits in moving to a collective insolvency procedure in place of traditional, individualistic debtor-creditor law. These benefits are not limited to improving creditor welfare, but advantage society as a whole.

Moreover, by conceiving of the insolvent firm as a "pool," one is naturally drawn to see everything in liquidation terms. A firm operating as a going concern does not pay from its asset pool, but rather pays from the income it generates. Insolvency law is as much about restructuring as it is about liquidation, and it is not clear that liquidation is necessarily the correct starting point for all analyses in this area.

Where, then, is the line between these two types of law? That is, what makes an insolvency law an *insolvency law*?

---

[12] Donald R. Korobkin, Rehabilitating Values: A Jurisprudence of Bankruptcy, 91 *Colum. L. Rev.* 717, 772 (1991).

[13] *Century Services Inc.* v. *Canada (Attorney General)*, 2010 SCC 60, [2010] 3 S.C.R. 379, at ¶ 22.

The issue is one that courts continue to struggle with in the context of chapter 15 of the Bankruptcy Code, where a foreign insolvency proceeding can be "recognized" – that is, given effect under US law – only if it is "a collective judicial or administrative proceeding in a foreign country."[14] While the second half of the definition is self-evident – France counts, Freedonia does not – what it means to be a "collective" procedure is often uncertain.

In the chapter 15 context, courts considering whether a proceeding is "collective" often state that the key question is whether the proceeding "is one that considers the rights and obligations of all creditors. This is in contrast, for example, to a receivership remedy instigated at the request, and for the benefit, of a single secured creditor."[15]

There is, of course, a good bit of space between a proceeding that addresses "all creditors" and one that addresses a single creditor.[16] In the United States, it is quite common for prepackaged chapter 11 cases – where bondholders agree to a reorganization plan before the case is filed – to convert bondholders to shareholders while leaving all other creditors, especially trade creditors, untouched. Few would doubt that this is nonetheless a "collective" proceeding.

In addressing "collectivity," it arguably makes more sense to consider if the proceeding adjusts one or more classes of creditors, as contrasted with a proceeding that works as a collection device for a single creditor or with respect to a single debt.[17] Thus, some forms of receiverships clearly are within the scope of this book because they represent a comprehensive restructuring of at least an entire class of debt, while other receiverships will not be covered, except in contrast to general receiverships, because I view them as simply one more tool in the debt collection toolbox.[18]

---

[14] 11 U.S.C. § 101(23).

[15] *In re Betcorp Ltd.,* 400 B.R. 266, 281 (Bankr. D. Nev. 2009).

[16] What it means to "consider" the rights of creditors is also more than a bit vague.

[17] *In re Gold & Honey, Ltd.,* 410 B.R. 357, 370 (Bankr. E.D.N.Y. 2009). ("The Israeli Receivership Proceeding is primarily designed to allow FIBI to collect its debts, and is not a scheme of arrangement or a winding up proceeding, both of which are instituted by a debtor for the purposes of paying off all creditors with court supervision to ensure evenhandedness.")

[18] I also avoid those receiverships that are unrelated to debtor-creditors matters, but instead involve things like regulatory enforcement.

That is, there is necessarily a good deal of line drawing involved here.[19] And some of it is frankly a pure exercise of writer's privilege. I will attempt to draw the line between what is necessary to separate core functions and policies in insolvency law and everything else.

A particularly difficult case is presented by syndicated bank loans. If the loan was made by a single bank, efforts to collect or restructure the debtor's obligations on the loan clearly would fall outside of "insolvency law." Does that answer change when the loan is broken up among dozens of lenders, who may in turn sell their pieces of the loan to other investors, mostly not banks, some of which would never have any contact with the debtor company, at least until default?

This begins to look more like a class of creditors rather than a single creditor. A restructuring of this class that is effectuated according to the terms of the loan – shades of the 1980s law-and-economics dream here – I view as not implicating insolvency law. Thus, when the loan agreement provides that a deal agreed to by two-thirds of the loanholders will be binding on the rest is outside of my field of vision in this book.

But if that same deal is imposed upon the loanholders by statutory law or regulation, I suddenly become interested. That is, my focus here is more on the insolvency process that is imposed by law, and less on the process that is simply facilitated by law.

Lots of laws also attempt to steer the outcome of a future insolvency proceeding, but I likewise do not view them as being insolvency procedures themselves.[20] For example, Article 8 of the Uniform Commercial Code, the state law regarding transfers of investment securities, contains elaborate provisions regarding the priority of various ownership interests in securities upon a stockbroker's insolvency. This has led some to term Article 8 an "insolvency law in disguise," although I do not treat it as such in the present work.

On the other hand, my wanderings through state law have disclosed myriad specialized receivership statutes. Many are clearly designed to forestall insolvency proceedings of more general applicability – most

---

[19] Cf. *Schlesinger* v. *State of Wisconsin*, 270 U.S. 230, 241 (1926). (Holmes, J. dissenting) (The "great body of the law consists in drawing such lines, yet when you realize that you are dealing with a matter of degree you must realize that reasonable men may differ widely as to the place where the line should fall.")

[20] See Ronald J. Mann, The Rise of State Bankruptcy-Directed Legislation, 25 *Cardozo L. Rev.* 1805 (2004).

often those under the federal Bankruptcy Code – from taking hold in a specific industry, or with regard to particular types of firms. I nonetheless view these as insolvency laws, although the line between priority and fully fledged insolvency law might be subtler than this suggests, particularly if the goal of the receivership is to protect some favored group of creditors within the debtor company's capital structure.

The potential sources of American insolvency law are also more diverse than might appear at first blush. Certainly, my search began with federal and state statutes. But then there is the common law of receiverships, compositions, and assignments for the benefit of creditors. In several jurisdictions, including sometimes the federal courts, these procedures appear but fleetingly in court rules, if at all. In other cases – for example, chapter 7 cases of commodity brokers – the statute provides a skeletal outline of the procedure, while rules enacted by the Commodity Futures Trading Commission (CFTC) provide all the real detail of how the process might actually work.

Cutting in the other direction, and as will be discussed in more detail in Chapter 3, several states have statutes on the books that are of questionable applicability. On the face of it, they seem to apply to business insolvency but close examination reveals that the primary remedy is to offer the debtor a discharge – from debtors' prison. Certainly, these statutes would not apply to a corporate debtor – perhaps only a bankruptcy professor would spend time imagining what it would look like to apply such a statute to Lehman Brothers.

Likewise, many of these state statutes date from an age when federal bankruptcy statutes were hardly permanent. While the Supreme Court's preemption jurisprudence with regard to the Bankruptcy Code is unclear and dated, a plausible argument could be made that most state insolvency statutes are in a kind of suspended animation, waiting for a future that may never come, namely the day when Congress repeals the Bankruptcy Code and fails to replace it.[21]

---

[21] *Stellwagen* v. *Clum*, 245 U.S. 605, 613, 615 (1918).

> In view of this grant of authority to the Congress it has been settled from an early date that state laws to the extent that they conflict with the laws of Congress, enacted under its constitutional authority, on the subject of bankruptcies are suspended. While this is true, state laws are thus suspended only to the extent of actual conflict with the system provided by the Bankruptcy Act of Congress.

In the United States, we face the added challenge that things we might clearly call "insolvency laws" do not necessarily require the debtor to be insolvent. The Bankruptcy Code is the most obvious and direct example.[22]

Section 109 of the Code has no insolvency requirement for filing bankruptcy, save for that in chapter 9, which applies only to municipalities.[23] This contrasts with the law of almost every other jurisdiction.

For example, the Companies' Creditors Arrangement Act, Canada's equivalent of chapter 11, defines a "debtor company" to include only those companies that are insolvent or have committed "acts of bankruptcy," as defined under section 42(1) of the Canadian Bankruptcy and Insolvency Act, which means either being insolvent or engaging in what amounts to either a fraudulent transfer or a preference.[24]

In contrast, under the American Bankruptcy Code there is not even a requirement that the debtor have any assets to be distributed to its creditors.[25]

Section 109 of the Code also contains no requirement that the debtor be either a US citizen, a legal resident, or otherwise legally domiciled in the United States.[26] Foreign corporations file under chapter 11 with some regularity, either independently or as subsidiaries of American parent companies already in chapter 11.[27]

Nonetheless, there seems no doubt that the Bankruptcy Code and other laws that apply in advance of formal insolvency should be included within the scope of this discussion. Thus, the precise contours of the "law of failure" are somewhat uncertain, and surely subject to

---

[22] Karen Gross & Matthew S. Barr, Bankruptcy Solutions in the United States: An Overview, 17 *N.Y.L. Sch. J. Int'l & Comp. L.* 215 (1997).

[23] 11 U.S.C. § 109(c)(3). *Connell v. Coastal Cable T.V., Inc.* (In re Coastal Cable T.V., Inc.), 709 F.2d 762, 764 (1st Cir. 1983); see also *In re Johns-Manville Corp.*, 36 B.R. 727, 736 (Bankr. S.D.N.Y. 1984). ("Accordingly, the drafters of the Code envisioned that a financially beleaguered debtor with real debt and real creditors should not be required to wait until the economic situation is beyond repair in order to file a reorganization petition.")

[24] Companies Creditors' Arrangement Act, R.S., 1985, c. C-36 § 2 (1); see also Bankruptcy and Insolvency Act, R.S.C. 1985, c. B-3 §42(1). Cf. Israel Treiman, Acts of Bankruptcy: A Medieval Concept in Modern Bankruptcy Law, 52 *Harv. L. Rev.* 189 (1938).

[25] *Vulcan Sheet Metal Co. v. North Platte Irrig. Co.*, 220 F. 106, 108 (8th Cir. 1910).

[26] In re Arispe, 289 B.R. 245 (Bankr. S.D. Fla. 2002); In re Merlo, 265 B.R. 502 (Bankr. S.D. Fla. 2001); In re Xacur, 216 BR 187 (Bankr. S.D. Tex. 1997).

[27] Oscar Couwenberg & Stephen J. Lubben, Corporate Bankruptcy Tourists, 70 *Bus. Law.* 719 (2015).

some debate. Nonetheless, my focus is on the insolvency laws of the nation, as outlined above.

So, we have a workable definition of insolvency for our tour of American business insolvency law, but the careful reader will note that I have studiously avoided defining what I mean by "business." Our tour of business insolvency law will involve the consideration of laws that apply to at least one class of creditors of *for-profit* business enterprises. In some cases, particularly with respect to partnerships, the interaction of the insolvency law with the law that created the business enterprise will also be of interest.

As noted earlier, American law presently provides a plethora of business entities for the would-be entrepreneur. That leaves an equally broad array of entities that might experience financial distress.

While I occasionally note a special receivership provision for co-operatives, or something of that ilk, my focus is on the for-profit firm. Thus, I steer away from charitable and religious entities, and even some not-for-profit enterprises, like hospitals or universities, that operate in something of a gray zone. And I organize most of the discussion around the two most basic entities of American business law: corporations and partnerships. Sometimes I talk about limited liability companies too.

American statutory corporate law seemingly varies quite a bit. The famous Delaware General Corporation Law provides myriad examples of how to express a concept in a particularly confusing way or how to write a phenomenal run-on sentence.[28] Those states that follow the Model Business Corporation Act have statutes of greater readability, without necessarily greater clarity. New York and California provide something in between.

But, at heart, there is little substantive difference in American corporate law as actually applied.[29] And thus, once we get to the point of insolvency, a corporation's state of incorporation – New York, New Jersey, or other – rarely matters, unless the state has a unique, applicable insolvency statute.

---

[28] Several examples of both can be seen in Del. Code Ann. tit. 8, § 251.

[29] California presents some interesting differences on the point of cumulative voting, but those rules are largely countermanded by the insolvency regimes I consider in this book.

With partnerships, on the other hand, it matters a good deal on which side of the Hudson the entity was formed.

Partnership law in the United States is based on one of two model statutes – both designed to replace the common law of partnership.[30] Most states, including New Jersey and other important jurisdictions like California, have adopted the Revised Uniform Partnership Act (RUPA). But the older Uniform Partnership Act (UPA), dating from 1914, remains in force in New York and a handful of other states. Because of New York's importance in commerce matters, its continued adherence to the UPA matters a lot, even if more states have gone over to the newer law.

In the insolvency context, the difference between New York and New Jersey law is stark. Both the UPA and the RUPA follow a basic rule that partnership creditors have first crack at the partnership assets upon insolvency.[31]

But the older UPA in force in New York follows the traditional "jingle rule,"[32] with regard to partnership creditors' ability to get at the partner's personal assets. That rule, as an early author explained, might be made to run like some jingle, "firm estate to firm creditors, separate estate to separate creditors, anything left over from either goes to the other."[33]

---

[30] Louisiana provides an additional wrinkle here, with a partnership law that limits the partner's liability to a proportionate share of the total liability. La. Civ. Code Ann. art. 2817. This is not the result of any ancient French influence, but rather a 1980 revision to the partnership law, which extended a rule previously applicable to non-commercial partnerships (an impossibility under the common law) to cover all partnerships. See Magan Causey, Limited Liability for General Partnerships: Another Louisiana Anomaly? 66 *La. L. Rev.* 527, 537–8 (2006):

> [T]here are no documented reasons for the strange liability choice in either the comments to Civil Code article 2817 or Act 150 of the 1980 revisions that created the anomaly. Today, partnerships engaged in the same commercial activity that pre-revision commercial partnerships were involved in enjoy limited liability rather than solidary [i.e., joint and several] liability for no apparent reason.

[31] Scott Rowley et al. Rowley on Partnership 758 (2d ed. 1960).

[32] Uniform Partnership Act § 40(h).

[33] F. D. Brannan, The Separate Estates of Non-Bankrupt Partners in the Bankruptcy of a Partnership under the Bankrupt Act of 1898, 20 *Harv. L. Rev.* 589, 592 (1907).

A catchy advertisement, to be sure. Each type of creditor obtains a priority claim against their primary debtor, and a subordinated claim against the secondary debtor. The rule was at one time followed throughout the common law world.[34]

But it has also been criticized for a very long time.[35] The late Frank Kennedy observed that the superficial symmetry of the rule "involves a serious departure from the basic rule of the common law of partnerships that the separate property of each partner is as fully liable for the payment of partnership debts as for his individual debts."[36]

Thus, the newer RUPA eradicates the jingle rule. Partnership creditors continue to have first priority against the partnership entity itself, but all creditors have equal claims against the individual partners.

The end result is that our examination of state insolvency law will necessarily involve consideration of not only the insolvency statutes, but also the type of business entity to which they might apply.

There are, of course, other legal entities, including limited partnerships, limited liability companies, and limited liability partnerships. While for governance purposes most of these look more like partnerships, from an insolvency perspective they are largely treated more like corporations. Most significantly, with these entities, as with corporations, liability typically begins and ends with the firm. Only in old-fashioned general partnerships (and with regard to the general

---

[34] See generally J. J. Henning, Criticism, Review and Abrogation of the Jingle Rule in Partnership Insolvency: A Comparative Perspective, 20 *S. Afr. Mercantile L.J.* 307 (2008).

[35] See *Bell* v. *Newman*, 1819 WL 1861, at *4 (Pa. 1819). ("It is very remarkable, that although this be the undoubted rule in cases of bankruptcy, yet no one can tell how it came to be so, nor is it approved by the present Chancellor of England (Lord Eldon), who submits to it only because he found it established by his predecessor.") See also *id.* at *5. ("It is not easy to discover the equity of excluding a creditor of the partnership from all share of the separate estates of the partners, until the separate debts are paid, nor of excluding a separate creditor from all share of his debtor's joint property, until the joint debts are paid, because the truth is, that persons who trust the partners, either in their separate or partnership character, generally do it, on the credit of their whole estates, both joint and separate.").

[36] Frank Kennedy, A New Deal for Partnership Bankruptcy, 60 *Colum. L. Rev.* 610, 631 (1960). But see Richard Squire, The Case for Symmetry in Creditors' Rights, 118 *Yale L. J.* 806, 838 n. 82 (2009) (terming Kennedy's criticism of the rule "misleading," because the partnership creditors are merely subordinated, rather than barred from recovery).

partners of limited partnerships) do we have to consider the role that the owners play in the law of failure.

One fundamental attribute of a corporation is that the ownership (equity) and most management rights are distinct from one another. In general, in partnerships, particularly smaller ones, owners are often the managers. And these owner-managers face personal liability if the business goes wrong. That necessarily will have effects on the insolvency of the entity.

The "new" business entities do draw us back to partnership law on the question of taxation, however. Section 61(a)(12) of the United States Tax Code provides that gross income includes "[i]ncome from discharge of indebtedness." For a corporation, that income is the entity's problem to deal with.

For partnerships, and related entities like limited liability companies (and even subchapter S corporations),[37] that income from the cancellation of debt can flow through to the owners. The total amount of cancellation of indebtedness income realized by the partnership is allocated among the partners of the partnership, and the partners are required to include the income in their gross income on their personal tax returns. Once again, this will influence the operation of insolvency law, and the choice of which insolvency mechanism to use.

Our focus remains with the entity throughout.[38] But it is also important to remember the incentives of those who control the entity.

Thus, we commence our review of American business insolvency law. The early stages are descriptive: we want to understand the full scope of study. The later stages turn more to an evaluation of the terrain. I consider the overall themes and the ways in which the law of failure might be improved.

Without getting too bogged down in broader theoretical debates about insolvency law – which tend to turn insolvency law into either a glorified debt-collection utensil or a solution to all (or most) of

---

[37] That is, regular corporations that have elected to be taxed as if they were partnerships under the US Tax Code. Shareholders of S corporations report the flow-through of income and losses from the corporation on their personal tax returns and are assessed tax at their individual income tax rates.

[38] See James W. M. Moore & Philip W. Tone, Proposed Bankruptcy Amendments: Improvement or Retrogression? 57 *Yale L.J.* 683, 710 (1948).

society's problems[39] – we will consider the substantive ends to be pursued by insolvency law or processes. Business insolvency law necessarily involves both public and private concerns, and we cannot evaluate the state of the law without illuminating these several interests and measuring the law against them.

The ultimate question is, "Does the law of failure effectively serve the goals that seemingly motivate it?"

---

[39] Vanessa Finch, The Measures of Insolvency Law, 17 *Oxford J. Legal Stud.* 227, 242 (1997).

2 THE FEDERAL LAW OF BUSINESS INSOLVENCY

Any sketch of the federal law of business failure must begin with the Bankruptcy Code, and its chapters 7 and 11. Indeed, these provisions are so prominent that they tend to obscure other insolvency systems of relevance on our tour.

The Bankruptcy Code has been the federal insolvency law of general applicability since its enactment in 1978. The need for a new bankruptcy law was widely recognized by the late 1960s, but the Vietnam War, Watergate, and other distractions of the age kept Congress from acting in a timely manner. When the Code was finally enacted, the *New York Times* declared that the "reform law, though not perfect, is well worth the years of effort and the last-minute compromises that brought it about."[1]

The Bankruptcy Code is enacted under and subject to any limits of the power bestowed on Congress by the Bankruptcy Clause of the Constitution. Specifically, article I, section 8, clause 4 of the Constitution provides that Congress shall have the power to enact "uniform laws on the subject of Bankruptcies throughout the United States."

Section 109 of the Code initially funnels most businesses into chapter 7. Under that section, a debtor must be a person, or a municipality, but those are not our concern here. Person "includes individual, partnership, and corporation." Partnership is, interestingly, an undefined term in the Code. Corporation, on the other hand, is defined, and

---

[1] Rescuing Bankruptcy From Bankruptcy, *N.Y. Times*, Dec. 1, 1978, at A26.

includes some things that most people would think were partnerships. In particular, a corporation for Bankruptcy Code purposes includes:

1. an association having a power or privilege that a private corporation, but not an individual or a partnership, possesses;
2. a partnership association organized under a law that makes only the capital subscribed responsible for the debts of such association;
3. a joint-stock company;
4. an unincorporated company or association; or
5. business trust.

But it expressly does not include a limited partnership, a term that is also not defined in the Code. Under this definition of corporation, a limited liability partnership or LLP has been held to be a "corporation" and not a partnership for Bankruptcy Code purposes.[2] A similar analysis finds a limited liability company to be a corporation for bankruptcy purposes.

In *In re C-TC 9th Ave. Partnership* the Second Circuit held that a dissolved but not-yet-wound-up partnership could not invoke chapter 11 because

> the primary purpose of chapter 11 is to enable businesses to reorganize and emerge from bankruptcy as operating enterprises, and New York partnership law prohibits [a dissolved partnership] from engaging in any business other than liquidation. There can be no opportunity to rehabilitate an entity that, by law, no longer exists except for the purposes of liquidation.[3]

The case might be distinguished as turning on New York law, which clings to the old-fashioned notion that the departure of any partner automatically commences the dissolution and winding up of a partnership. And unlike RUPA, the UPA in place in New York does not provide for the "undoing" of a dissolution. Even so, since chapter 11 can be used to liquidate a corporation, we might wonder why the same could not be said for a partnership.

---

[2] In re Dewey & LeBoeuf LLP, 518 B.R. 766, 777 (Bankr. S.D.N.Y. 2014).
[3] *In re C-TC 9th Ave. P'ship*, 113 F.3d 1304, 1308 (2d Cir. 1997).

Similarly, it is still the case that under state law, the bankruptcy of a partner will cause that person to withdraw from the partnership. In RUPA states, the partner in question will typically be "bought out" by the remaining partners. In UPA states, as well as under the limited liability company laws of some states, this purports to cause the disbanding of the entity.

Many courts reject the Second Circuit's *9th Ave. Partnership* analysis. And further the purported automatic dissolution of an entity upon a bankruptcy filing is typically held to be barred by one of two provisions of the federal Bankruptcy Code.[4]

Note that the Code's definition of "corporation" also sweeps in other odd-ball business entities, including, somewhat puzzlingly, "unincorporated" companies or associations. That is, a corporation includes things that are not incorporated, just so long as it is not a partnership.

Joint stock companies, essentially partnerships with tradable shares and other corporate-like features grafted on,[5] were widely used when incorporation was difficult or required action by the legislature, but the advent of easy incorporation, and entities like limited liability companies and limited liability partnerships,[6] make such companies exceedingly rare.[7] Nonetheless, if one wanders into the bankruptcy court, the Code slams it into the corporation box and we are off and running. The same basic rule applies to most other business forms: if it is not a partnership or a limited partnership, it will be called a corporation for purposes of the Bankruptcy Code.[8]

---

[4] Sections 541(c) or 365(e). See generally Sally S. Neely, Partnerships and Partners and Limited Liability Companies and Members in Bankruptcy: Proposals for Reform, 71 *Am. Bankr. L.J.* 271 (1997).

[5] *Chapman* v. *Barney*, 129 U.S. 677, 682 (1889). See also N.Y. Gen. Ass'ns Law § 2 ("The term 'joint stock association' includes every unincorporated joint stock association, company or enterprise having written articles of association and capital stock divided into shares, but does not include a corporation or a business trust.")

[6] Cf. *Galt* v. *United States*, 175 F. Supp. 360, 362 (N.D. Tex. 1959).

[7] American Express was one of the last publicly traded joint stock companies. *Mason* v. *Am. Exp. Co.*, 334 F.2d 392, 399 (2d Cir. 1964). Foreign joint stock companies occasionally appear in American insolvency cases. Whether the term "joint stock company" has the same meaning abroad is often unclear.

[8] See In re Tidewater Coal Exch., 280 F. 638, 643–4 (2d Cir. 1922). ("It is sufficient that the Exchange is an association of individuals in pursuit of a common business object, under a control agreed to by all its members, and capable of having debtors and creditors,

Eligibility to file under chapter 7 is also a key component of determining if a debtor-company might be able to file a petition under the legendary chapter 11. In most cases, if the company can file a chapter 7 petition, it can also proceed under chapter 11 instead.

But there are several exceptions. As an initial matter, three subparts of section 109 bar railroads and an eclectic mix of what we might roughly term "financial institutions," both foreign and domestic, from filing chapter 7 petitions. But not all financial institutions are excluded – for example, certain stockbrokers and commodity brokers are permitted to file chapter 7 petitions, and indeed there are special sub-parts of chapter 7 to deal with them. Casinos, money transmitters, non-depository banks, agreement corporations,[9] and some foreign insurance companies are also eligible to file without restriction.[10]

and which is neither a corporation, nor a partnership, nor a joint-stock company. It is 'an unincorporated company' within the meaning of the act, and as such can be adjudicated a bankrupt.")

[9] As explained by the district court in *Rose Hall, Ltd.* v. *Chase Manhattan Overseas Banking Corp.*:

> In 1916, the National Banking Act was amended to authorize national banks to invest in the stock of a bank or corporation chartered under either federal or state law and "principally engaged in international or foreign banking ... either directly or indirectly through the agency, ownership, or control of local institutions in foreign countries." Act of Sept. 7, 1916, 36 Stat. 752, 755–6 (1916), 12 U.S.C. § 601. These corporations could be formed only under state law and approval of the Federal Reserve Board of Governors was required for national banks to acquire stock in these state-chartered corporations. As such these became known as "agreement corporations."
>
> Few agreement corporations were formed and, in an effort to stimulate and facilitate trade with Europe after the First World War, Congress temporarily amended the Federal Reserve Act by adding section 25a to provide for investment in either banking or financing operations. Act of September 17, 1919, 41 Stat. 285–6 (1919), 12 U.S.C. § 601. Later in 1919, Congress promulgated the Edge Act which granted permanent authority to national banks to participate in banking or financing corporations. The Edge Act brought these financing and banking corporations under more direct supervision of the Federal Reserve Board of Governors by authorizing their incorporation under federal charter.
>
> Under these two legislative schemes – the National Banking Act and the Edge Act – two types of corporations have evolved: first, state chartered agreement corporations and second, federally chartered Edge Act corporations.
>
> 576 F. Supp. 107, 161 n. 78 (D. Del. 1983), aff'd 740 F.2d 956 (3d Cir. 1984). I found fourteen currently active agreement corporations when researching this book.

[10] Under section 109(3)(A), foreign insurance companies are prohibited from bankruptcy only if "engaged in such business in the United States."

Just because something is called a "bank" does not mean it is necessarily excluded from the Bankruptcy Code either. In 2012, Arcapita Bank filed a chapter 11 petition in New York.[11] In papers filed with its bankruptcy petition, its officers explained that it was a Bahraini closed joint stock company, and that it was "not a domestic bank licensed in the United States, nor does it have a branch or agency in the United States as defined in section 109(b)(3)(B) of the Bankruptcy Code."[12] Therefore it asserted it could file a chapter 11 case, even though it had the magic word "bank" in its legal name. The only motion to dismiss in the case (which was denied), had nothing to do with the debtor's status as a bank.

And likewise, with special permission of the Federal Reserve, certain multilateral clearing organizations can file under a special subpart of chapter 7. Precisely where one might encounter a "multilateral clearing organization" – at the car wash? – is hard to discern from any study of the Bankruptcy Code.[13]

Any business that can get into chapter 7 can also get into chapter 11, except for the stockbrokers and commodity brokers who must stay in chapter 7. Railroads are also allowed into chapter 11, while most financial institutions are still excluded.

But then petitions are permitted by "an uninsured State member bank." The membership referenced here is in the Federal Reserve System, and the insurance in question is that offered by the Federal Deposit Insurance Corporation (FDIC). Apparently this bit of the Bankruptcy Code applies to a single, very important piece of financial infrastructure. Also allowed into chapter 11 are corporations "organized under section 25A of the Federal Reserve Act, which operates, or operates as, a multilateral clearing organization." Those again.

They can file chapter 7 petitions only with Fed approval, but chapter 11 petitions are fair game, even in the face of Fed objections. As noted, I leave all of the federal law of financial institution insolvency for another chapter.

---

[11] In re Arcapita Bank B.S.C.(C), et al., 12-bk-11076 (Bankr. S.D.N.Y. Mar. 19, 2012).

[12] Strictly speaking, there is no definition in section 109(b)(3)(B) – perhaps better to say the debtor is not a "bank" as meant by section 109(b), because it is not a depository bank, but rather an investment bank.

[13] We come back to them in Chapter 4.

Putting those finance entities to one side, what do we have left?

All business debtors, be they partnerships, corporations, or what-not, can file chapter 7 petitions, save railroads. In addition, railroads and all other businesses can file under chapter 11, although the rules for railroads are somewhat different. This congressional preoccupation with railroads seems more than a bit peculiar, and it surely must have already been doubtful even in 1978, when the current Code was enacted. Certainly back in the nineteenth century, and even in some parts of the country right up through the Second World War, railroads were special. They represented the only practical link between many communities and the larger world.

As such, courts developed a kind of common law rule that railroads could not liquidate.[14] That rule was carried over into the New Deal's section 77, which applied to railroad bankruptcy cases from the 1930s until the enactment of the current Bankruptcy Code.

But by 1978, the railroad industry had been devastated by the post-war development of both government-funded interstate highways and air travel.[15] The notion that a railroad could not be permitted to fail was surely suspect.[16] Nonetheless, this relatively ancient history carries through to today's law, albeit with some ability to liquidate after the railroad has spent five years flailing about in chapter 11.[17]

Any business bankruptcy case begins with the filing of a petition. A voluntary petition, filed by the debtor-company itself, immediately triggers an "order for relief." That is, the court need not do anything, the company is immediately under the protection of the bankruptcy system.

Section 303 of the Bankruptcy Code provides that an involuntary case may be commenced under chapter 7 or 11 against a company

---

[14] *Continental Ill. Nat'l Bank & Trust Co.* v. *Chicago, R.I. Ry. Co.*, 294 U.S. 648, 671–2 (1935).

[15] *Blanchette* v. *Connecticut Gen. Ins. Corps.*, 419 U.S. 102, 108 (1974). ("A rail transportation crisis seriously threatening the national welfare was precipitated when eight major railroads in the northeast and midwest region of the country entered reorganization proceedings under s77 of the Bankruptcy Act ...") See also 45 U.S.C. § 701(a).

[16] It was a few years before deregulation of the railroad industry, and the drafters of the Code likely sought to avoid a distracting fight with the Interstate Commerce Commission and members of Congress who wanted to protect rail service within their districts.

[17] 11 U.S.C. § 1174. Instead of converting the railroad's chapter 11 case to a chapter 7 case, the chapter 11 case proceeds "as if" it were a chapter 7 case.

that may be a debtor under the chapter under which such case is commenced. Thus, a corporation might be involuntarily placed into either chapter 7 or chapter 11, while a railroad could only be involuntarily shoved into chapter 11.

An exception to that general rule is that an involuntary case may not be commenced against a corporation that is "not a moneyed, business or commercial corporation." But we are not really concerned with those in any event.

An involuntary case, filed by creditors against the company, does not trigger immediate protection. Instead, the court holds a trial to determine whether to issue an order for relief. The debtor-business continues to operate as normal until the court rules. Assuming, of course, normal operations are possible for a firm with a bankruptcy petition hanging over its head.

If the petition is contested, the Code provides that an order for relief should be entered only if the debtor is not generally paying its undisputed debts as they become due. Alternatively, the appointment of a trustee, receiver or other similar agent under insolvency law can support an involuntary bankruptcy case – thus connecting several of the insolvency mechanisms studied in this book with the federal Bankruptcy Code.[18] As we shall see, pre-emption – either in the formal constitutional sense[19] or in the sense of a federal bankruptcy case overwhelming another form of insolvency procedure[20] – looms large in the world of business failure.

If the debtor is a partnership, one or more general partners can file an involuntary petition. The thinking is that general partnerships are the one instance where the continued operation of the debtor might result in further liability for the petitioning owners (the partners).

---

[18] In re Quality Laser Works, 211 B.R. 936, 943 (B.A.P. 9th Cir. 1997). Further, once a receiver obtains knowledge that a debtor has commenced a bankruptcy case, the receiver must cease from making "any disbursement from, or take any action in the administration of, property of the debtor, proceeds, product, offspring, rents or profits of such property, or property of the estate, in the possession, custody or control of" the receiver, unless the "action ... is necessary to preserve such property." 11 U.S.C. § 543(a).

[19] "This Constitution, and the Laws of the United States which shall be made in Pursuance thereof ... shall be the supreme Law of the Land; ... any Thing in the Constitution or Laws of any state to the Contrary notwithstanding." U.S. Constitution, article VI, clause 2.

[20] Straton v. New, 283 U.S. 318, 331 (1931).

If a majority of the partners are running up the partnership's debts, the minority partners will be personally liable, so an involuntary petition is a way to allow them to stop their personal bleeding.

This does give partners a mechanism to put their firm into bankruptcy that is lacking in other businesses. A minority of a corporation's board have no standing – unless the directors are also unpaid creditors – to force the company into bankruptcy. Same with any group of shareholders. The special power is also strictly limited to its terms – limited partners, for example, may not force a limited partnership into bankruptcy.[21]

Indeed, it is interesting to note that neither state nor federal law provides a clear answer to the question of who controls a business entity's authority to file for bankruptcy.[22] For example, who can authorize a Delaware corporation to file a bankruptcy petition? Neither the Bankruptcy Code nor the Delaware General Corporation Law provides a clear answer.[23] The nearest thing to a definitive answer comes from Justice William O. Douglas, writing long ago in a case under the Bankruptcy Act:

> The District Court in passing on petitions filed by corporations under Chapter X must of course determine whether they are filed by those who have authority so to act. In absence of federal incorporation, that authority finds its source in local law ... But nowhere is there any indication that Congress bestowed on the bankruptcy court jurisdiction to determine that those who in fact do not have the authority to speak for the corporation as a matter of local law are entitled to be given such authority and therefore should be empowered to file a petition on behalf of the corporation.[24]

---

[21] In re Cold Harbor Assocs., L.P., 204 B.R. 904, 916 (Bankr. E.D. Va. 1997); In re Royal Gate Assocs., Ltd., 81 B.R. 165, 167 (Bankr. M.D. Ga. 1988). But see In re Taylor & Assocs., L.P., 193 B.R. 465, 475 (Bankr. E.D. Tenn. 1996) (stating that limited partners were entitled to be petitioning creditors where they held contract and tort claims).

[22] This is not a new problem. Power of Directors to Institute Voluntary or Involuntary Bankruptcy Proceedings Without Stockholders' Consent, 50 *Harv. L. Rev.* 662 (1937).

[23] Some states provide clearer statutory answers regarding non-profit corporations. E.g., 15 Pa. Stat. and Cons. Stat. Ann. § 5903.

[24] *Price* v. *Gurney*, 324 U.S. 100, 107 (1945).

As a result, courts have applied general principals of agency law.[25] Corporate officers do not have any implicit authority to file; they need express authorization by the board.[26] Remarkably, while a board typically needs shareholder approval to proceed with extraordinary transactions, filing a bankruptcy petition is not considered to require such approval.[27] Rather, a board acting alone can put the company into either a chapter 7 or chapter 11 case.[28]

This is practical, even if it does not quite conform to the overall conceptual structure of corporate law. That is, if a merger, sale of all assets, or dissolution and winding up requires shareholder approval, why not a bankruptcy petition? Under current law, a bankruptcy petition is treated more like a bylaw amendment than a dissolution or other terminal event in the corporation's life.

The board does have an obligation to act in the best interests of the corporation, which, if insolvent, may require acting in ways that are against the interests of the shareholders.[29] Shareholder approval would both delay the availability of bankruptcy protection – especially in a public company, where shareholder votes mean complex and expensive proxy statements – and potentially give the shareholders an extortionate hold over otherwise appropriate action.

On the other hand, we must remember that a federal bankruptcy petition can be filed for a solvent corporation. And the shareholders' ability to participate in the case is plainly somewhat less than their ability to vote as a class under state law.[30] There is clearly some risk of foul

---

[25] In re Nica Holdings, Inc., 810 F.3d 781, 790 (11th Cir. 2015); *Hager* v. *Gibson*, 108 F.3d 35, 40 (4th Cir. 1997).

[26] In re *Stavola/Manson Elec. Co., Inc.*, 94 B.R. 21, 24 (Bankr. D. Conn. 1988).

[27] The rule used to be that a board could file a bankruptcy petition without shareholder approval only if the board could likewise initiate an assignment for the benefit of creditors without shareholder approval. Garrard Glenn, The Law Governing Liquidation § 41 (1935). As noted in Chapter 3, in many states – notably Delaware, California, and New York – it is thought that an assignment requires shareholder approval under current law. Nonetheless, no modern bankruptcy court looks to state assignment law to answer this question. Indeed, it would appear that the Supreme Court cut the connection between assignments and bankruptcy in 1933. *Royal Indem. Co.* v. *Am. Bond & Mortg. Co.*, 289 U.S. 165, 171 (1933).

[28] In re Giggles Rest., Inc., 103 B.R. 549, 553 (Bankr. D.N.J. 1989).

[29] See *Quadrant Structured Prod. Co.* v. *Vertin*, 102 A.3d 155, 176 (Del. Ch. 2014).

[30] Cf. Chaim J. Fortgang & Thomas Moers Mayer, Trading Claims and Taking Control of Corporations in Chapter 11, 12 *Cardozo L. Rev.* 1, 64 (1990).

play, although perhaps that is best left to the "duty of loyalty" under state corporate law.

The courts' decision to forego a shareholder vote makes a lot of practical sense, but it would certainly be better if this policy choice were made express by the legislature, state or federal.

The debtor or its creditors (in an involuntary case) choose either chapter 7 or chapter 11 although that choice might be later altered by conversion to the other chapter. And sometimes cases are dismissed. Conversion does not create a "new" date of the filing of the petition, commencement of the case, or order for relief.[31] Dismissal results in orders and judgments being vacated, avoided liens and transfers being reinstated, and property revesting in whoever had it before the bankruptcy was commenced.[32]

When the case proceeds, federal law gives American bankruptcy courts exclusive jurisdiction "of all property, wherever located, of the debtor as of the commencement of such case, and of property of the estate."[33] This broad jurisdictional grant is matched by the equally broad language used in defining property of the bankruptcy estate, which consists of "all legal and equitable interests of the debtor in property as of the commencement of the case," and consists of all such property "wherever located and by whomever held."[34]

While eligibility and commencement are virtually unrestricted, and the jurisdiction of the court quite broad, the Code has three mechanisms that somewhat limit the scope of American bankruptcy cases. These are the court's abstention power in section 305, the court's power to dismiss a chapter 11 case for cause in section 1112(b) and the rules that govern co-ordination of concurrent US and foreign cases in sections 1528 and 1529.

Under both chapters 7 and 11, the estate is protected by the "automatic stay" – a statutory prohibition on taking estate assets, that is triggered by the order of relief. Creditors are paid from the estate, and the automatic stay prohibits attempts to collect outside that process.

---

[31] 11 U.S.C. § 348(a).
[32] 11 U.S.C. § 349.
[33] 28 U.S.C. § 1334(e)(1).
[34] 11 U.S.C. § 541(a).

A chapter 7 bankruptcy case invokes bankruptcy in the traditional sense. A trustee is appointed to take charge of the debtor's assets, which are transferred to a bankruptcy "estate," much like the estate of someone who has shuffled off this mortal coil. Those assets of the estate are turned into cash, and the proceeds distributed to creditors. Nearly every developed economy has a bankruptcy provision like this, and many developing economies inherited something that looks like this from their former colonial rulers.

The trustee's command is to maximize the return to creditors and the trustee's compensation is structured accordingly: she receives a percentage of the amount distributed to creditors, both secured and unsecured. Thus, the greater the return to creditors, the more the chapter 7 trustee may receive as compensation.

Unsecured creditors and shareholders rarely receive anything by way of distributions in a chapter 7 case.[35] And the company that files a chapter 7 case can never escape. There is no discharge of the company; it simply peters out or is dissolved under non-bankruptcy law.[36]

In a partnership case, the automatic stay only applies to the debtor entity itself, and not the constituent partners.[37] They have to file their own, personal bankruptcy cases if they want protection from creditors. In chapter 7, the jingle rule is overridden by federal law, and the partnership trustee participates in partner bankruptcies on the same level as other unsecured creditors, no matter what state the partnership was formed in.[38] The trustee also benefits from special powers to freeze the assets of non-bankrupt partners until it becomes clear how much they owe.

Importantly, these provisions are contained within chapter 7. Thus, in a chapter 11 case involving a partnership neither the debtor nor the

---

[35] Stephen J. Lubben, Business Liquidation, 81 *Am. Bankr. L.J.* 65 (2007).

[36] 11 U.S.C. § 727(a)(1).

[37] The federal bankruptcy laws have adopted an entity theory – at least in part, there are some inconsistencies (e.g., 11 U.S.C. § 101(32)(B)) – since the 1898 Bankruptcy Act. As I note later, this inconsistency is at least partially due to the adoption of the Code in 1978, before any of the proposed refinements to partnership law had made their way into actually enacted laws.

[38] 11 U.S.C. § 723.

trustee, if there is one, has any express ability to freeze partner assets.[39] Moreover, in chapter 11 the jingle rule arguably applies in those states that still operate under the UPA.[40] Thus, a New York partnership could be subject to the jingle rule under state law, not subject to it when an involuntary chapter 7 case is filed against it, and subject to it again if it successfully converts to chapter 11.

The primary effect on the partnership creditors of all this is on their ability to collect from individual partners. This will mainly come into play in those cases where partners attempt to obtain a release from their personal liability in the partnership's chapter 11 case, in exchange for a contribution made to the entity's bankruptcy plan. In the case of a New York partnership, those partners can rightly tell partnership creditors that they have but a subordinated claim against them under the jingle rule.

Moreover, the federal "repeal" of the jingle rule is often overstated.[41] The repeal only applies in the case where the partnership is in chapter 7 *and* the partner is in a case under chapter 7 of the Code as well. If neither condition obtains, normal state law would instead apply. For example, if the partnership is in chapter 11, or the individual partners stay out of bankruptcy, then the jingle rule has not been repealed in those states who still adhere to it.

This is a function of the indirect way in which repeal was achieved. Section 723(c) provides that the trustee "is entitled to distribution in such partner's case under section 726(a) of this title the same as any other claim of a kind specified in such section." Thus we need not only a chapter 7 trustee, operating under section 723 for the benefit of a bankrupt partnership, but also a partner-debtor who is subject to a distribution of assets under section 726. If the partner is not in

---

[39] The bankruptcy court still has whatever equitable power it may have to try to freeze such assets.

[40] Subject to the requirement in section 1129(a)(7) that every plan provide at least much as a hypothetical chapter 7 case – although it is important to remember that this would be a hypothetical chapter 7 of the partnership, and not the partners. Frank R. Kennedy, Partnerships and Partners under the Bankruptcy Code: Claims and Distribution, 40 *Wash. & Lee L. Rev.* 55, 61 (1983).

[41] Henry Hansmann et al., Law and the Rise of the Firm, 119 *Harv. L. Rev.* 1333, 1381 (2006) (stating that the jingle rule "remains in effect in England today, and was in force in the United States until 1978").

bankruptcy herself, the relevant provision is section 723(a), which does nothing to the jingle rule under state law.[42]

Moreover, there is an argument to be made that the debtor-trustee in a partnership chapter 11 could not exercise statutory rights to compel capital contributions from individual partners.[43] As noted earlier, federal law prohibits triggering of dissolution solely because of the bankruptcy filing of a partner, and a similar analysis would prohibit the dissolution and winding up of a partnership because of a bankruptcy filing by the partnership itself.[44] Under both the UPA and RUPA, the partners' obligation to fund the entity's shortfalls only comes into play once dissolution has been triggered.[45]

Under the RUPA, "[e]ach partner is entitled to a settlement of all partnership accounts upon winding up the partnership business ... A partner shall contribute to the partnership an amount equal to any excess of the charges over the credits in the partner's account." But this obligation comes in a provision that is expressly applicable to the winding up process. Therefore, even in states that have gone over to the newer form of partnership law, there will continue to be an issue as to whether property of the estate in chapter 11 cases includes claims against general partners for the deficiency in partnership assets to pay partnership liabilities.[46]

Partnership agreements may provide that partners are required to contribute further capital for ongoing operations of the entity. Such contractual arrangements should be enforceable by debtor or trustee, but that leaves a lot turning on the partnership agreement drafted long before the onset of financial distress.

---

[42] If the partner is solvent, the jingle rule is irrelevant in any event.

[43] This is already less attractive than proceeding under section 723, because in jingle rule states the capital contribution claim would come after all of the partner's individual creditors.

[44] The case law is a mass of confusion. Some courts held that the filing of a case under the Bankruptcy Code by a partner does not dissolve the partnership. In re Safren, 65 B.R. 566 (Bankr. C.D. Cal. 1986); In re Rittenhouse Carpet, Inc., 56 B.R. 131 (Bankr. E.D. Pa. 1985); In re Cardinal Industries, Inc., 105 B.R. 834 (Bankr. S.D. Ohio 1989). Contra In re Minton Group, Inc., 27 B.R. 385 (Bankr. S.D.N.Y. 1983), aff'd, 46 B.R. 222 (S.D.N.Y. 1985); In re Harms, 10 B.R. 817 (Bankr. D. Colo. 1981); In re Sunset Developers, 69 B.R. 710 (Bankr. D. Idaho 1987); In re Phillips, 966 F.2d 926 (5th Cir. 1992).

[45] The relevant provisions are UPA § 40(a) and RUPA § 807(b).

[46] Cf. In re Granite Partners, L.P., 194 B.R. 318, 339 (Bankr. S.D.N.Y. 1996).

In general, chapter 11 invokes much of the same language as chapter 7, but it truly is a different animal. Just as in chapter 7, the filing of a petition creates a bankruptcy estate made up of all the company's assets, formally separate from the pre-bankruptcy debtor-company.

But there is normally no trustee in chapter 11, or rather the debtor-company acts as if it were the trustee, under an arrangement known as "debtor in possession." The debtor, that is, is in possession of its own bankruptcy estate. The debtor, or "DIP" to use the lingo, runs the show.[47]

No other major jurisdiction goes quite so far. The closest analogue to chapter 11 is Canada's Companies' Creditors Arrangement Act, or CCAA, which applies to companies with debts over $5 million (Canadian).[48] The goal of the CCAA is approval of a plan of arrangement that restructures the company's debt package.

And while the CCAA leaves company management in place during a restructuring, in all cases the company is also subject to oversight by a court-appointed monitor.[49] The monitor's role is substantial, and suggests the degree to which even Canada is unwilling to accept chapter 11's broad deference to extant management:

> The minimum duties of the monitor include … reviewing cash-flow statements, appraising the financial state of affairs of the debtor company, advising the court of material adverse changes of the debtor company's finances, attending court proceedings, advising the court if, in the monitor's opinion, it would be more beneficial for creditors to proceeds under the [Bankruptcy and Insolvency Act], advising the court on the reasonableness of any compromise or arrangement that is proposed and filing reports to the court.[50]

In other jurisdictions, especially in Europe, there is often talk of embracing "chapter 11," but never of embracing the idea of the DIP, which is sometimes referred to with strong language and general derision. References to giving Captain Edward Smith – of the *RMS Titanic* – "another

---

[47] "DIP" is used without any apparent condescension.
[48] CCAA § 3(1). The CCAA is codified at R.S.C. 1985, ch. C-36, and available at https://goo.gl/v7ncsX.
[49] CCAA § 11.7
[50] Kevin P. McElcheran, *Commercial Insolvency in Canada 270–71* (3d ed. 2015).

try" also commonly arise in connection with foreigners' discussion of the DIP.

Under chapter 11 the DIP continues to operate its business, with no court oversight of routine operations. The ultimate goal is creditor approval of a reorganization plan that will revamp the company's capital structure, and often its operations as well.

In the meantime, the debtor-firm can sell off parts of its assets, or even all its assets. While state corporate law provides for assets sales as well, assets sold under federal bankruptcy law are less apt to be tainted by lingering liabilities incurred by the selling company.[51] In theory, this could be done in chapter 7 as well, but the separation of company management between the pre-bankruptcy board of directors and the post-bankruptcy trustee does not often assist such a move. Instead, a chapter 7 bankruptcy trustee is commonly dealing with a business that has ceased operations upon bankruptcy, if not earlier.

Under both chapters of the Bankruptcy Code, trustees and DIPs exercise special bankruptcy powers that non-insolvent companies could only dream of. Contracts and leases are sorted between those that the company would like to consider assets, and those the company would like to treat as debts. The latter are paid the same partial recoveries that creditors typically receive in chapter 11 cases – one common rule of thumb being that unsecured creditors obtain about a 45 percent recovery in chapter 11.[52]

Maintaining the going concern value of a business through chapter 11 can have a positive effect on other stakeholders: employees' jobs may be saved, customers' supply chains are not interrupted, and vendors do not lose a client. Ideally, the debtor's assets are also worth more as a going concern than in liquidation. These benefits come with a cost, however.

In a broad sense, chapter 11 costs more than chapter 7. This additional cost is the price creditors and other stakeholders pay for the greater recovery they typically obtain in chapter 11.

---

[51] See In re Motors Liquidation Company, 2017 BL 239623 (Bankr. S.D.N.Y. July 12, 2017).

[52] Although the growth of multiple layers of secured debt in capital structures may be putting some downward pressure on this old standard.

The direct costs of chapter 11 – the professional fees, mostly – are higher than chapter 7. Other costs are more indirect, but equally real. A large national retail company may use chapter 11 to reject leases at locations that are no longer profitable. The landlord's claims for breach of the lease are capped in bankruptcy, effectively forcing the lessor to pay for the lessee's restructuring. A similar effect can be seen when pension benefits are cut to save existing jobs. These are essentially policy motivated redistributions of value, with the aim of increasing overall value.

Other indirect costs include the time lost by both creditors and the debtor's employees when engaging in the chapter 11 process. This operates as a drag on the normal operations of both parties.

In chapter 11, a committee comprising the larger unsecured creditors is appointed to protect the interests of all unsecured creditors. The committee has standing to appear throughout the case and the debtor must consult with the committee on all important matters, including the plan. But the committee itself represents a cost: the estate pays for the committee's professionals, and a hostile or aggressive committee can drive up the cost of the DIP's own professionals.

Within bankruptcy, the estate is reshaped with a package of tools commonly referred to as "avoiding powers." Some, like the ability to reverse fraudulent transfers, exist under fundamental debtor-creditor law. Section 548 of the Code provides, for example, that a debtor may avoid a "constructive" fraudulent conveyance of the debtor's property that was made within two years of the bankruptcy where the debtor received less than a reasonably equivalent value in exchange and either was insolvent on the date of the transaction or became insolvent as a result.[53] Analogous provisions are found under the common or statutory law of all states. But many of the avoiding powers are unique to the bankruptcy system.

For example, the trustee, and thus the DIP as well, acquires a hypothetical lien on all the debtor's property.[54] This means that any other would-be secured creditors, who have not yet finalized their own liens before bankruptcy, will be bumped behind the trustee acting on behalf

---

[53] 11 U.S.C. §548(a)(1)(B).
[54] 11 U.S.C. § 544(a)(1).

of all creditors. The putative secured creditor becomes an unsecured creditor, and all benefit from the collateral.

The exercise of these avoidance powers, particularly the federal and state fraudulent transfer powers, become a bit confused when applied to general partnerships. Section 101(32) indicates that a partnership is insolvent when "the sum of such partnership's debts is greater than the aggregate of ... (i) all of such partnership's property, exclusive of property" fraudulently transferred, "and (ii) the sum of the excess of the value of each general partner's non-partnership property," again exclusive of fraudulently transferred property, "over such partner's non-partnership debts." Insolvency is a key issue in many fraudulent transfer actions, but this definition comes perilously close to adopting the old aggregate theory of partnership. Why should we care about the partner's assets, when claim is (at least nominally) against the entity?

Moreover, it raises the possibility in a chapter 11 case, where the debtor-trustee has little clear power to act against the individual partners, that the actions of the individual partners could still be quite important. If the excess value in the property of the general partner suffices to make the partnership solvent, what the partner does with that property is of great interest to the debtor and its creditors.

But the partner's individual property is not property of the entity's bankruptcy estate, and thus not subject to avoidance under the Bankruptcy Code or control in general by a bankruptcy court. It is more than a bit confusing, and reflects the Code's awkward position in relation to the development of partnership law. In 1978, when the Code was enacted, the old 1914 UPA was still in force in most states, but had been under strong academic attack for years. Unfortunately, the move to the new RUPA would not get underway until the 1980s, leaving the Code with one foot in the new world of partnership, while also having to reflect the law that was actually in force in 1978.

The confusion is further illustrated by the special avoidance provision in the Code for partners. Under this provision, any transfer of partnership assets and any obligation incurred by the partnership:

- made or incurred within two years of the bankruptcy filing;
- made to or in favor of a general partner of the debtor;
- if the debtor was insolvent on the date of the transfer, or was rendered insolvent by the transfer

is automatically avoidable.[55] Intent to defraud is not an element. Consent of the partners is immaterial. Even an exchange of "reasonably equivalent value" for the partnership's property does not prevent the avoidance of the transfer.[56]

Writing shortly after the Code's enactment, Richard Levin proclaimed that the "likely result is that the increased recovery to partnership creditors by avoidance of the transfer will be greater than the reduced recovery from the estate of the individual partners, as long as the administrative expense of recovering the transfer is not great."[57] Even putting administrative costs to one side, it is not clear how this could be so, given that the recovery provision is not limited to transfers that we would call "fraudulent" under any metric.

The provision seems to simply allow the shifting of money from one set of creditors to another, solely because it was shifted once already. It is a policy judgment in favor of the entity's creditors, and against the individual's creditors. In jingle-rule states it has a real effect because it gets partnership creditors out from under the rule's subordination. But what is the justification for that in the absence of a transfer that could be avoided under normal avoidance rules?

The waning role of general partnerships in American commercial life removes any pressure on Congress to address the situation. The Bankruptcy Reform Act of 1994 amended section 723 to address the issue of limited liability partnerships, and dispel any notion that the trustee could collect funds from individual partners who had no such liability under state law. Given that most courts have deemed limited liability partnerships to be "corporations" under the Bankruptcy Code,

---

[55] 11 U.S.C. § 548(b). ("The trustee of a partnership debtor may avoid any transfer of an interest of the debtor in property, or any obligation incurred by the debtor, that was made or incurred on or within 2 years before the date of the filing of the petition, to a general partner in the debtor, if the debtor was insolvent on the date such transfer was made or such obligation was incurred, or became insolvent as a result of such transfer or obligation.")

[56] The partner does get the benefit of section 548(c) ("a transferee or obligee of such a transfer or obligation that takes for value and in good faith has a lien on or may retain any interest transferred or may enforce any obligation incurred, as the case may be, to the extent that such transferee or obligee gave value to the debtor in exchange for such transfer or obligation").

[57] Richard B. Levin, An Introduction to the Trustee's Avoiding Powers, 53 *Am. Bankr. L.J.* 173, 182 (1979).

it was a sensible if perhaps needless change. It represents the only effort by Congress to address the Code's treatment of debtor-partners since 1978.[58]

Given the power of chapter 11, there is some temptation for business debtors to try to use chapter 11, while not appearing to do so, and thus avoiding the "taint" of bankruptcy. This is the American "prepack," which is a shortened version of an earlier slang description of these cases as "prepackaged chapter 11 cases."[59]

To understand prepacks, we have to step back and discuss another method of corporate reorganization known as an "exchange offer." When a distressed company has bonds outstanding, an exchange offer is the most likely, if not the only, option to complete an out-of-court restructuring. A prepack brings the restructuring "in court," for a very brief period of time, to get the benefits of chapter 11.

As the name suggests, an exchange offer is an offer to bondholders to swap existing bonds for something new, with the goal of resolving the debtor's financial problems. Thus, bonds might be exchanged for stock, or new debt that matures long in the future.

To take a recent example, in early 2017 retailer J. Crew Group, Inc. offered to exchange more than $560 million of its outstanding pay-ment-in-kind (PIK) notes[60] for $250 million in new 13 percent senior secured notes due in 2021, issued and guaranteed by a newly created subsidiary holding J. Crew's intellectual property, as well as $190 mil-lion of preferred stock and 15 percent of the common equity. That is, new debt (in a lesser amount) and some equity too.

Not surprisingly, holders of J. Crew's outstanding secured term loan complained about the transfer of the IP to the new subsidiary, and brought a lawsuit. The retailer approached its term loan lenders with a debt restructuring proposal to drop the lawsuit, in exchange for a 10 percent principal paydown of the term loan. Several hedge funds

---

[58] A more substantive reform effort in the mid-1990s did not gain traction. Morris W. Macey & Frank R. Kennedy, Partnership Bankruptcy and Reorganization: Proposals for Reform, 50 *Bus. Law.* 879 (1995).

[59] They should be distinguished from their British counterparts. In the United Kingdom, a "prepack" is more like an American "363 Sale," as described later in the chapter.

[60] Meaning that interest payments are paid with further debt, and no actual cash is paid until maturity.

that already owned the PIK notes reportedly purchased large stakes in the term loan, with the aim of taking this offer and further ensuring J. Crew's offer with regard to the PIK notes would go forward. Sharp elbows all around to be sure, but in July 2017 J. Crew disclosed that 99.85 percent of its $566.5 million PIK notes had been tendered into the exchange offer, and that the lawsuit had been dismissed.

Exchanges of public securities are governed by various regulations under the 1933 Securities Act, the 1934 Exchange Act, and the Trust Indenture Act of 1939. Most relevant for these purposes, the Trust Indenture Act requires that *all* holders consent to any change in timing or amount of interest and principal payments.

This means that exchange offers – standing alone – are purely consensual restructuring tools. A variety of techniques can be used to induce participation in the exchange. For example, bondholders are often asked to consent to the repeal of all covenants that can be changed by majority rule – typically this consent is given just before the bondholder swaps into a new security. Other exchange offers fund a cash offer for outstanding (non-callable) unsecured bonds by means of a secured bank loan. Either structure attempts to make remaining in the old debt instrument somewhat painful. But in the end, a bondholder that wants to hold out can do so.

This potentially leaves the debtor company with an annoying "stub" of old debt outstanding, in addition to whatever new securities are issued as part of the exchange offer. For example, in the case of J. Crew – where 99.85 percent of its $566.5 million PIK notes were tendered – 0.15 percent of the notes remain outstanding. In some cases the outstanding amount is even more substantial: 10 or 15 percent, perhaps. The prepack attempts to fix this problem.

A prepack is essentially an exchange offer that is run through a quickie chapter 11 case, to bind all bondholders to the terms of the deal. The Bankruptcy Code overrides the Trust Indenture Act, thus any and all terms of an outstanding bond issue can be changed if approved by the Code's voting majorities – two-thirds in amount and a majority in number of the bondholders.[61] In exchange for a month or so in bankruptcy, the defects of the exchange offer are cured.

---

[61] 11 U.S.C. § 1126(c).

This, of course, assumes that the debtor's problems are financial, rather than operational. For the latter, a "real" chapter 11 case will likely be in order.

But for a company with a simple problem of overabundant indebtedness – the targets of leveraged buyouts, like J. Crew, being obvious examples – several choices are on the table. First, the company may simply solicit approval of an exchange offer and then reassess its options if the exchange offer is not approved by a sufficient number of bondholders. Second, the issuer may combine the solicitation of approval of an exchange offer with the solicitation of approval of a prepackaged bankruptcy plan of reorganization, as a kind of backup in case the exchange offer does not get sufficient traction. Third, the issuer may solicit approval of a prepackaged bankruptcy plan that effectuates the securities exchange without even attempting an exchange offer – that is, cut to the chase.

Taken as a whole, the package of tools offered by the Bankruptcy Code – a stay against creditor action, an ability to recover preferential payments, which both promotes equity and reduces the chances of runs on the debtor, and an ability to revamp the debtor's operations by rejecting burdensome contracts and selling assets – provide a kind of baseline for comparison with other insolvency systems we will encounter on this tour.

The joint effects of the automatic stay, followed at the end of the case by a discharge of pre-bankruptcy debts, also provide another important feature of Bankruptcy Code which other insolvency systems seek to replicate, especially those that aim to save an existing business, rather than liquidate it.

During the bankruptcy case, the automatic stay protects the assets of the newly created estate from individual creditor action. After the bankruptcy case is over – at least in a chapter 11 case, where the debtor survives – the debtor's pre-bankruptcy debts are discharged by statute. That is, the pre-bankruptcy debts are no longer collectable against the debtor-firm. This discharge is the modern successor to the original discharge under English and colonial insolvency law, which was much more literal in application: it let the debtor-merchant out of debtors' prison.

In partnership cases, non-debtor partners frequently seek to be released at the time the plan is confirmed for the debtor partnership.

This has been approved in many cases, especially when it is deemed necessary to facilitate the payments by the partners to the partnership to carry out the plan.

In railroad cases, fourteen special Bankruptcy Code provisions – sections 1161 through 1174 – apply. Conversely, several other provisions of the Code do not apply.[62]

A "railroad" is defined in section 101(44) as a "common carrier by railroad engaged in the transportation of individuals or property or owner of trackage facilities leased by such a common carrier." That sweeps wider than the board-game, stripy overalls conception of "railroad."

For example, the Las Vegas Monorail, which filed a "normal" chapter 11 case back in 2010, arguably should have been subject to the special railroad provisions.[63] The parties agreed to look the other way, perhaps in part because under section 1163 the appointment of a trustee is mandatory in all railroad reorganization cases.[64] Trustees increase the cost of bankruptcy too.

Another notable feature of railroad chapter 11 cases is that the court is expressly instructed to consider the public interest. While one would hope that judges would generally hesitate to take action that flies in the face of the public interest, the statutory provision provides an explicit basis to resist the antisocial impulses of creditors.

Both the railroad and general provisions of chapter 11 have their roots in the equity receiverships of the nineteenth century. Receiverships, which are still used today, typically are collection devices for a secured creditor, who fears that the debtor is destroying the very asset that supports the creditor's debt.[65] For example, a lender with a mortgage against an apartment building might obtain a receiver to collect the rents and manage the building if the debtor was allowing the building to waste away.[66] When the federal government is

---

[62] 11 U.S.C. § 1161.

[63] See In re Las Vegas Monorail Co., 429 B.R. 770 (Bankr. D. Nev. 2010).

[64] The case is discussed in brief in Melissa B. Jacoby, What Should Judges Do in Chapter 11?, *2015 U. Ill. L. Rev.* 571, 581–2 (2015).

[65] See *CitiMortgage, Inc.* v. *Hubener*, 345 S.W.3d 193, 197 (Tex. App. 2011). See also *Hotel 71 Mezz Lender LLC* v. *Falor*, 926 N.E.2d 1202, 1212 (N.Y. 2010).

[66] See Colo. Rev. Stat. § 38-38-601.

owed money, it has a special power to request such a receiver in federal court.[67] There is also a long history of using receiverships when businesses violate federal law.[68]

Receivers were first used against railroads – the first large corporate debtors – in their traditional sense, including to collect money owed on secured mortgage bonds issued by the railroad.[69] But by the 1840s New York courts, based in part on special railroad statutes enacted in that state, were extending receiverships to provide equitable recoveries to all creditors. Thus, when a New York trial court pronounced a traditional receivership for a single creditor, the appellate court explained that

> the order appealed from should have extended the receivership to all the property and effects of the corporation, instead of limiting it to so much of such property and effects as would be sufficient to pay the debt and costs of the complainant merely.[70]

Within a few years, it seems that receiverships were commonly used to pay off the creditors of distressed railroads.[71] A similar early case from Georgia shows that this antebellum experimentation with a broader use of receiverships was not confined to the Empire State.[72]

By the Gilded Age, the basic ritual of the railroad receiverships had become well understood, and was often applied to all types of large corporations.[73] Because a secured creditor could only obtain a receiver to control the property covered by their mortgage – and railroad mortgages tended to be granted over specific lines or railyards whenever

---

[67] 28 U.S.C. § 3103.

[68] *United States* v. *Am. Tobacco Co.*, 221 U.S. 106, 186–7 (1911).

[69] *Pullan* v. *Cincinnati & C. Air-Line R. Co.*, 20 F. Cas. 32, 38 (C.C.D. Ind. 1865); *State* v. *N. Cent. Ry. Co.*, 18 Md. 193, 217 (1862); *Coe* v. *Columbus, P. & I.R. Co.*, 10 Ohio St. 372, 381 (1859).

[70] *Morgan* v. *N.Y. & A.R. Co.*, 1843 WL 4814 (N.Y. Ch. 1843).

[71] *Pentz* v. *Hawley*, 1845 WL 4301 (N.Y. Ch. 1845). See also *Mann* v. *Pentz*, 3 N.Y. 415, 419 (1850). These New York receiverships seem to have been based on special receivership statutes enacted within that state.

[72] *Macon & W.R. Co.* v. *Parker*, 9 Ga. 377, 393 (1851). ("It is admitted to be now an established rule of Chancery practice, that for the purpose of marshaling the assets of an insolvent debtor's estate, that the executor or administrator may file his bill and obtain a decree not only for the purpose of reducing the property to money, but also of ascertaining the order in which the debts are to be paid; and, that this done, all the creditors will be restrained from prosecuting their respective claims at Law.")

[73] E.g., *Leadville Coal Co.* v. *McCreery*, 141 U.S. 475 (1891); *Davis* v. *Gray*, 16 U.S. 203, 219 (1872).

the road might need further financing – it was quickly understood that these creditors should not make the first move.

Instead, an unsecured creditor would sue first, and at the same time seek the appointment of a receiver to take charge of all the debtor-railroad's property.[74] Ideally, the creditor would be a resident of some state other than the home state of the railroad, so that the jurisdiction of the federal courts could be invoked, with jurisdiction over an entire district and, in the case of circuit judges, perhaps some neighboring states too, whereas state courts were often limited to jurisdiction within the county of their appointment.[75]

Normally, an unsecured creditor cannot obtain a receiver until the creditor has received a final judgment on its debt, a receiver being more in the nature of a remedy than an end in itself. But if the defendant railroad were to file an answer admitting the validity of the debt, and its inability to pay the same, the courts felt comfortable moving quickly to the remedy stage.[76] The various mortgage holders would then appear, and file their claims for receiverships too. Often the same receivers would be appointed in all the suits.

The process ultimately led to an agreed-upon restructuring, under which the assets of the railroad would be sold in a foreclosure sale, and most creditors would agree to take securities in a new corporate entity that purchased the assets in the sale. There was no discharge in these receivership proceedings, but the objecting creditors' claims were against the old corporation that no longer had any assets. Dissenters were left with their proportionate share of the foreclosure sale proceeds, and little else.

In some senses, the railroad receivership process was akin to the modern English company administration under the Insolvency Act 1986. This is the core of English corporate insolvency

---

[74] 3 Clark on Receivers § 855 (3d ed. 1959).

[75] *Kingsport Press* v. *Brief English Sys.*, 54 F.2d 497 (2d Cir. 1931) contains a good description of the process, including the debtor's communication with its petitioning creditors and the ultimate appointment of the debtor's president as receiver.

[76] For a good overview of the procedure, see 3 Clark on Receivers, at page 1339. Eventually this process of "consent receivers" was adopted by the state courts too. See *New England Theatres, Inc.* v. *Olympic Theatres, Inc.*, 287 Mass. 485 (1934).

practice – supplemented by a robust "scheme of arrangement" system that facilitates workouts before default.[77]

Under administration, an administrator – typically from an accounting firm – takes charge of the debtor's assets. The administrator may be appointed in two ways: by court order upon application of the debtor, its directors or one or more of its creditors, or out of court, either by the debtor or its directors, or by the holder of a qualifying floating charge over the debtor's assets. The process

> is essentially a temporary measure which either lays the foundations for the rescue of the company ... or for the winding up on a more favourable basis ...[78]

Shortly after commencement, an "administration proposal" is sent to stakeholders. The administration proposal contains details regarding the administrator's appointment and how the administrator proposes to achieve a reorganization, and a general statement of the company's affairs. Included in each creditor's copy of the proposal will be an invitation to a creditors' meeting, which must be held within ten weeks of the commencement of administration.

Proposals can be accepted, modified and then accepted, or rejected. If they are rejected, the administrator is required to turn to the court to seek further directions, and in all events is required to send a report of the outcome of the meeting to the court. If accepted, the administrator manages the company's affairs, business, and property in accordance with the proposal.

Of course, the English system benefits from being codified, whereas the nineteenth century equity receivership process was largely court driven, and thus subject to disruption by each level of appellate process.[79]

---

[77] Oscar Couwenberg & Stephen J. Lubben, Corporate Bankruptcy Tourists, 70 *Bus. Law.* 719, 724 (2015). Schemes of Arrangement are found in the Companies Act 2006, Part 26, sections 895–901. Schemes can be used for restructurings or to implement an agreed upon moratorium that will facilitate a fuller reorganization. Approval requires a vote of 75 percent by value and a majority in number of the members of each scheme class.

[78] Andrew Keay & Peter Walton, *Insolvency Law: Corporate and Personal* 95 (2003).

[79] Before 2003, English law contained a procedure – "administrative receivership" – that was more like a traditional American receivership for secured creditor collection, and unlike the equity receivership process in that the receiver was under neither an obligation to rescue the business nor an obligation even to attempt to rescue it.

Assent to the American process was manifested by depositing securities with the creditors' committee, which then used those securities as the key consideration to purchase the debtor's assets. In addition, a small amount of cash would usually be paid to provide dissent bondholders with an "upset price" equal to the estimated liquidation value of the company. In other cases, the dissenters would be bought out by the committee to facilitate an entirely consensual plan.

As one court explained the process:

> When a non-depositing bondholder objects to confirmation solely on the ground that the reorganization committee's bid, though not grossly inadequate, was substantially short of the fair value, the answer is that his co-owners of the common mortgage and the common decree offered him the opportunity to deposit his bonds and to share equally with them the benefits of the purchase ...
>
> A reorganization plan is somewhat like an insurance policy, or a bill of lading, against which there is no protection except through legislative control of the insurance and railroad companies' offerings. The solitary and distant bondholder must accept the organization plan or let it alone, as it is written. When the unitary property of a single company of the kind in question is to be reorganized, the persons who assume or accept the committeeship, realizing the equality of all bondholders and recognizing that no bondholder has any right to preferential treatment, usually offer a plan that will give the common owners of the mortgage equal benefits through the foreclosure, usually become nothing but the agency through which the bondholders act for their mutual protection. In such a reorganization, if a bondholder does not come through the foreclosure as well off as any other bondholder, it is his own fault.[80]

The need to carefully stage-manage this process and its sequencing often led to cries of "collusion."[81] No doubt many of the receiverships

---

[80] *Inv. Registry* v. *Chicago & M.E.R. Co.*, 212 F. 594, 610–11 (7th Cir. 1913).

[81] In re Reisenberg, 208 U.S. 90, 110 (1908). ("In this case we can find no evidence of collusion, and the circuit court found there was none. It does appear that the parties to the suit desired that the administration of the railway affairs should be taken in hand by the circuit court of the United States, and to that end, when the suit was brought, the defendant admitted the averments in the bill, and united in the request for the appointment of receivers.") See also In re Paramount-Publix Corp., 10 F. Supp. 504, 508 (S.D.N.Y. 1934). ("The familiar old cry of 'collusion' in a consent equity receivership is advanced again here, but, as usual, it had not any merit.")

operated to "squeeze out" the small players at the expense of the insiders. But is not clear that the selection of a "friendly" unsecured creditor to get the process underway, often pointed to in support of such claims of collusion, really played the central role in such squeeze outs that critics claimed. And small creditors continue to get squeezed out even under modern, enlightened chapter 11.[82]

Even when the limitations of state court jurisdiction were avoided by putting the receivership into the federal court system, the process was cumbersome and expensive.[83] For example, ancillary receiverships had to be filed in every district – beyond the main proceeding – where the debtor had assets.[84] Sometimes the same receiverships might be appointed in these ancillary cases, but often a local attorney was also named as co-receiver, driving up the cost. And the sale process was susceptible to what today we might call successor liability claims – claims asserted against the new railroad by creditors of the old railroad who were not addressed by the receivership.

By at least the 1920s, practitioners were increasingly worried that the receivership process was also venerable to strike suits and "holdup artists."[85] The latter would demand special treatment in exchange for letting the receivership proceed. Increasingly sophisticated objecting

---

[82] Diane Lourdes Dick, Grassroots Shareholder Activism in Large Commercial Bankruptcies, 40 *J. Corp. L.* 1, 15 (2014). See also Roger S. Foster, *The Investor Pays* by Max Lowenthal. New York: Alfred A. Knopf, 1933, pp. 406; 43 *Yale L.J.* 352 (1933) (book review).

[83] *Ecker* v. *W. Pac. R.R. Corp.*, 318 U.S. 448, 469 (1943). ("Since railroads could not take advantage of the Bankruptcy Act ... their financial adjustments for years had been carried out in equity receiverships under judicial control. These were cumbersome, costly and privately managed with inadequate consideration for the public interest in a soundly financed transportation system.")

[84] Federal Practice Respecting Foreign Receiverships, 43 *Harv. L. Rev.* 805, 806–7 (1930). New York was (and still is) among the few states with a statute that permits out of state railroad receivers to "perform, within this state, the duties of his office not inconsistent with the laws of this state, and may sue and be sued in the courts of this state." N.Y. R.R. Law § 146. The same statute also provides for quick recognition of out of state foreclosures on railroad mortgages.

[85] Somewhat later, one student-author noted that "[n]o field of corporate affairs has been more attractive to the striker than reorganization." Extortionate Corporate Litigation: The Strike Suit, 34 *Colum. L. Rev.* 1308, 1317 (1934). Even earlier, a noted restructuring lawyer worried that "it is not exaggeration to say that the Supreme Court has simply placed a dangerous weapon in the hands of those guerillas who hang about the outskirts of reorganizations and endeavor to levy tribute as a condition of abating the nuisance of their presence." Adrian H. Joline, Railway Reorganizations, 4 *Brief* 1, 20 (1902).

creditors combined with increasingly skeptical – or at least less deferential – courts in ways that caused many to doubt the continued usefulness of equity receiverships.[86]

All of that came to a head during the Great Depression, when the need for a viable insolvency system for large businesses became too stark to ignore. Congress responded by codifying the railroad receivership process in 1933,[87] and providing a similar process for other corporations in 1934.[88] These two statutes are the seeds from which today's chapter 11 grew.[89]

Indeed, beginning with these two statutes, the use of receiverships as a reorganization tool began a swift decline. As the authors of the leading civil procedure treatise note, in "the twentieth century … the scope of federal equity receivership in this country diminished sharply as the scope of bankruptcy practice and other statutory receiverships have enlarged … the most frequently used form of federal equity receivership, known as the consent receivership, has all but disappeared."[90]

The question is whether these 1930s statutes and their successors entirely prohibited the further use of equity receiverships as a kind of corporate insolvency process in federal court. In the immediate wake of the statutes' enactment, some courts held that consent receiverships were still permissible.[91] The expectation was that receiverships would slowly fade away, given the more attractive statutory option, but that did not preclude the occasional use of consent receiverships.

---

[86] E.g., *First Nat. Bank of Cincinnati* v. *Flershem*, 290 U.S. 504, 517 (1934).

[87] Act of March 3, 1933, chap. 204, 47 Stat. 1474 (1933).

[88] Act of June 7, 1934, chap. 424, 48 Stat. 211 (1934).

[89] In 1938 the Chandler Act was adopted (52 Stat. 840). Section 77, relating to railroads, was retained, and Chapter X, Corporate Reorganizations, replaced former section 77B. Both section 77 and the Chandler Act were replaced by the current Bankruptcy Code in 1978.

[90] Charles Alan Wright et al., History and Purpose of Rule 66, 12 Fed. Prac. & Proc. Civ. § 2981 (2d ed.). See also Bankruptcy – Railroad Reorganization – Reorganization Under Consent Receivership Held Improper Where Statutory Reorganization Provisions Are Applicable, 57 *Harv. L. Rev.* 1114 (1944). ("Since the enactment of § 77, however, the railroads and their creditors have practically abandoned the use of equity receiverships in favor of the statutory system, so that the court in the [New England Coal & Coke Co.] case may have gone as far as necessary to assure the continuance of the recent railroad reorganization practices.")

[91] *Guaranty Trust Co. of New York* v. *Seaboard Airline Ry.*, 53 F. Supp. 672 (E. D. Va. 1943).

Other courts, including the Second Circuit Court of Appeals, held that the new statutes completely forbade any further use of the equity receivership process.[92] Receiverships pending before the statutes were enacted could continue, if the parties so desired, but it was said to be improper to commence new receiverships.[93]

On the other hand, during the rail crisis of the 1970s, Congress defined "railroad in reorganization" to mean not only railroads reorganizing under section 77 of the Bankruptcy Act, but also those in "an equity receivership or equivalent proceeding," which might suggest some belief that equity receiverships were, or at least could be, still in use in the 1970s.[94] And neither the text of the present chapter 11, nor old section 77 before it expressly indicate any actual intent to bar the use of equity receiverships.[95] Indeed, there was some possibility of failed section 77 cases ending up in a receivership.[96]

As we will see in a coming chapter, equity receiverships are still frequently used in connection with stock and commodity broker insolvencies, and in investment fraud cases.[97] The courts in these cases rarely address the old case law regarding the transition from equity to statute, but we might distinguish these SEC and CFTC cases as involving regulatory concerns not present in the more general use of receiverships as a reorganization mechanism. Moreover, as indicated, there are good reasons to doubt the authority against receiverships that does exist. And thus the broader question remains unanswered.

In theory, then, a debtor and its creditors, outside these specific regulatory contexts, might try to address insolvency through a general receivership, filed either by an unsecured creditor or by a secured creditor with a blanket lien on all the debtor's assets.[98] With regard to

[92] *New England Coal & Coke Co.* v. *Rutland R. Co.*, 143 F.2d 179, 185 (2d Cir. 1944).

[93] *Badenhausen* v. *Guar. Trust Co. of N.Y.*, 145 F.2d 40, 51 (4th Cir. 1944).

[94] 45 U.S.C. § 702(16).

[95] 49 Stat. 911, 921–2 (1935).

[96] Order Transferring Railroad Reorganization from Bankruptcy to Equity Reversed, 103 U. Pa. L. Rev. 966 (1955).

[97] E.g., *Liberte Capital Grp., LLC* v. *Capwill*, 248 F. App'x 650, 652 n.2 (6th Cir. 2007).

[98] Max Lowenthal, The Railroad Reorganization Act, 47 *Harv. L. Rev.* 18 (1933). ("Section 77 does not abolish the old procedure. In consequence, if directors, bankers, or lawyers advising or having influence over a railroad board prefer the old procedure, they may arrange for an equity receivership of the old type. Whether they will succeed depends upon the judge to whom they apply.")

the former, we might worry that the consent receivership process is so long forgotten that any modern effort would necessarily involve a degree of collusion that might even exceed that of the "good old days." It is hard to imagine a modern district court judge joining in these efforts.[99]

Those provisos aside, federal courts could reorganize a company through a receivership, and the federal court enjoys a jurisdictional advantage over its state counterpart because the old ancillary receivership process is now greatly simplified.[100] Indeed, one hears of such receiverships – typically based on diversity among the parties – in the stories told at bankruptcy conferences. Finding actual proof of their existence is more challenging. But maybe they are out there.

One example might be seen in the case of Auster Acquisitions, LLC, a Chicago produce wholesaler.[101] When it began to experience financial distress, it was beset by claims under the Perishable Agricultural Commodities Act, the vegetarian counterpart to the Packers and Stockyards Act of 1921, which I discuss later in this chapter. In short, that law provides for a kind of robust priority for farmers who sell to produce dealers.

Faced with the looming dismemberment of its collateral, and the possibility that management might simply walk away from the business, the company's secured lender moved for "the appointment of a receiver to marshal the assets of Auster in an orderly fashion pursuant to Federal Rule of Civil Procedure 66."

In early 2011, the court "entered a consent order appointing the Receiver and authorizing him to liquidate and distribute Auster's assets to the holders of allowed claims on a pro-rata basis pursuant to court order."[102] In 2014, the receiver was discharged.

---

[99] *Gilchrist* v. *General Elec. Capital Corp.*, 262 F.3d 295, 304 (4th Cir. 2001). ("While it is true that the district court has broad equity power, any attempt to use that power to supervise a complex corporate liquidation, in the absence of special circumstances, would ultimately be more clumsy and expensive than long-established bankruptcy procedures.")

[100] 28 U.S.C. § 754.

[101] *C.H. Robinson Worldwide, Inc.* v. *Auster Acquisitions, LLC et al.*, Docket No. 1:11-cv-00105 (N.D. Ill. Jan. 07, 2011).

[102] Note that the receiver was charged dealing with all claims, making this case somewhat broader than the more common receiverships used by secured creditors to protect their interests.

Given some sense that receiverships are less costly than chapter 11 cases, and that chapter 11 costs are rising, federal receiverships might become more common.[103] Whether receiverships are actually cheaper than chapter 11 cases is unclear, given the lack of directly comparable data. But in the above-mentioned vegetable case, the receiver and counsel charged the estate some $370,000 in fees, plus another $74,000 in expenses, to distribute about $800,000 to creditors, with the unvalued residue turned over to the secured lenders.

If representative, that does not seem much better than what could be achieved in chapter 11. And the threat of an involuntary bankruptcy filing – or even a voluntary filing by the company's board, if the receivership order does not swiftly take away their power over the company – remains a potent issue.

On the other hand, recent chapter 11 practice has moved toward a model that looks like an equity receivership. Rather than negotiate a full reorganization plan, by the mid-1990s it had become common to sell all the debtor's assets under a quick "363 sale" – named for section 363 of the Code – and then distribute the sale proceeds under a chapter 11 plan that provided for the liquidation of the debtor. In the high-profile *General Motors* and *Chrysler* chapter 11 cases, the quick sale process looked even more like the old receivership process, because the purchasing companies were newly created entities, backed by the United States and Canadian governments.

Nevertheless, the degree to which these cases, and chapter 11 practice in general, has moved back to the old days is easy to overstate. Modern chapter 11 sales are always subject to an open auction process – whereas the railroads of old were typically sold in sales with very limited opportunities to counterbid – and the transparency inherent in modern chapter 11 is beyond anything that J. P. Morgan and his advisors would have ever tolerated in the "good old days."

Moreover, even the automotive cases were not that unique if one considers that most well-advised asset buyers, be they public or

---

[103] But complaints about the cost of receiverships are equally common, although the frequent use of receiverships in fraud cases might somewhat skew the analysis. E.g., Scott Daugherty, Payout disputes remain as Wextrust saga nears an end, Virginia Pilot (Jan. 12, 2015), at https://goo.gl/OvutCq.

private, purchase assets through a newly created subsidiary. Indeed, in or out of bankruptcy, deals are routinely done with "triangular" structures that cabin the liability exposure of the acquiring firm in the new subsidiary.

As noted, to the extent federal court receiverships are still used today, they tend to be based on diversity of citizenship between the plaintiff and the defendant and an amount in controversy exceeding $75,000.[104] But in a few cases there might be a direct, federal cause of action.[105]

For example, in actions to appoint receiver of a ship registered in the United States, the federal courts will have jurisdiction regardless of the amount in controversy or the citizenship of the parties.[106] When the government holds the mortgage, the Transportation Secretary can be appointed as receiver.[107] Ironically, in one of the handful of reported decisions under these receivership provisions, a court of appeals complained that "[w]hat happened here is all too reminiscent of what used to happen in the former and unlamented federal equity receiverships of railroads."[108] In particular, the court felt that the government had delayed foreclosing on its mortgage, while allowing the ship in question to continue to operate at the expense of other creditors.

In all cases, the goal of a receivership used as restructuring tool is much like that in bankruptcy: consolidate control over the debtor's assets in a party that will act in the interests of all creditors. Consolidation is achieved not only by empowering one party to act for all, but also by preventing action by others. In bankruptcy, this is done by the dual effects of the automatic stay and the creation of the bankruptcy estate, in a receivership the federal court obtains jurisdiction over the debtor's property, enjoins action without the court's consent

---

[104] 28 U.S.C. § 1332(a). See also *Hoagland ex rel. Midwest Transit, Inc.* v. *Sandberg, Phoenix & von Gontard, P.C.*, 385 F.3d 737, 738 (7th Cir. 2004). "The appointment of a receiver in a diversity case is a procedural matter governed by federal law and federal equitable principles." *Aviation Supply Corp.* v. *R.S.B.I. Aerospace, Inc.*, 999 F.2d 314, 316 (8th Cir.1993).

[105] *Cagan* v. *Intervest Midwest Real Estate Corp.*, 774 F. Supp. 1089, 1093 (N.D. Ill. 1991).

[106] 46 U.S.C. § 31325(c), (e).

[107] 46 U.S.C. § 50305(a). And the Secretary has the power to veto the appointment of anyone else as receiver.

[108] *Nw. Marine Works* v. *United States*, 307 F.2d 537, 542 (9th Cir. 1962) (decided under 46 U.S.C. § 952, the predecessor to 46 U.S.C. § 31325(e)).

and, in the case of an old-style equity receivership, oversees the transfer of the debtor's assets to an entity beyond the reach of creditors.

Beyond receiverships and bankruptcy, and the law of financial institutions I address elsewhere, federal insolvency law becomes a bit sparse. One special provision provides for the restructuring of overstretched pension plans[109] – not exactly *business* insolvency law; more like its second derivative.

The word "insolvency" or its variants (e.g., insolvent) appears in more than 200 provisions in the US Code, although in some cases that includes notes and other material that is not strictly speaking "the law." Almost forty of those references come in title 11 – the Bankruptcy Code. A similar number of provisions relate to SIPA[110] and Dodd-Frank's "orderly liquidation authority."

Most uses of the word are not what we would call "insolvency laws." For example, one of the first references to insolvency requires the Commodities Futures Trading Commission to consider

> the existence of reasonable legal certainty in the event of the insolvency of the relevant derivatives clearing organization or 1 or more of its clearing members with regard to the treatment of customer and swap counterparty positions, funds, and property.[111]

This is related to the central clearing of swaps as part of the Dodd-Frank Act's reforms of derivative markets after the financial crisis. While the provision raises interesting questions for those of us who spend lots of time thinking about issues of insolvency, and prompts one to consider the laws that apply upon the insolvency of a clearinghouse or members of the same, it is not itself an "insolvency law."[112]

Perhaps somewhat closer is the Packers and Stockyards Act of 1921,[113] although the act is really aimed to protect livestock sellers from the effects of their counterparties' insolvency. Meat packers

---

[109] 26 U.S.C. § 418E. See also 26 U.S.C. § 432; 29 U.S.C. § 1426

[110] The "Securities Investor Protection Act of 1970." 15 U.S.C. § 78aaa. Covered in a future chapter.

[111] 7 U.S.C. § 2(h)(2)(D)(ii)(V). The SEC is given a similar task by 15 U.S.C. § 78c-3(b)(4)(B)(v).

[112] Accord 7 U.S.C. § 7a-1(c)(2(G)(i) (requiring clearinghouses to have rules to address a member's insolvency).

[113] 7 U.S.C. §§ 181-229.

whose average annual purchases of livestock exceed $500,000, and "every other person operating as a dealer" must maintain a bond as a means of protecting livestock sellers. All livestock buyers must pay for purchased animals quickly – typically within a day – and dealers are required to maintain a statutory trust for the benefit of unpaid sellers. The Agriculture Secretary also has strong powers to enjoin buying by insolvent dealers, and otherwise force market participants to address their financial distress.[114] But the statute does not itself provide for any sort of debt adjustment.[115]

Other similar federal statutes allow Gallaudet University to access the corpus of its endowment, if needed to avoid insolvency,[116] while another provides similar protection to the Helen Keller National Center.[117] Yet another provides the government with special priority in any insolvency proceeding outside the Bankruptcy Code.[118] But all are really about avoiding the consequences of insolvency, rather than addressing insolvency itself.

The Treasury Secretary has the authority to regulate companies that give surety bonds under federal statutes. The Secretary is instructed to revoke the surety corporation's license if the company becomes insolvent – the companies are required by the same statute to file quarterly financial reports.[119] Again, not so much an insolvency law as it is a law to keep insolvency at arm's length.

More promising is the statute which acknowledges the Federal Election Commission's ability to formulate rules regarding "the orderly liquidation of an insolvent political committee."[120] But it does not appear that the Commission has ever enacted such rules, even if such a committee were considered a business.[121]

---

[114] E.g., 7 U.S.C. § 228a.
[115] Many of the financial protections outlined above also do not apply to "swine packers." Perhaps the pig buyers have better lobbyists? I leave the requisite snarky remark to the reader's ingenuity.
[116] 20 U.S.C. § 4357(d)(3)(B)(i).
[117] 29 U.S.C. § 1907(d)(3)(B)(i).
[118] 31 U.S.C. § 3713.
[119] 31 U.S.C. § 9305(c), (d).
[120] 52 U.S.C. § 30103(d)(2).
[121] West Virginia is apparently the only state with similar provisions in its law. W. Va. Code § 3-8-4a(b).

In short, the general federal law of business insolvency is rather sparse. Sure, the Bankruptcy Code is a dominant force in this area, but it is also a rather grand and expensive business insolvency tool. For smaller businesses, state law alternatives could provide a more attractive solution.

But the federal Constitution stands in the way. While we will examine myriad state statutes in upcoming chapters, all must deal with the reality of the Contracts Clause – article I, section 10, clause 1, which provides that "No State shall ... pass any ... Law impairing the Obligation of Contracts."

From early days, this was held to bar application of state insolvency laws to contracts that were signed before the state statute was passed.[122] Such state insolvency laws are also limited to addressing contracts and creditors that are within the jurisdiction of the state court – a contract signed in London with a British creditor would be outside the reach of a state insolvency law, unless the creditor voluntarily came within the jurisdiction.[123]

Debtors, too, are only subject to the insolvency laws of their state of residence – thus a partnership insolvency proceeding would only directly bind the partners within the state.[124] That means that only the insolvency laws of key commercial jurisdictions – New York and California, for example – are apt to be useful to larger businesses.

As summarized by the New York Court of Appeals, in an age when these topics were all the rage:

> under the decisions of the supreme court of the United States it must now be held, that a discharge under an insolvent law of this state, will not be a bar even in this state, to an action on a contract made or debt contracted in another state between parties residing there at the time; nor will it discharge a debt contracted within this state by a citizen of the state, as against a creditor who is a citizen

---

[122] *Sturges* v. *Crowninshield*, 17 U.S. 122 (1819).

[123] *Baldwin* v. *Hale*, 68 U.S. 223, 234 (1863). ("Insolvent laws of one State cannot discharge the contracts of citizens of other States, because they have no extra-territorial operation, and consequently the tribunal sitting under them, unless in cases where a citizen of such other State voluntarily becomes a party to the proceeding, has no jurisdiction in the case. Legal notice cannot be given, and consequently there can be no obligation to appear, and of course there can be no legal default.")

[124] *Schmidt* v. *Ellis*, 38 A. 382, 382 (N.H. 1897).

of another state. Bankrupt and insolvent laws of a foreign nation, or of a sister state having no force here, statutory assignments made under the authority of these laws, are not recognised by our courts, as having any validity, or as affecting any property of the bankrupt or insolvent in this state.[125]

Prospective state insolvency laws have been upheld, subject to the same jurisdictional limitations outlined above.[126] On the other hand, some cases from the early era suggested that states could alter creditors' remedies without triggering the Clause.[127] Small erosions of contract rights were regarded as permissible, but large deviations were not, even though the Clause speaks of all impairments in absolute terms.

Where exactly this line falls is still unclear. Moreover, it has long been (convincingly) argued that any jurisdictional limits on state insolvency laws should be a function of due process, rather than the Bankruptcy or Contracts Clauses, which were the subjects of these early decisions.[128] Nonetheless, the Supreme Court has never overruled its far-reaching early nineteenth century insolvency jurisprudence.

Recent case law regarding the interaction of state insolvency laws and the Contracts Clause has been sparse, given that a broadly applicable federal bankruptcy law has been in effect since the late 1890s. Outside the insolvency context, during the New Deal the court indicated that the Clause – like the Commerce Clause and the Due Process

---

[125] *Hoyt* v. *Thompson*, 5 N.Y. 320, 349–50 (1851) (citations omitted). See also Corporations – Reorganization – Effect Upon Claims of Non-Resident Creditors, 43 *Harv. L. Rev.* 1154, 1155 (1930) ("… the rule is well settled that such creditors, who were not served within the jurisdiction, and have not voluntarily appeared in the proceedings, are not affected").

[126] *Ogden* v. *Saunders*, 25 U.S. 213 (1827) (contract was properly discharged under New York state law insolvency proceeding enacted before the contract was signed, and such proceeding did not offend federal bankruptcy powers). What part of the Constitution supports the geographic limits on state insolvency laws remains a bit vague – especially when we remember this was before any federal due process clause applied to state governments. David P. Currie, The Constitution in the Supreme Court: The First Hundred Years, 1789–1888 at 154–5 (1985). ("Justice Johnson composed a mysterious cadenza [to Ogden v. Saunders, noting the geographic limitation] … It seems certain that this section was not based upon the contract clause; to determine what it was based on is appreciably more difficult …")

[127] See, e.g., Joseph Story, Commentaries on the Constitution of the United States § 1385 (2d ed. Boston, MA: C.C. Little and Brown, 1851).

[128] See generally Hollis R. Bailey, A Discharge in Insolvency, and Its Effect on Non-Residents, 6 *Harv. L. Rev.* 349 (1893).

Clause of the 14th Amendment, as applied to economic matters[129] – was more flexible than previously indicated.[130] In short, the state and federal legislature would be granted substantial deference when exercising traditional police powers, despite the strict language of the Contracts Clause.

In one of the more recent Supreme Court cases on the Clause generally, the court explained that examination of state laws under the Clause involves a three-part inquiry:

- whether a statute represents a "substantial impairment" of contract rights;
- if so, whether the law serves a "significant and legitimate public purpose," such as "the remedying of a broad and general social or economic problem";
- and, finally, whether the means of serving that purpose are "reasonable" and "appropriate." On this point, the Supreme Court suggested strong deference to legislative justifications.[131]

How this new reformulation interacts with the earlier case law on the specific issue of state insolvency laws is uncertain, although the suggestion in some of the more recent cases that broad regulatory measures are permissible, while those that target contracts specifically are not, may indicate that state insolvency laws remain problematic for Contracts Clause purposes.[132]

In addition, state insolvency laws are often subject to challenge on the basis that they have been pre-empted by the federal Bankruptcy Code.[133] Again, the case law in this area is rather confused, but a few basic principles can be distilled.

First, there is no dormant Bankruptcy Clause, in contrast to the dormant Commerce Clause. When Congress does not use its bankruptcy powers, the states retain the right to legislate in the area.

---

[129] E.g., *West Coast Hotel* v. *Parrish*, 300 U.S. 379 (1937); *Nebbia* v. *New York*, 291 U.S. 502 (1934).

[130] *Home Bldg. & Loan Ass'n* v. *Blaisdell*, 290 U.S. 398, 428–30 (1934).

[131] *Energy Reserves Grp., Inc.* v. *Kansas Power & Light Co.*, 459 U.S. 400, 412-13 (1983). See also *Gen. Motors Corp.* v. *Romein*, 503 U.S. 181, 186 (1992).

[132] *Exxon Corp.* v. *Eagerton*, 462 U.S. 176, 192 (1983).

[133] *Cattle Raisers Loan Co.* v. *Doan*, 86 S.W.2d 252, 255 (Tex. Civ. App.), writ refused, 86 S.W.2d 1082 (Tex. 1935).

Next, when Congress does utilize its bankruptcy power, the states are precluded from enacting laws that provide debtors with a discharge.[134]

And finally, traditional state insolvency laws that do not provide a discharge are permissible. For example, assignments for the benefit of creditors and receivership statutes are generally permissible.[135]

What this summary does not address – because it remains unclear – is what features of a state law beyond a discharge may cause it come into conflict with the Bankruptcy Code.[136] In a series of cases the Supreme Court has noted that "one of the principal requisites of a true bankruptcy law" is that it operates "for the benefit of the debtor in that it discharges his future acquired property from the obligation of existing debts."[137] But it has not provided any further guidance.

For example, recall that the old railroad receiverships did not involve a discharge per se, but achieved something similar through the sale of assets, free from most liabilities, to a new corporation. If state receivership laws start to mimic the federal Bankruptcy Code in all respects save the formal matter of giving a discharge, but provide for something similar, might they "cross the line" to such a degree that the Supreme Court would strike them down? The answer is unclear, in large part because the Court has not waded into this area in decades.

So our tour moves on, and looks at these state insolvency laws in more detail.

---

[134] *Int'l Shoe Co.* v. *Pinkus*, 278 U.S. 261, 265–6 (1929). ("Congress did not intend to give insolvent debtors seeking discharge, or their creditors seeking to collect claims, choice between the relief provided by the Bankruptcy Act and that specified in state insolvency laws. States may not pass or enforce laws to interfere with or complement the Bankruptcy Act or to provide additional or auxiliary regulations.")

[135] *Pobreslo* v. *Joseph M. Boyd Co.*, 287 U.S. 518 (1933).

[136] See generally Alan J. Feld, The Limits of Bankruptcy Code Preemption: Debt Discharge and Voidable Preference Reconsidered in Light of Sherwood Partners, 28 *Cardozo L. Rev.* 1447 (2006) (arguing that discharge is the only basis for preemption).

[137] *Stellwagen* v. *Clum*, 245 U.S. 605, 616 (1918).

3   STATE BUSINESS INSOLVENCY LAW

Until the Bankruptcy Act was signed into law by President William McKinley in the summer of 1898, the federal law of business failure consisted of three laws, each of brief duration.[1] But it is important to recollect that throughout the first half of its existence, save for during the Civil War, the federal government was almost a non-entity, which did little more than run the post office and collect tariffs.[2] Seen in this broader context, the congressional hesitation to use the powers granted by the Bankruptcy Clause becomes more understandable.

As a result, modern state insolvency law rests on a foundation of more than a century during which such law was the primary source of American business insolvency law. This law takes a variety of forms, and each state differs in fine detail, but two key clusters of law in this area are assignments and receiverships. And then there is the law that creates business entities, which often also provides for statutory rules regarding the entity's dissolution.

The most basic form of state business insolvency law is the composition. Compositions have a long history. For example, in Benjamin Franklin's *Autobiography*, he describes a friend:

> He had formerly been in business at Bristol, but failed in debt to a number of people, compounded and went to America. There, by a

---

[1] All of this history is discussed in detail in Stephen J. Lubben, A New Understanding of the Bankruptcy Clause, 64 *Case W. Res. L. Rev.* 319 (2013). For a brief historical overview of the comparable Canadian insolvency law, see Janis Sarra, *Creditor Rights and the Public Interest* 10–17 (2003).

[2] See Daniel Okrent, Last Call: The Rise and Fall of Prohibition 54–5 (2010) (in 1910, 30 percent of federal revenue came from liquor taxes, with the remainder from the tariff).

close application to business as a merchant, he acquired a plentiful fortune in a few years. Returning to England in the ship with me, he invited his old creditors to an entertainment, at which he thank'd them for the easy composition they had favoured him with, and, when they expected nothing but the treat, every man at the first remove found under his plate an order on a banker for the full amount of the unpaid remainder with interest.

These lucky creditors were atypical, as their surprise attests. The legislative history to the 1978 Bankruptcy Code addressed the role of compositions, as contrasted with the Code:

> Most business arrangements, that is, extensions or compositions (reduction) of debts, occur out-of-court. The out-of-court procedure, sometimes known as a common law composition, is quick and inexpensive. However, it requires near universal agreement of the business's creditors, and is limited in the relief it can provide for an over-extended business. When an out-of-court arrangement is inadequate to rehabilitate a business, the bankruptcy laws provide an alternative. An arrangement or reorganization accomplished under the Bankruptcy Act binds non-consenting creditors, and permits more substantial restructuring of a debtor's finances than does an out-of-court work-out ... When a petition is filed, all creditor actions against the debtor are stayed. The stay gives the debtor the opportunity to bring all of its creditors together for discussion, explanation of the debtor's financial problems, and negotiation.[3]

In short, composition agreement is an agreement made between a debtor and two or more of its creditors whereby the creditors agree to be paid a specified amount, often on a deferred schedule, in full satisfaction of the amount that is owed to them.[4] But a composition is something more than a series of agreements between the debtor and its creditors to accept something less than what is owed. Instead, a composition is a joint agreement among all the consenting creditors and the debtor.[5]

---

[3] H.R. Rep. No. 95-595, at 220–1 (1977).

[4] *Hyman* v. *Sabic Innovative Plastics US, LLC*, No. FSTCV086001098S X08, 2011 WL 2611805, at *4 (Conn. Super. Ct. June 8, 2011).

[5] *Cadle Co.* v. *Int'l Bank of Commerce*, No. 04-06-00456-CV, 2007 WL 752260, at *3 (Tex. App. Mar. 14, 2007).

A composition agreement supplants all the former obligations of the debtor and creates a binding contract among all. And once a debtor has fully performed – in particular, paid the agreed portion of the claims – the debtor cannot be sued for the original debt.[6]

A composition, particularly one that involves payments over time, may utilize a trustee or payment agent, both to distribute payments to participating creditors and to collect future payments from the debtor for distribution. In this sense, they begin to resemble assignments.

Assignments – also known as general assignments or, more formally, assignments for the benefit of creditors[7] – have been used as a business insolvency tool for centuries, and with regard to incorporated entities for more than a century.[8] Although formally limited to business liquidations, they can be combined with a going concern sale of the debtor's assets.

When the sale is to a new entity organized by the debtor's insiders, an assignment essentially works as a reorganization tool.[9] More broadly, assignments "reflect the policy favoring general assignments for the benefit of creditors (which contemplate the ratable distribution to creditors of the assignor's assets) over attachment (which permits an unsecured creditor to establish a priority over other unsecured creditors)."[10]

But as with all state law, assignments are limited in scope by the geographic boundaries of the state itself. Personal property might be moved within the jurisdiction, but real estate is another matter entirely.[11]

---

[6] *Schild* v. *Quality Furs, Inc.*, 170 N.Y.S.2d 107, 108 (App. Term 1957).

[7] General assignments, as opposed to partial assignments, which tend to involve the assignment of specific assets to satisfy a creditor. Bruce H. Greenfield, Partial Assignments for the Benefit of Creditors, 49 *Yale L.J.* 1325 (1940). Some states prohibit partial assignments, e.g., Iowa Code Ann. § 681.1; Mo. Ann. Stat. § 426.010; Wash. Rev. Code Ann. § 7.08.010, although we might wonder about the effectiveness of such a prohibition.

[8] In Alabama, assignments are referred to as "express trust[s] … for the payment or security of debts." Ala. Code § 19-3-20.

[9] Edward R. Morrison, Bargaining Around Bankruptcy: Small Business Workouts and State Law, 38 *J. Legal Stud.* 255 (2009).

[10] Cal. Civ. Proc. Code § 493.020 (1977 Law Revision Commission comments). See also Wis. Stat. Ann. § 128.03.

[11] Some states nonetheless try to include such property within their assignments. Ohio Rev. Code Ann. § 1313.16.

They are also vulnerable to involuntary bankruptcy petitions.[12] Section 303(h)(2) of the Bankruptcy Code provides that an involuntary petition may be filed within a period of 120 days after the making of an assignment for the benefit of creditors. And even if the assignment makes it past 120 days, it still may be disturbed by a filing under section 303(h)(1), which permits an involuntary petition when the creditor can show that the debtor is not generally paying its debts as they become due. Any business which has made an assignment for the benefit of creditors is always not paying its debts as they become due, since it has no assets with which to do so.

Likewise, assignments are often of little use to a publicly traded company. The assignment will arguably constitute a transfer of substantially all assets, requiring shareholder approval.[13] In a publicly traded company this invokes the federal proxy rules, with all their attendant cost. In a private company, on the other hand, board and shareholder approval might involve the same group of individuals.

That is, at least, the traditional analysis. In days of yore, corporate statutes were often much more skeletal and courts routinely found that boards had the inherent power to assign the company's assets without shareholder approval.[14] And if we actually look at the relevant statutory provisions, we find they vary a lot, depending on the state in question. In Washington it appears that boards can still assign without shareholder consent,[15] in Illinois they clearly may not,[16] and in Delaware, and many other places, it is a bit unclear. In particular, Delaware requires a shareholder vote whenever the corporation wants to "sell, lease or exchange all or substantially all of its property and assets."[17] Is a transfer

---

[12] See In re O'Reilly & Collins, 2013 WL 4548260, at *1 (Bankr. N.D. Cal. Aug. 26, 2013).

[13] David S. Kupetz, Assignment for the Benefit of Creditors: Effective Tool for Acquiring and Winding Up Distressed Businesses, Bus. L. Today, November 2015, at 1.

[14] E.g., *Sargent v. Webster*, 54 Mass. 497, 503 (1847); *Calumet Paper Co. v. Haskell Show-Printing Co.*, 45 S.W. 1115, 1115 (Mo. 1898).

[15] Wash. Rev. Code Ann. § 23B.12.010.

[16] 805 Ill. Comp. Stat. 5/11.60. Accord Cal. Corp. Code § 9631; NY Bus. Corp. L. § 909.

[17] Del. Code Ann. tit. 8, § 271. ("Every corporation may at any meeting of its board of directors or governing body sell, lease or exchange all or substantially all of its property and assets, including its goodwill and its corporate franchises, upon such terms and conditions and for such consideration, which may consist in whole or in part of money or other property, including shares of stock in, and/or other securities of, any other corporation or corporations, as its board of directors or governing body deems expedient and for the

to an assignee a sale, lease or exchange?[18] Arguably no, especially when contrasted with laws in other states that also expressly include "transfers," but then again, the overall structure of the Delaware General Corporation Law suggests shareholders should have a vote here, given that they provide an independent check on management in all other significant transactions. The Delaware courts tend toward statutory literalism, but it would still be a bold attorney who advised a client to proceed with an assignment without a shareholder vote.

The issue is sometimes clearer with regard to partnerships, depending on which jurisdiction the partnership was formed in. Under the old 1914 UPA, still in force in New York and a few other states, assignments require unanimous consent of the partners.[19] The newer RUPA then muddies the waters by repealing the specific list of actions requiring unanimous consent, and instead throwing the court back on the question of whether or not a particular action is outside the ordinary course of business.[20] Presumably an assignment always will be non-ordinary course, but the RUPA reduces the certainty of the UPA in this regard. Newer is not necessarily better.

Before the New Deal, assignments were often made to a creditors' committee who then acted as the assignee.[21] The invention of federal securities laws effectively put an end to this practice as well, because the committee would typically issue creditors "certificates of deposit" in exchange for their claims.[22] The 1933 Securities Act included "certificates of deposit" among the securities that could only be sold with a registration statement.[23] And again, soliciting creditors could itself invoke the proxy rules under the 1934 Securities Exchange Act. Less formal committees of large creditors could still act as an assignee, but

---

best interests of the corporation, when and as authorized by a resolution adopted by the holders of a majority of the outstanding stock of the corporation entitled to vote thereon.")

[18] See In re E.T. Russell Co., 291 F. 809, 815 (D. Mass. 1923).

[19] UPA § 9(3)(a). See also N.Y. P'ship Law § 20.

[20] RUPA § 301. See, in particular, the official and author comments.

[21] *Peabody* v. *Tenney*, 30 A. 456, 457 (R.I. 1893). In a somewhat related vein is a New York statute that allows boards of trade or chambers of commerce to act as assignees in that state. N.Y. Not-for-Profit Corp. Law § 1410(c)(1).

[22] A good description of the process, in a related context, can be found in *La Salle Nat. Bank* v. *Britton*, 119 N.E.2d 486, 488 (Ill. App. Ct. 1954).

[23] 15 U.S.C. § 77b(1).

in doing so the creditor would be taking on fiduciary duties to all other creditors, and thus members of the committee would more likely defer to a third-party assignee.[24]

In many states, financial institutions are expressly prohibited from making an assignment; while in most others, one would expect that attempting such a move would quickly attract the attention of regulators.[25] In New Hampshire, both "banking and railroad corporations" are prohibited from making assignments – railroads are still different in the Granite State.[26]

Partnership assignments are more complex than corporate assignments, and the law in many jurisdictions is quite old and confused. For example, some states have case law requiring all partners to assign their property along with partnership property.[27] In others, individual property of the partners need not be included in an assignment for the benefit of creditors.[28] In both cases, the opinions tend to date from an era when the presidents had beards, and thus predate both uniform partnership acts currently in use. An argument could be made that this case law no longer applies – because it represents an outdated conception of what a partnership entails – although until the issue is addressed by court or statute, particularly in states with the former sort of case law, requiring all partners to assign along with the firm, it would tend to discourage any assignments by partnerships.

The basic mechanism in all assignments is a contract that transfers all the company's assets to somebody else – either an individual or another legal entity.[29] The recipient of the assets – the "assignee" – agrees to liquidate them and distribute the proceeds to creditors, in exchange for a fee.[30] The assignee is typically selected by the debtor, which may be preferable to a chapter 7 bankruptcy trustee that is otherwise a stranger to the debtor's business.

---

[24] Cf. *Family Sav. & Loan Ass'n Shareholders' Protective Comm.* v. *Stewart*, 241 Md. 89, 215 A.2d 726 (1966).

[25] E.g., Minn. Stat. Ann. § 49.013; Mo. Rev. Stat. § 361.330.

[26] N.H. Rev. Stat. Ann. § 568:49. Cf. 39 Pa. Stat. Ann. § 161.

[27] *Still* v. *Focke*, 2 S.W. 59, 63 (Tex. 1886).

[28] *Drucker* v. *Wellhouse*, 8 S.E. 40, 43 (Ga. 1888).

[29] E.g., *Wafra Capital Partners, L.P.* v. *Prime Leasing, Inc.*, No. 03 C 4687, 2004 WL 432490, at *1 (N.D. Ill. Jan. 28, 2004).

[30] Fla. Stat. Ann. § 727.101; 39 Pa. Stat. Ann. § 71.

TRUST AGREEMENT AND ASSIGNMENT FOR THE BENEFIT OF CREDITORS
OF MYCOM NORTH AMERICA, INC. AND XEREX, INC.

THIS TRUST AND AGREEMENT AND ASSIGNMENT FOR THE BENEFIT OF CREDITORS ("Trust Agreement") is made and entered into this 11th day of April 2016, by and between MYCOM NORTH AMERICA, INC. ("Mycom") and XEREX, INC. ("Xerex," and together with Mycom, "Assignors"), each a Delaware corporation, located at 1080 Holcomb Bridge Road, Building 200, Suite 350, Roswell, Georgia 30076, and Development Specialists, Inc., an Illinois corporation located at 70 West Madison Street, Suite 2300, Chicago, Illinois 60602-4250 (hereinafter referred to as the "Trustee-Assignee").

WITNESSETH:

WHEREAS, the Assignors are indebted to various persons, corporations, and other entities and are unable to pay their debts in full, and has decided to discontinue their business, and are desirous of transferring their property and assets to an assignee for the benefit of their creditors pursuant to Delaware law so that the property and assets transferred may be expeditiously liquidated and the resulting proceeds be fairly distributed to their creditors without any preference or priority, except such preference or priority as is established and permitted by applicable law;

NOW, THEREFORE, in consideration of the Assignors existing indebtedness to their creditors, the express undertakings of the Trustee-Assignee and the mutual covenants contained herein, it is hereby AGREED:

1. **Creation and Object of Trust.** There is created a trust (the "Trust") the name of which is the "**MYCOM Trust**" and the object of which is be the orderly liquidation of the

We see an example above. As explained by the First District Appellate Court of Illinois:

The assignment passes the legal and equitable title to the property absolutely, beyond the control of the assignor. An assignment for the benefit of creditors, therefore, is simply a unique trust arrangement in which the assignee (or trustee) holds property for the benefit of a special group of beneficiaries, the creditors.[31]

But assignment law is subject to seemingly endless variation, and we see an early example of this with the selection of the assignee. In North Carolina, the assignee can be replaced by vote of one-quarter in number and 50 percent in amount of the creditors.[32] While in Washington, two creditors can call a meeting at which a majority – in both number and value of claims – of the creditors attending in person or by proxy can select a new assignee.[33] In Ohio, creditors holding more than $1,000 in claims can petition for the election of a new assignee.[34] And in South Carolina they can appoint a co-assignee if they so desire.[35]

The assignee holds the assets in trust for all creditors, thus moving the assets out of the reach of unsecured creditors.[36] Because the debtor-company remains liable for all of its debts after the assignment, this is apt to be more useful to limited liability entities – corporations and the like – and less useful to partnerships and other entities where the owners are ultimately responsible for the firm's debts.

Of course, the last comment largely turns on the true extent of individual liability under state law – in states with generous homestead exemptions, for example, a partnership assignment might still make sense. That makes the antiquated state of law with regard to partnership assignments, as noted earlier, all the more troublesome.

Some states attempt to create a discharge within the assignment process, which might expand the utility of the process to unincorporated firms.[37] Texas, for example, provides that a debtor is "discharged from liability on the claim of a consenting creditor unless the consenting creditor does not receive at least one-third of the amount allowed on his claim against the assigned estate."[38] A creditor is deemed to have

---

[31] *Illinois Bell Telephone Co.* v. *Wolf Furniture House, Inc.*, 157 Ill. App. 3d 190, 195, 509 N.E.2d 1289, 1292 (Ill. App. 1987) (internal citations and quotations omitted).

[32] N.C. Gen. Stat. § 23-6.

[33] Wash. Rev. Code Ann. § 7.08.030(5).

[34] Ohio Rev. Code Ann. § 1313.05.

[35] S.C. Code Ann. § 27-25-40.

[36] Secured creditors retain their liens on the assets.

[37] Ariz. Rev. Stat. Ann. § 44-1032; Va. Code Ann. § 55-159.

[38] Tex. Bus. & Com. Code § 23.10.

consented if it accepts a distribution from the assignee, a provision that would seem to be susceptible to attack on pre-emption grounds, inasmuch as the creditor of a corporation is effectively obliged to give the discharge to get any recovery on its claim.[39]

On the other hand, in Massachusetts, a majority of creditors must consent to the assignment process for it to proceed.[40] This undoubtedly limits the utility of assignments in the Commonwealth.

Originally assignments were a common law creation, and they remain such in several states.[41] In these states the assignment process is apt to be rather opaque, as the process develops in private, under state contract law, at least until some cock-up requires the parties to come to court.

Starting in the late 1800s and early 1900s many states codified the process. Indeed, it is common to find similar language among the various state statutes. In many cases these were originally based on either the Field Code of New York, or California's version of the same, which has since been repealed.[42] That said, given more than a century since enactment, many statutes that start from a common root have nonetheless grown in different directions.

For example, while the statute originally enacted by the Dakota Territory formed the basis for several assignment statutes throughout the middle of the country – from Oklahoma to Montana – South Dakota's current statute contains a provision allowing the assignee to recover preferential payments to creditors made within four months of the assignment.[43] Assignees in other states in the region have no such power.

Somewhat confusingly, Pennsylvania has two assignment statutes: a "new" act from 1901,[44] and the old act, parts of which date from as early as 1843.[45] Both are in effect.

---

[39] Id. § 23.30. See also Ariz. Rev. Stat. Ann. § 44-1037.
[40] Mass. Gen. Laws Ann. ch. 203, § 41. See also Ala. Code § 19-3-22.
[41] Key examples include Connecticut, Illinois and Hawaii. Illinois had an assignment statute from 1877 until 1939, and caselaw from that period may guide assignments in the present day. As discussed below, California has a mixed system of a few statutory provisions, filled in by mostly common law.
[42] *Credit Managers Assn.* v. *Nat'l Indep. Bus. All.*, 209 Cal. Rptr. 119, 121 (Ct. App. 1984).
[43] S.D. Codified Laws § 54-9-13.2.
[44] Pa. Stat. Ann. tit. 39, §§ 1–154.
[45] Id. §§ 161–327.

Just less than half of the states give assignees the power to recover preferential payments. Often that power looks back at payments made within four months of the assignment, as in South Dakota, giving the assignees somewhat more power than a federal bankruptcy trustee operating under a ninety-day limit.[46]

Some states limit assignments to insolvent debtors, or, as Indiana quaintly puts it, those "in embarrassed or failing circumstances."[47] As a result, assignments in these states are subject to limitations not found in the Bankruptcy Code, assuming creditors raise the solvency issue. At the very least, litigating the issue of insolvency could incinerate any cost advantage the state assignment process might have over its federal counterpart.

In some of these "code" states the assignee's fee is limited to what could be charged by an executor on a will.[48] West Virginia is among the states that grant the assignee – or trustee, as they are termed there and some other places as well – a commission based on a schedule, combined with the possibility of additional compensation if the creditors consent.[49] Other states leave the fee up to the court;[50] while the common law states apparently leave the fee to bilateral negotiation amongst the parties.

Some states require the assignment to be filed with the local trial court, or at least the clerk of the court.[51] In others, the assignment, and perhaps an inventory of the property assigned, are recorded as if they were real estate deeds.[52] In some jurisdictions, the assignee has to make both kinds of filings,[53] while in other states, particularly those that still allow common law assignments, no filing is required at all. California – which since 1980 has operated under a largely common law system,

---

[46] N.Y. Debt. & Cred. Law § 15; N.J. Stat. § 2A:19-3; N.C. Gen. Stat. § 23-3. But see Cal. Civ. Proc. Code § 1800 (ninety-day lookback period); S.C. Code Ann. § 27-25-20 (same).

[47] Ind. Code Ann. § 32-18-1-1(a). See also Okla. Stat. Ann. tit. 24, §§ 31-32.

[48] Okla. Stat. Ann. tit. 24, § 48; S.D. Codified Laws § 54-9-14.

[49] W. Va. Code § 38-13-16.

[50] Mich. Comp. Laws Ann. § 600.5255; Tenn. Code Ann. § 47-13-110 (but with an upper cap of 5 percent of the assets distributed).

[51] N.C. Gen. Stat. § 23-2; 10 R.I. Gen. Laws § 4-2; Vt. Stat. Ann. tit. 9, § 2153; Wis. Stat. Ann. § 128.05.

[52] Ga. Code Ann. § 18-2-43; N.J. Stat. § 2A:19-4; Tex. Bus. & Com. Code § 23.08; Va. Code Ann. § 55-156.

[53] Ky. Rev. Stat. Ann. § 379.020

framed by a few statutory provisions[54] – is the most notable example of the latter.[55] In Illinois, which operates a pure common law system, it is apparently common to file the assignment with the county recorder nonetheless.

In several jurisdictions where the assignment process has been codified, common law assignments are still permissible.[56] Thus, an assignment that fails to comply with the statute will often be analyzed instead under the common law rules.[57]

This can result in substantial differences in treatment, even with a single state. For example, Colorado's assignment statute[58] applies to any "person," which is defined as individuals, partnerships, associations or corporations.[59] In a properly commenced assignment for the benefit of creditors under the Colorado statute, a mortgage or deed of trust or other security interest cannot be foreclosed within one year of the assignment without a court's permission. A common law assignment provides no such protection.[60]

The approach to asset sales also varies widely between the states. In many jurisdictions, the assignee is given virtually unfettered discretion to sell assets at public auction, while needing court approval only to conduct private sales.[61] Some require court approval for all sales.[62] And in other cases the only prohibitions on the assignee relate to real estate.[63]

Some states require assignee bonds equal to the value of the estate.[64] Some even require a bond of twice the value of the debtor's assets.[65] Rhode

---

[54] Previously California had both statutory and common law assignments, but the statutory assignment process was rarely used.

[55] Cal. Civ. Proc. Code § 1802 (providing that the assignee will give notice to creditors of the assignment, and the claims bar date as set by the assignee).

[56] *Bumb* v. *Bennett*, 333 P.2d 23 (Cal. 1958). As noted, California has since largely repealed its assignment statute.

[57] *Damaskus* v. *McCarty-Johnson Heating & Eng'g Co.*, 295 P. 490, 491 (Colo. 1931).

[58] Colo. Rev. Stat. Ann. §§ 6-10-101 to 6-10-154.

[59] Id. § 6-10-101.

[60] See *Markoff* v. *Barenberg*, 368 P.2d 964, 965 (Colo. 1962) (inviting the creditor on remand to argue that the statute, if it applied, was preempted by the Bankruptcy Act); see also *McKelvy* v. *Striker*, 116 P.2d 921, 921 (Colo. 1941).

[61] Ind. Code Ann. § 32-18-1-10; 10 R.I. Gen. Laws § 4-7.

[62] Md. Code Ann., Com. Law § 15-103; Mo. Ann. Stat. § 426.310; N.M. Stat. Ann. § 56-9-40. See also Ark. Code Ann. § 16-117-404.

[63] Iowa Code Ann. § 681.24.

[64] Tenn. Code Ann. § 47-13-101

[65] Ark. Code Ann. § 16-117-401; Iowa Code Ann. § 681.7; N.M. Stat. Ann. § 56-9-8.

Island requires a bond of $1,000,[66] regardless of the size of the debt-or's estate, while others leave the amount of the bond to the discretion of the court,[67] or even the clerk,[68] and several others have no bonding requirements whatsoever.

In some states the assignments statutes have been revised relatively recently, often with the effect of creating a mini-bankruptcy system. Courts oversee the process, but the assignee gains the ability to bring avoidance actions on behalf of all creditors,[69] and sometimes even the ability to reject contracts and impose caps on the damages resulting from that breach of the original deal.[70]

These sorts of statutes do raise the question of how many bits of the federal Bankruptcy Code can be grafted onto state assignments before a court declares the latter a disguised state bankruptcy law, pre-empted by its federal counterpart.[71] In 2005, the Ninth Circuit Court of Appeals struck down California's preference statute, applicable in assignments, as pre-empted by the Code.[72] The decision was widely panned, and ignored by those courts that could.[73] But certainly the solitary focus of constitutional pre-emption analysis cannot be a discharge, especially when discharge is of minor concern to a limited liability entity.[74] The more vital question, which I will return to, is when

---

[66] 10 R.I. Gen. Laws § 4-1.

[67] N.Y. Debt. & Cred. Law § 6; Ohio Rev. Code Ann. § 1313.01; N.J. Stat. § 2A:19-10; Vt. Stat. Ann. tit. 9, § 2154.

[68] W. Va. Code § 38-13-2.

[69] E.g., Md. Code Ann., Com. Law § 15-101(d). ("All preferences, payments, transfers, and obligations made or suffered by the insolvent which are fraudulent, void, or voidable under any act of the Congress of the United States relating to bankruptcy are fraudulent, void, or voidable, respectively, under this subtitle to the same extent that they would be fraudulent, void, or voidable under applicable federal bankruptcy law.")

[70] Fla. Stat. §§ 727.108(5), 109(6), 112(6).

[71] See generally Michelle M. Harner, Rethinking Preemption and Constitutional Parameters in Bankruptcy, 59 *Wm. & Mary L. Rev.* 147 (2017).

[72] *Sherwood Partners, Inc.* v. *Lycos, Inc.*, 394 F.3d 1198, 1206 (9th Cir. 2005).

[73] E.g., *Credit Managers Ass'n of California* v. *Countrywide Home Loans, Inc.*, 50 Cal. Rptr. 3d 259, 264 (Ct. App. 2006). But see *Windmill Health Prod., LLC* v. *Sensa Prod.*, No. C-15-0574 MMC, 2015 WL 6471180, at *4 (N.D. Cal. Oct. 27, 2015). The Sherwood Partners case does mean that out of state defendants can remove actions brought by the assignee to federal court, on the basis of "diversity" among the parties, and then move to dismiss them. *Dev. Specialists, Inc.* v. *Shedrain Corp.*, No. 2:12-CV-7718-SVW-AGR, 2012 WL 12903636, at *1 (C.D. Cal. Dec. 19, 2012).

[74] In re Wisconsin Builders Supply Co., 239 F.2d 649, 652 (7th Cir. 1956).

and why the federal government should assert the sole right to act regarding business failure.

As a general rule, those jurisdictions with older assignment statutes tend to have systems that would seem to be less attractive to all concerned, as compared with locations that either have newer statutes or common law assignment systems that retain their inherent flexibility. Given the degree of variation among the states on assignments, it is unsurprising that the use of assignments varies widely by state.[75] If a business is fortunately located in a jurisdiction with useful assignment law – in statutory or common law form – the assignment process provides a viable substitute for bankruptcy, provided the debtor largely does business within the confines of that jurisdiction.

Frustration must surely arise when the local law is less than useful, especially by virtue of being out of date. Assignees in Indiana, to take but one example, are required to hire appraisers. But the statute limits the appraisers' compensation to $1 per day.[76]

Perhaps less onerous, but equally amusing, particularly in an online world, is the Missouri statute that requires assignees to publicly process creditors' claims for at least three days, from at least 9 a.m. to 5 p.m.[77] Notice of the get-together is to be published in a local newspaper, of course. All "creditors who, after being notified as aforesaid, shall not attend at the place designated during the said term, and lay before the assignee the nature and amount of their demands, shall be precluded from any benefit of said estate."

Assignments are close cousins of receiverships, and indeed in Washington State a relatively recent revision to the statutes automatically converts assignments into a kind of receivership.[78] A "receiver is not in a strict sense the assignee of the corporation, but he is the officer of the court appointed to impound the corporate assets, and administer them for the benefit of all interested therein."[79]

The primary distinction is that receivers are always appointed by courts. Historically, appointment was always in aid of some other

[75] See generally Ronald J. Mann, An Empirical Investigation of Liquidation Choices of Failed High Tech Firms, 82 *Wash. U. L. Q.* 1375 (2004).
[76] Ind. Code Ann. § 32-18-1-21. See also N.M. Stat. Ann. § 56-9-16 (four dollars per day).
[77] Mo. Ann. Stat. § 426.180.
[78] Wash. Rev. Code Ann. § 7.08.030.
[79] Walter S. Jones, A Treatise on the Law of Insolvent Failing Corporations § 405 (1908).

action brought by a secured or judgment creditor.[80] In addition, receiverships can be commenced involuntarily, by a creditor or shareholder, whereas assignments by their nature require the debtor to consent to the transfer of assets.[81] And while debtors pick their assignees creditors, or sometimes the courts, pick the proposed receiver.[82]

In 2010, a Delaware chancery court judge noted that, in his experience, state court receiverships came in three basic flavors:

> The first type is brought by a single creditor seeking the appointment of a receiver under a loan document or because the debtor is insolvent. The second type seeks the dissolution of an alternative entity and the concomitant appointment of a receiver. The last type is a catch-all for efforts by practitioners to employ the flexible receivership remedy in creative circumstances.[83]

The receiver acts as an officer of the court that appointed the receiver and is subject to its direction.[84] The court that appoints the receiver will by order determine the range of powers and duties of the receiver, and the process by which claims against the receivership estate will be determined.[85]

Many states have statutes that provide for receiverships generally.[86] In other jurisdictions, the power of a court to appoint a receiver is contained in a rule of procedure,[87] which sometimes tracks the text of Federal Rule 66, which itself refers courts to "historical practice."

In California, receiverships are encompassed in the California Code of Civil Procedure (CCP) sections 564 to 570 and the California Rules of Court sections 3.1175 to 3.1184. While the provisions of the CCP governing a receiver's powers and duties are broadly worded,

---

[80] *C. E. Dev. Co.* v. *Kitchens*, 264 So. 2d 510, 514 (Ala. 1972).

[81] 1 Clark on Receivers § 44 (3d ed. 1959). But see 39 Pa. Stat. Ann. § 31 (provision under assignment law for the creditor to institute proceedings when the debtor fails to do so).

[82] *Casa Bella Landscaping, LLC* v. *Lee*, 890 N.W.2d 875, 877 (Mich. App. 2016).

[83] Honorable J. Travis Laster, The Chancery Receivership: Alive and Well Receivership Proceedings in the Court of Chancery Are Re-Emerging As a Viable Alternative to Bankruptcy for Some Businesses, *Del. Law.*, 12 (Fall 2010).

[84] Miss. Code. Ann. § 11-5-161.

[85] N.Y. C.P.L.R. 6401. See also Wis. Stat. Ann. § 128.14.

[86] E.g., Alaska Stat. Ann. § 09.40.240; Cal. Civ. Proc. Code § 564; Kan. Stat. Ann. § 60-1301; Mich. Comp. Laws Serv. § 600.2926; Miss. Code Ann. § 11-5-151; W. Va. Code, § 53-6-1. See also NY City Civ. Ct. Act § 1508.

[87] Arkansas Rules of Civil Procedure, Rule 66; Massachusetts Rules of Civil Procedure, Rule 66; Mich. Ct. R. 2.622; Pa.R.C.P. No. 1533.

CCP section 564 specifies the exclusive circumstances under which a receiver may be appointed. None really picks up a simple case of insolvency, making it clear that receivers are but ancillary tools in the Golden State.

In other states, the general equitable power of a court to appoint receivers is supplemented by a series of more specific statutes. For example, in Pennsylvania, the general power to appoint equity receivers is governed by Civil Procedure Rule 1533,[88] while other statutes cover receivers for corporations[89] or limited liability companies.[90] Even when statutory, the precise powers and duties of the receiver are often left rather vague.

That is, in many general receivership cases the common law will play a key role.[91] Normally receiverships under statute are more likely to be viable as independent actions, while common law – or more aptly, equity – receiverships still tend to be supplementary to some other cause of action.[92]

In many states, a receiver's authority principally comes from the order of the court appointing the receiver.[93] Beyond the limited statutory regime and the appointment order, case law, much of it many decades old, guides a receiver.

As with assignments, the receivership statutes in many states also come with cobwebs. For example, Massachusetts sets the priorities of claims in a receivership:

- "First, debts due the United States or debts due, or taxes assessed, by the commonwealth or a county, city or town therein."
- Second, certain debts for wages "due an operative, clerk or servant for labor," up to $100.
- Third, debts to physicians for services to an individual debtor, up to $50.[94]

---

[88] Pa.R.C.P. No. 1533.

[89] 15 Pa. Stat. and Cons. Stat. Ann. § 5985.

[90] Id. § 8872(e).

[91] *Premier Farm Credit, PCA* v. *W-Cattle, LLC*, 155 P.3d 504, 519 (Colo. App. 2006).

[92] *Spivery-Jones* v. *Receivership Estate of Trans Healthcare, Inc.*, 91 A.3d 1172, 1180 (Md. 2014).

[93] *McCray* v. *Lawrence Street Associates, LLC*, 2014 WL 10962263 (Pa. Super. Ct. 2014).

[94] Mass. Gen. Laws Ann. ch. 206, § 31.

A state court receivership involves the appointment of an individual or company as receiver who then supplants the debtor-firm's management, and proceeds to run the firm for some limited period of time for the benefit of its various stakeholders, namely its creditors.[95] Because the assets are now under court control, outside collection activity ceases. In those states with more elaborate receivership statutes, there is often an express statutory stay. The appointing order will also grant the receiver the authority to obtain financing, operate the business in the ordinary course of business, hire financial advisors, attorneys, and accountants, and sell the assets subject to further order of the court.

Indeed, the ultimate objective is a sale conveying the debtor's assets free of encumbrances, with such attaching to the proceeds of sale in the order of their priority.[96] While some state statutes specifically provide for sales free and clear of liens, claims, and encumbrances,[97] in other states, the court order approving the sale conveys the assets lien free.

In some cases, the ability of the receiver to sell "free and clear" is in doubt. For example, in Pennsylvania, old case law seems to allow such sales, but practitioners express some doubt on the point.[98] Likewise in California, attorneys worry that a receiver cannot sell assets in the face of the debtor's objection. In both jurisdictions, and likely others, the receivership is often paired with a foreclosure or execution sale to ensure that the sale is indeed "free and clear." Doing so obviously makes receiverships somewhat more expensive, and thus less useful, in these jurisdictions.

There is also little case law about how such a sale order might interact with court-created successor liability doctrines, meaning that there is some additional risk in using a receivership to effectuate a sale, as compared with a 363 sale under federal bankruptcy law.[99]

---

[95] Minn. Stat. Ann. § 576.29. See also *Selheimer* v. *Manganese Corp. of Am.*, 206 A.2d 28, 30 (Pa. 1965).

[96] Wash. Rev. Code Ann. § 7.60.260.

[97] Del. Code Ann. tit. 8, § 297; Ga. Code Ann. § 9-8-6; Mo. Ann. Stat. § 515.640.

[98] *Baird* v. *Moshannon Coal Mining Co.*, 178 A. 19 (Pa. 1935)

[99] But see *John T. Callahan & Sons, Inc.* v. *Dykeman Elec. Co.*, 266 F. Supp. 2d 208, 222 (D. Mass. 2003). ("The present asset sale ... occurred under the auspices of the state receivership proceeding and the Rhode Island court's approval of that sale. Such a sale is more akin to a sale of assets free and clear of any 'interest' in the property of the debtor under the Bankruptcy Code. See 11 U.S.C. § 363(f) ... In such circumstances, any exercise by

Receiverships, like most other state-law insolvency proceedings, are always apt to being overtaken by an involuntary bankruptcy filing.[100] Alternatively, in some cases such a receiver can provide a means for overcoming governance problems that block voluntary bankruptcy petitions.[101]

But what if the debtor cannot file for bankruptcy protection? In the past, the case law was reasonably clear that state insolvency proceedings could apply to such debtors, subject to the limitations imposed by the Contracts Clause.[102]

In more modern times, the range of debtors that are neither subject to the federal Bankruptcy Code nor some specialized regulatory regime is quite limited. For a time, Puerto Rico and its municipal entities was one such example,[103] although now Congress has enacted a new bankruptcy provision for the territory and its municipalities.

Another possible example are marijuana-related businesses in those states where cannabis has been legalized. Several bankruptcy courts have ruled that a marijuana business cannot use federal bankruptcy for protection from creditors.[104]

Thus, there is an opening here for use of state receiverships, provided a willing receiver can be found. There have been some already, most notably in Washington, California and Arizona.[105] In Colorado,

the Rhode Island court of that power of sale would have been valid to extinguish Harrier's successor liability to Callahan.")

[100] Paula Whitney Best, Corporate Receiverships and Chapter 11 Reorganizations, 10 *Cardozo L. Rev.* 285, 298 (1988).

[101] E.g., In re Monterey Equities-Hillside, 73 B.R. 749 (Bankr. N.D. Cal. 1987) (bankruptcy petition filed by the receiver for limited partnership, in the face of the general partner's opposition).

[102] Samuel Williston, The Effect of A National Bankruptcy Law Upon State Laws, 22 *Harv. L. Rev.* 547, 550, 555–6 (1909) (questioning this doctrine).

[103] Under the 1941 law that created PREPA, the Commonwealth's public power company, and the utility's bond documents, there is the possibility of appointing a receiver when the utility defaults on its debts. See P.R. Laws Ann. tit. 22, § 207.

[104] E.g., In re Arenas, 535 B.R. 845, 852 (10th Cir. BAP 2015). ("[S]hort of exposing him to physical harm, nothing could be more burdensome to the Trustee's administration than requiring him to take possession, sell and distribute marijuana Assets in violation of federal criminal law.") But see In re Olson, No. 3:17-BK-50081-BTB, 2018 WL 989263, at *7 (B.A.P. 9th Cir. Feb. 5, 2018) (Tighe, J. concurring). ("Although debtors connected to marijuana distribution cannot expect to violate federal law in their bankruptcy case, the presence of marijuana near the case should not cause mandatory dismissal.")

[105] See Dominique R. Scalia, Washington's First Marijuana Receivership Reaches A Successful Conclusion, *NWLawyer* 36 (Jul–Aug. 2017).

the question has been confused by the Medical Enforcement Division's claim that receivers must obtain the requisite licenses, although we might wonder if such a move intrudes too much on a court's inherent powers to appoint a receiver.[106]

In addition to the general receivership power of state courts, several states have receivership statutes expressly aimed at insolvent companies.[107] New Jersey, for example, has enacted separate statutes providing for receivers for insolvent corporations,[108] partnerships,[109] and limited partnerships.[110] Texas has a single statute that allows the appointment of receivers for all insolvent "domestic entities,"[111] which means any business formed under the Texas Business Organizations Code, be it corporation, partnership, or whatnot.[112]

Some of the corporate receivership statutes are comparatively ancient, yet quite developed, reflecting a time before an attractive federal corporate bankruptcy option.[113] For example, Nevada's statute dates from 1925, and boldly vests the receiver with all "real and personal property of an insolvent corporation, wheresoever situated."[114] The shareholders have the power to reorganize and recapitalize the corporation,[115] while the receiver can sell assets free of liens.[116]

Delaware's corporate law has provided for the appointment of receivers for insolvent corporations since 1891, predating the more famous 1899 adoption of the State's first modern corporation law.[117]

---

[106] *N.Y. Title & MTG Co.* v. *Polk Arms*, 186 N.E. 35, 37 (N.Y. 1933).

[107] Conn. Gen. Stat. § 52-507; Kan. Stat. Ann. 17-6901; Okla. Stat. Ann. tit. 18, § 1106; 15 Pa. Stat. and Cons. Stat. Ann. § 1985; Tenn. Code Ann. § 48-24-303. See *Jacobson-Lyons Stone Co.* v. *Silverdale Cut Stone Co.*, 370 P.2d 68, 75 (Kan. 1962). Somewhat closer to a collection action are those statutes that allow appointment of a receiver when a corporation fails to pay a judgment. Fla. Stat. Ann. § 56.10; Mass. Ann. Laws ch. 156, § 51; Minn. Stat. Ann. § 316.05; N.Y. Bus. Corp. Law § 1201. See also Tenn. Code Ann. § 29-12-107.

[108] N.J. Stat. Ann. § 14A:14-2.

[109] N.J. Stat. Ann. § 42:4-7.

[110] Id. § 42:3-20.

[111] Tex. Bus. Orgs. Code § 11.404.

[112] *Spiritas* v. *Davidoff*, 459 S.W.3d 224, 235 (Tex. App. 2015).

[113] Beyond those examined in the text, Rhode Island and Oklahoma are further examples of jurisdictions with heavily codified corporate receivership statutes.

[114] Nev. Rev. Stat. Ann. § 78.640.

[115] Id. § 78.655.

[116] Id. § 78.700.

[117] Act of March 25, 1891, chapter 181; 19 Del. Laws, p. 359.

Under section 291, a Delaware receivership can be initiated by any creditor, whereas under the Bankruptcy Code it takes three or more entities, each having non-contingent claims to accomplish an involuntary bankruptcy. Recent case law suggests that insolvency alone will not result in a receivership under the statute, rather the petitioning party must show some additional need.[118] In the past the statute appears to have been used with greater regularity and employed with greater liberality, again perhaps reflecting the lack of a workable federal corporate bankruptcy system.[119]

Others represent more recent attempts to provide a state law alternative to chapters 7 and 11. Washington's statute was revised in 2004 and again in 2011 to create a system where the receivership is protected by an automatic stay and the receiver has the power to assume and assign executory contracts and leases.[120] The receiver's ability to assume and reject contracts, always part of general practice under equity receiverships, is thus codified.[121] Other sections provide for continued utility service to the debtor,[122] and post-receivership financing.[123]

Taken as a whole, it looks a lot like a bankruptcy statute – to similar effect is the recently enacted Missouri Commercial Receivership Act.[124] As with the recent vintage assignment statutes discussed earlier, it bears considering at what point these newly robust state receivership laws might go "too far," and blunder into federal territory.[125]

---

[118] *Badii* v. *Metro. Hospice, Inc.*, No. 6192-VCP, 2012 Del. Ch. LEXIS 71, at *25 (Ch. Mar. 12, 2012).

[119] E.g., Josiah Marvel, Delaware Corporations and Receiverships 231–74 (4th ed. 1929). To be sure there was a federal bankruptcy law that applied to corporations by this point, but it only allowed liquidation under a chapter 7-style proceeding.

[120] Wash. Rev. Code Ann. ch. 7.60.

[121] Id. § 7.60.130.

[122] Id. § 7.60.120.

[123] Id. § 7.60.140.

[124] Mo. Ann. Stat. § 515.500 (effective Aug. 2016). See, e.g., Mo. Ann. Stat. § 515.585. ("A receiver may assume or reject any executory contract or unexpired lease of the debtor upon order of the court following notice and a hearing, which shall include notice to persons party to the executory contract or unexpired lease to be assumed or rejected.")

[125] In re Wisconsin Builders Supply Co., 239 F.2d 649, 651 (7th Cir. 1956). ("Of course, it is possible that state legislation may go so far as to change the general assignment into a state insolvency system in conflict with or covering the same subject matter as the

The appointment of receivers for insolvent corporations is common, especially in those states with express statutes on point, the same cannot be said for partnerships. One practice guide profoundly proclaims that "It is doubtful as to whether a court of equity should entertain an action for the appointment of a receiver of an insolvent partnership."[126] Such matters, the authors opine, are best left to bankruptcy courts. And Ralph Clark, who literally authored the book on receivers, wrote many years ago that "the appointment of a receiver of a partnership nearly always follows, or occurs at the same time as, a dissolution of the partnership."[127]

Conversely, even modern courts seem reluctant to appoint a receiver in routine partnership dissolution cases.[128] But what of a restructuring – or at least a controlled sort of liquidation? That is, can a receivership be used as a bankruptcy substitute in the case of a partnership, like often is done with a corporation?

Clark himself noted that

> The courts appoint consent receivers of railways, street railways, public utility corporations, and also of private corporations, also a partnership.[129]

Thus, in the glory days of equity receivers, there was some action on this front. The parallel decline of receiverships and general partnerships no doubt has depressed the number in recent years.

If a partner is subject to a state court receivership in a state that still adheres to the UPA – New York again represents the most obvious example – the existence of the jingle rule under state law, and its repeal under chapter 7 of the Bankruptcy Code, could encourage involuntary bankruptcy petitions. In particular, creditors of the insolvent

---

Bankruptcy Act and where that occurs such legislation is held to be superseded by the paramount federal law.")

[126] § 12.4. Appointment of receivers of partnerships, 31 Mass. Prac., Equitable Remedies § 12.4 (3d ed.).

[127] Ralph E. Clark, Contingent and Immature Claims in Receivership Proceedings, 29 *Yale L.J.* 481, 489–90 (1920).

[128] *Scharff* v. *SS & K P'ship*, 590 N.Y.S.2d 243, 245 (App. Div. 1992); see also *Rogers* v. *McDonald*, 163 S.E.2d 719, 722 (Ga. 1968).

[129] 1 Clark on Receivers § 188 (3d ed. 1959) (footnotes omitted). Clark cites *U S Radiator Corp.* v. *Doody*, 5 F. Supp. 471, 472 (E.D. Pa. 1933) as an example of a partnership consent receivership.

partnership may find it to their advantage to initiate an involuntary case so as to avoid having their claims against the partners subordinated to the claims of non-partnership creditors. This presumes, as discussed in Chapter 2, that the partners are also in chapter 7.

What of the newer, partnership-like entities? The Delaware Limited Liability Partnership Act and the Limited Liability Company Act contain provisions for the appointment of receivers in the context of a dissolution, but nothing like the provisions for insolvent corporations that we noted above.

The Delaware LLC statute allows courts to supplement the Act with "the rules of law and equity, including the rules of law and equity relating to fiduciary duties and the law merchant,"[130] but at least one Delaware court has refused to use that provision to appoint a receivership for an insolvent limited liability company.[131] Presumably, the LLC founders could include use of the corporation receivership provisions in the governing documents, but we might doubt how often we would see such pessimistic foresight.

On the other hand, in states like Texas where the receivership provisions apply to business entities generally,[132] it would seem likely that a receivership could be used to rehabilitate a distressed limited liability company.[133]

It is often said that state court receiverships are "cheaper" than comparable federal bankruptcy proceedings. Certainly, the out-of-pocket cost to the debtor-firm is lower, but that begs the question of whether the overall cost has simply been relocated to others. For example, the cost of creditors' committees in chapter 11 cases is often substantial.[134] The debtor is responsible for both the committee's own professionals, as well as the costs the debtor's professionals incur through interactions with the committee. But is the absence of a committee in a receivership a true cost saving, or does it simply allow the debtor more freedom to abuse the now unrepresented creditors?

---

[130] Del. Code Ann. tit. 6, § 18-1104.
[131] *Ross Holding & Mgmt. Co.* v. *Advance Realty Grp., LLC*, No. CIV.A. 4113-VCN, 2010 WL 3448227, at *5 (Del. Ch. Sept. 2, 2010).
[132] Tex. Bus. Orgs. Code Ann. § 11.404.
[133] Accord Ohio Rev. Code Ann. § 2735.01.
[134] Stephen J. Lubben, The Chapter 11 Attorneys, 86 *Am. Bankr. L.J.* 447, 466–71 (2012).

Other related statutes in this area provide for the appointment of a receiver for an insolvent corporation as part of the larger corporate law and the process of dissolution thereunder.[135] And the dissolution process itself can work as an insolvency system, particularly for smaller businesses.

For example, under section 14.30 of the Model Business Corporations Act, a court can order the dissolution of a corporation in a proceeding by a creditor if it is established that:

1. the creditor's claim has been reduced to judgment, the execution on the judgment returned unsatisfied, and the corporation is insolvent; or
2. the corporation has admitted in writing that the creditor's claim is due and owing and the corporation is insolvent.[136]

That is, under circumstances that would have warranted the commencement of an equity receivership in the old days, a creditor can exercise a power that is normally in the hands of shareholders or the state attorney general.

Through whichever route dissolution is begun – either voluntarily by the shareholders and the board, or involuntary imposed by the court – the company continues to exist only to take care of certain final matters that, collectively, are known as "winding up" the company.[137] Key among the winding-up tasks are meeting the corporation's liabilities and, if possible, distributing any remaining corporation assets to stockholders.[138]

There is no filing with a court, and even the filing with the secretary of state's office might be somewhat skeletal.[139] Below is an example from

---

[135] Ala. Code § 10A-2-14.32; Del. Code Ann. tit. 8, § 279; Me. Rev. Stat. tit. 13-C, § 781; Md. Code Ann., Corps. & Ass'ns § 3-414; Miss. Code Ann. § 79-4-14.32; N.Y. Bus. Corp. Law § 1113. See Del. Code Ann. tit. 6, § 18-805 (LLC provision); N.Y. Gen. Ass'ns Law § 9 (joint stock associations).

[136] See, e.g., Colo. Rev. Stat. § 7-114-301 (enacted version of MBCA 14.30); La. Rev. Stat. Ann. § 12:1-1430 (same); N.M. Stat. Ann. § 53-16-16 (same); N.C. Gen. Stat. § 55-14-30 (same); Or. Rev. Stat. Ann. § 60.661 (same).

[137] Del. Code Ann. tit. 8, § 278.

[138] Tex. Bus. Orgs. Code § 11.053.

[139] For example, in Delaware dissolution becomes effective once the certificate of dissolution is accepted and date-stamped by the secretary of state in accordance with Section 103 of the DGCL.

California, where under section 1900 of the Corporate Code the need for a shareholder vote can be avoided simply by "holding out" and not conducting any business for at least five years. The company in question was a holding company that owned a bank taken over by the FDIC.[140]

For a variety of reasons, Judge Learned Hand was undoubtedly correct when he proclaimed that: "Dissolution is a heroic remedy for a public corporation."[141] Above all, many of the state law failure tools require shareholder approval, while filing a federal bankruptcy petition is considered within the power of the board in most companies. But for a smallish company, the dissolution mechanism – with creditors notified of their one, last chance to claim part of the debtor's assets – works as a pretty good substitute for a chapter 7 liquidation, particularly if the debtor-company benefits from limited liability.[142]

Attempts to reorganize around a corporate dissolution are apt to run into problems, however, as the law is clear that a purchaser from a dissolved and wound-up corporation can often be held to account for its predecessor's actions. Indeed, much successor liability law was developed in the specific situation where a debtor-company sold all its assets to a new firm that operated what appeared to be the same business in a new corporate shell.[143] Australia has recently introduced "Director Identity Numbers" to allow creditors to track "phoenix activity" – the practice of transferring assets from a near insolvent company to a new company with the same directors and shareholders, which then continues to undertake substantively the same business – which is seen as fraud on creditors. While the government is considering other reforms related to phoenix activity, one thought is that the identification numbers will allow regulators to have directors of multiple failed companies banned from acting as directors in future.

A few American states also include provisions in their corporate codes that allow dissenters to be bound to the terms of a workout agreement, provided notice of such a prospect is included in the company's charter.[144] The case law on these sorts of provisions is sparse, but transparency is also problematic. It is hard to know how often they are used, but there are some hints that, at least in Delaware, these

---

[141] Ex parte Relmar Holding Co., 61 F.2d 941, 942 (2d Cir. 1932).
[142] In re Krafft-Murphy Co., Inc., 82 A.3d 696, 702–04 (Del. 2013).
[143] E.g., *Ray* v. *Alad Corp.*, 560 P.2d 3, 6 (Cal. 1977).
[144] Del. Code Ann. tit 8, §§ 102(b), 302; Mich. Comp. Laws §§ 450.1205, 450.1204.

provisions are not entirely dead,[145] particularly in those instances where the debtor has a concentrated creditor group.[146]

The Sixth Circuit has ruled that Michigan's statute is pre-empted by ERISA,[147] but the court accordingly did not have to address the broader pre-emption question.[148] An intermediate Michigan state court opinion suggests that the provision, to the extent it binds dissenters, is indeed pre-empted by the Bankruptcy Code.[149]

At the very least, the Trust Indenture Act's requirement of unanimous bondholder consent to modifications of key payment terms would seem to take most larger companies out of the scope of these sorts of provisions.[150] The limited jurisdiction of most state courts could also become an issue in a proceeding under such a provision. Moreover, the use of these provisions is predicated on the corporate charter allowing it, which one Delaware attorney advises is uncommon these days.

Probably the biggest, and most well-known, corporation with such a provision in its charter is Wal-Mart. The eighth section of the company's restated certificate of incorporation sets forth the provision required by section 102 of the Delaware corporate law:

> Whenever a compromise or arrangement is proposed between this
> Corporation and its creditors or any class of them and/or between

---

[145] Holly Corp; Form 10-Q; EX-4.6; Note Agreement Of Holly Corporation; Filed: Dec. 14, 1995. ("The enforceability of the Note Agreement, the Notes and the Guaranty may be limited by ... applicable bankruptcy ... including without limitation, Section 302 of the Delaware General Corporation Law inasmuch as Article Ninth of the Company's Restated Certificate of Incorporation contains the language set forth in Section 102(b) of such Act.")

[146] E.g., In re R.A.B. Holdings, No. 903-N, 2005 BL 116165 (Del. Ch. Jan. 06, 2005); In re Treasure Bay Gaming & Resorts, No. 916-N, 2004 BL 32784 (Del. Ch. Dec. 16, 2004); see also In re R.A.B, Holdings, Inc. et al., 2004 WL 5385805 (Del. Ch.) (cover letter). ("All nine holders of the Enterprises notes and four of the six holders, owning 95% in value, of the Holdings notes are parties to the Agreement and have agreed to vote in favor of the proposed Compromise.")

[147] The Employee Retirement Income Security Act of 1974 (ERISA) is the primary federal law that regulates pension and health plans in private industry.

[148] *Michigan Carpenters Council Health & Welfare Fund* v. *C.J. Rogers, Inc.*, 933 F.2d 376, 383 (6th Cir. 1991).

[149] *Jerry Davidson, Inc.* v. *Michigan Nat. Bank*, 220 N.W.2d 714, 716 (Mich. App. 1974).

[150] But see Howard J. Kashner, Majority Clauses and Non-Bankruptcy Corporate Reorganizations-Contractual and Statutory Alternatives, 44 *Bus. Law.* 123, 136 (1988) (arguing that the intentions of the TIA are met by a court-supervised reorganization, even in a state court).

this Corporation and its stockholders or any class of them, any court of equitable jurisdiction within the State of Delaware may, on the application in a summary way of this Corporation or of any creditor or stockholder thereof, or on the application of any receiver or receivers appointed for this Corporation under the provisions of Section 291 of Title 8 of the Delaware Code or on the application of trustees in dissolution or of any receiver or receivers appointed for this Corporation under the provisions of Section 279 of Title 8 of the Delaware Code order a meeting of the creditors or class of creditors, and/or of the stockholders or class of stockholders of this Corporation, as the case may be, to be summoned in such manner as the said court directs. If a majority in number representing three-fourths in value of the creditors or class of creditors and/or of the stockholders or class of stockholders of this Corporation, as the case may be, agree to any compromise or arrangement and to any reorganization of this Corporation as consequence of such compromise or arrangement, the said compromise or arrangement and the said reorganization shall, if sanctioned by the court to which the said application has been made, be binding on all the creditors or class of creditors, and/or on all the stockholders or class of stockholders, of this Corporation, as the case may be, and also on this Corporation.[151]

The possibility of such a restructuring does not feature in a recent SEC filing related to Wal-Mart's debt sales.[152] There is also the interesting question of how this debt, issued under New York law, interacts with such a Delaware corporate law provision. And as applied to stockholders, it is unclear why this provision would be more helpful than a simple amendment of the certificate of incorporation, which would require but the vote of a majority of the outstanding shares.

In all cases of receivership under state law, the question of jurisdiction over a corporation of any substantial size must also loom large. While some states have receivership provisions purporting to reach as broadly as the Bankruptcy Code – for example, under the Pennsylvania corporation code, a receiver has exclusive jurisdiction

---

[151] https://goo.gl/iRo6ZV.
[152] The prospectus supplement dated April 1, 2014, issued in connection with an offering of €850,000,000 aggregate principal amount of 1.900 percent notes due 2022 and €650,000,000 aggregate principal amount of 2.550 percent notes due 2026.

over the corporation and all assets, "wherever situated"[153] – we might doubt the constitutionality of such a reach.

With that, our tour of state business insolvency law veers off the main road, to pick up a host of narrowly tailored insolvency provisions, and a few laws that can only be termed state bankruptcy codes. As we will see, it is often unclear if the latter were ever intended to apply to business entity debtors, or rather reflect a time when nearly all "persons" were genuine people.

Beginning with the former, grain elevators, nursing homes, and (in a recurring theme) railroads are among the industries most often the subject of specialized state insolvency regimes. But we also see cemeteries, apartment complexes, and utility companies in this part of our exploration. And we shall not neglect New Jersey's provisions for turnpikes and canals, or Nevada's special provisions regarding campground receiverships.

Begin with the always popular trains. At one point, most jurisdictions had elaborate statutes regulating both railroad operations, and the process of their failure.[154] In many jurisdictions, the statutes remain, potentially providing a tool for dealing with financial distress in a smaller, localized railroad.[155]

New Jersey retains an ornate railroad reorganization law on its books, in chapter 12 of its Public Utilities Code. Moreover, chapter 3, article 5 of the public utilities law provides a set of general rules for "any railroad, canal, turnpike, bridge or plank road … created by or under any law of this state" under the heading "Sale and Reorganization; Receivers."[156] Thus the statutes provide for even more ancient forms of transport, although one might doubt whether any plank road companies remain in the Garden State.[157]

These provisions codify the law which had developed to provide that the foreclosure-sale purchaser of the assets of a legislatively

---

[153] 15 Pa. Stat. and Cons. Stat. Ann. § 1985.
[154] E.g., Tex. Rev. Civ. Stat. Ann. art. 6421, repealed by Acts 2007, 80th Leg., ch. 1115, § 5(9), eff. Sept. 1, 2007.
[155] According to their trade association, such small railroads "operate 50,000 miles of track or nearly 40 percent of the national railroad network and handle in origination or destination one out of every four rail cars moving on the national system." www.aslrra.org/.
[156] E.g., N.J. Stat. Ann. § 48:3-23.
[157] http://eh.net/encyclopedia/turnpikes-and-toll-roads-in-nineteenth-century-america/.

chartered railroad essentially formed a new corporation, without further action by the state, with both the same burdens and benefits as the old.[158] Under the New Jersey statutes, the majority of purchasers

> may organize such new corporation by electing a president and board of six directors, to continue in office for one year succeeding such meeting, and annually thereafter, on the same day of the month, a like election for president and six directors shall be held to serve for one year. At such meeting such majority shall adopt a corporate name and corporate seal, determine the amount of the capital stock thereof, and shall have power and authority to make and issue certificates therefor to the persons in interest, to the amount of their respective interests therein, in shares of fifty dollars each.
>
> Such new corporation may then, or any time thereafter, create and issue preferred stock to such an amount, and at such times as they may deem necessary, and from time to time issue bonds at a rate of interest not exceeding six percent per annum, to any amount not exceeding their capital stocks and secure the same by a mortgage of the property, rights, powers, privileges and franchises of such corporation.[159]

In short, they are off and running without formal creation of a new entity, something that might have been useful in an era when a new railroad charter might have still required legislative action.

The statutes also provide for the appointment of receivers for insolvent transport companies, who are authorized to sell the company. Purchasers take it "free and clear of all debts, claims and demands of creditors, mortgagees or stockholders."[160] Consistent with the rule in foreclosure proceedings, the receiver can sell special charter rights as part of the sale.[161]

Ohio has special railroad provisions designed to act as an overlay to a traditional receivership. If two-thirds of creditors and shareholders

---

[158] Leonard A. Jones, Treatise on the Law of Corporate and Mortgages 590–1 (2d ed. 1890); see also *Boylan v. Kelly*, 36 N.J. Eq. 331, 335 (1882). New Jersey's statute was enacted in 1887. Statutes to this effect remain in force in a few other states. E.g., Mass. Ann. Laws ch. 160, § 55.

[159] N.J. Stat. Ann. § 48:3-24.

[160] Id. § 48:3-28.

[161] Id. § 48:3-29.

agree, a reorganization plan can become binding for any railroad that is at least partially within the State of Ohio.[162] The dissenters are entitled to the same treatment as the plan proponents, but are otherwise barred from any further recovery.[163] That last provision looks suspiciously like a discharge.

Railroad receiverships are not directly subject to special provisions in New York, but the commissioner of transportation has special oversight powers in such receiverships, including the ability to veto the reorganized company's proposed capital structure.[164] And an 1877 statute in Tennessee gives a special priority, over all liens, for "judgments and decrees, and executions therefrom, for timbers furnished and work and labor done on, or for damages done to persons and property in the operation of its railroad in this state."[165] The timber suppliers must have had very skillful lobbyists.[166]

And then there are the grain elevators. The basic insolvency problem for grain elevators – be they commercial or co-operative – is that when they fail, they are holding other people's property. Moreover, all property tends to be lumped together in a single, indistinguishable mass. In this respect, they are like stock and commodity brokers.

Many states have statutes providing that farmers with a valid receipt for placing their grain in the elevator have a claim to their proportionate share of the grain in the elevator at the time of failure.[167] Many states also provide for a priority claim against the elevator's estate for any shortfall. Since 1984, farmers have enjoyed a similar, albeit limited, priority under the federal Bankruptcy Code.[168]

Likely to help effectuate these provisions, several states provide for special receiverships of grain elevators.[169] In several cases the regulator

---

[162] Ohio Rev. Code Ann. §§ 4971.01, 4971.12.

[163] Id. § 4971.16.

[164] Commissioner of Transportation

[165] Tenn. Code Ann. § 65-10-112.

[166] See also Tenn. Code Ann. § 29-36-102. ("Any railroad contractor, the railroad contractor's agent or operatives, who wrongfully cuts down, appropriates, or otherwise injures or destroys any growing timber, or wood, or any fence rails, on ground not belonging to the railroad company, shall be liable in damages to the party injured.")

[167] E.g., Wyo. Stat. Ann. § 11-11-114.

[168] 11 U.S.C. § 507(a)(6).

[169] North Dakota also have such provisions for roving grain buyers, N.D. Cent. Code § 60-02.1-29, and hay buyers. N.D. Cent. Code § 60-03-13.

of elevators – often the Department of Agriculture – has the power to seek such a receivership upon learning that the elevator is in distress. [170] In some cases, an official from the regulator is marked as the receiver. [171]

Logically, these sorts of receiverships are always apt to be engulfed by a federal bankruptcy proceeding. For instance, on March 13, 2008, the state Agriculture and Forestry Commissioner was appointed receiver for the Central Louisiana Grain Co-operative. On 10 April, the co-operative filed a chapter 7 petition and the receivership was washed up. [172]

Nevertheless, there are some indications that state law alternatives are frequently pursued, although precisely how often is unclear. In the 1980s, there was a wave of grain elevator failures. [173] As part of a larger study of the topic, Marianne Culhane notes

> Some grain elevators are liquidated by state law insolvency proceedings and never result in a bankruptcy filing that would show up in the ... USDA statistics. Thus, the figures considerably understate the rate of elevator insolvency. An example of state law insolvency liquidation is the Coole-Reese elevator in Ashland, Nebraska, which lost its license in 1980 and has turned its assets over to a committee of creditors. [174]

And in a more recent case, an Ohio bankruptcy court abstained in favor of a state-law receiver who had already made progress in

---

[170] E.g., Ark. Code Ann. § 2-17-236 ("Whenever the commissioner shall become satisfied that the corporation cannot resume business or liquidate its indebtedness to the satisfaction of its creditors, the commissioner shall report the fact of its insolvency to the Attorney General. Immediately upon receipt of the notice, the Attorney General shall institute proper proceedings in the proper court for the purpose of having a receiver appointed."); Tenn. Code Ann. § 43-32-108.

[171] Ala. Code § 8-15-14; Mo. Rev. Stat. § 276.501; N.D. Cent. Code Ann. § 60-04-03.

[172] In re Cent. Louisiana Grain Co-op., Inc., No. 08-80475, 2014 WL 4345268, at *1 (Bankr. W.D. La. Aug. 28, 2014).

[173] Missouri Bean Farmer, Hero Of Drive For A New Bankruptcy Law, Is Freed, N.Y. Times (June 2, 1982). ("The jailing of Mr. Cryts was the latest episode in what has been a two-year battle over the ownership of two million bushels of grain and soybeans stored in 11 bankrupt elevators in Missouri and Arkansas. The dispute has widened to include the larger question of economic protection for farmers at a time when elevator bankruptcies have become commonplace.")

[174] Marianne B. Culhane, *Grain Elevator Insolvency Problems 1* (Creighton Univ. Sch. of Law ed., 1982).

rehabilitating and selling the debtor's business,[175] while Archer Daniels Midland was reported to have bought a grain elevator in Wisconsin from a receiver.[176]

In a broad sense, the solvency of any sort of quasi-fiduciary is apt to be of special concern to legislators. Thus, we also see a host of specialized insolvency procedures with regard to nursing homes and other related healthcare facilities.[177] For example, New Mexico's "Health Facility Receivership Act" broadly picks up not only nursing homes, but a variety of healthcare facilities from hospitals to childbirth centers.[178]

In many states, the power to appoint a receiver for a nursing home facility is confined to the "secretary" or "commissioner" of the state agency that regulates nursing homes, the "agency" or "department" itself, or the attorney general acting for either of the foregoing.[179] In Connecticut, a patient can file a request for a receivership with the regulator, and if the regulator then fails to act, the patient can proceed to court.[180] In Massachusetts, the attorney general, the Department of Public Health, or any "interested party" may file a petition in the Superior Court for the appointment of a long-term care facility receiver.[181]

Under these statutes insolvency or financial distress is an express or implied factor that would warrant appointment of a receiver, [182] but the primary concern is not creditor recoveries, but instead protection of residents.[183] In California, the commencement of such a receivership

---

[175] In re Archbold Elevator, Inc., Case No. 11-34894 (Bankr. N.D. Ohio Sept. 27, 2011).

[176] Rick Romell, Archer Daniels Midland acquires grain elevators from Olsen's Mill, J. Sentinel (Aug. 31, 2011).

[177] See, e.g., N.Y. Pub. Health Law § 2810; Conn. Gen. Stat. §§ 19a-542 to 19a-549. See also *Attorney Gen. v. M.C.K., Inc.*, 736 N.E.2d 373, 376 (Ma. 2000).

[178] N.M. Stat. Ann. § 24-1E-2.

[179] E.g., Ind. Code Ann. § 16-28-8-1; Md. Code Ann., Health-Gen. § 19-334; Mo. Rev. Stat. § 198.099. See also Mo. Rev. Stat. § 630.763 (mental health facility); N.Y. Mental Hyg. Law § 31.28. But see Colo. Rev. Stat. Ann. § 25-3-108(2). ("The department of public health and environment, the licensee or owner of a long-term health care facility, or the lessee of such facility with the approval of the owner may apply to the district court for the appointment of a receiver to operate the long-term health care facility ...")

[180] Conn. Gen. Stat. Ann. § 19a-542.

[181] Mass. Gen. Laws Ann. ch. 111, § 72M.

[182] Alaska Stat. Ann. § 18.20.370; Fla. Stat. Ann. § 400.126; Minn. Stat. Ann. § 144A.15; Tex. Health & Safety Code § 246.092.

[183] N.H. Rev. Stat. Ann. § 151-H:3. ("The purpose of a receivership created under this section shall be to safeguard the health, safety, and continuity of care to residents and to protect them from the adverse health effects and increased risk of death caused by abrupt

imposes a sixty-day automatic stay that broadly prohibits interference with the continued operations of the facility.[184] While in Massachusetts, receivers of long-term care facilities "shall not close the facility without leave of court."[185]

However, even in states that have these specialized statutes, they are not always used. For example, California's nursing home receivership statute can only be invoked by the regulator.[186] Thus, in one recent case where a chain of nursing homes was not paying its rent, the landlord sought the appointment of a receiver under the normal receivership provisions.[187] The landlord noted that while normally it might seek to evict a non-paying tenant, one could hardly do that in the case of a nursing home. This would seem to be precisely the kind of situation in which to invoke the special procedures, but the plaintiff was not a proper plaintiff under the statute.

In a somewhat related vein, continuing-care retirement communities allow seniors to live in an independent environment for as long as possible, and then receive nursing care within the same community when it is needed. Residents of these communities pay a large upfront entry fee in exchange for the promise of lifetime care, when and if needed. That obviously leaves the residents vulnerable to insolvency, since they pay well in advance of the provision of services.[188]

As a result, several states have enacted legislation to regulate continuing care retirement communities' financial viability.[189] Some are of questionable utility. For example, in Virginia regulators can issue a cease or desist order or an injunction if

---

or unsuitable transfer of residents.") See also Conn. Gen. Stat. Ann. § 19a-545; Mass. Gen. Laws Ann. ch. 111, § 72N.

[184] Cal. Health & Safety Code § 1327.5. See also Ark. Code Ann. § 20-10-913.

[185] Mass. Gen. Laws Ann. ch. 111, § 72O.

[186] Cal. Health & Safety Code § 1327.

[187] *Quality Care Properties Inc. et al.* v. *HCR III Healthcare LLC*, Docket No. BC672837 (Cal. Super. Ct. Aug. 17, 2017).

[188] See generally Nathalie D. Martin, The Insolvent Life Care Provider: Who Leads the Dance Between the Federal Bankruptcy Code and State Continuing-Care Statutes?, 61 *Ohio St. L.J.* 267 (2000).

[189] E.g., Ark. Code Ann. § 23-93-111; Mass. Gen. Laws Ann. ch. 93, § 76.

> A provider is bankrupt, insolvent, under reorganization pursuant
> to federal bankruptcy laws, or in imminent danger of becoming
> bankrupt or insolvent.[190]

If the community is already in a federal bankruptcy proceeding, such
an action is more likely to result in a debate about the scope of the automatic stay than anything else. And an order or injunction on the eve of
bankruptcy or insolvency might simply make that outcome inevitable.

Equally ineffective are provisions like those found in Arkansas:

> In the event of the bankruptcy or receivership of the provider
> resulting from the financial difficulties of the provider, the residents
> of the facility shall have a statutory lien on the real and personal
> property of the facility.[191]

As applied to bankruptcy proceedings, this provision was pre-empted
the very day it was enacted back in 1987.[192] And such pre-emption
provides an obvious reason for the community to favor a federal bankruptcy court over a state court receivership. No different are those
states who purport to provide a "preferred claim" – which sounds nice,
but is totally lacking in detail – in any insolvency proceeding involving
the community.[193] Perhaps more useful is a provision like Minnesota's,
which provides for a lien in favor of the resident upon their entry into
the community.[194]

Some states include special receivership proceedings for the communities among the regulatory toolbox.[195] These receiverships can
provide for either liquidation or reorganization of the community.[196]
In some states these are clearly designed to favor the residents, over

---

[190] Va. Code Ann. § 38.2-4925.
[191] Ark. Code Ann. § 23-93-113. See also N.J. Stat. Ann. § 52:27D-341 (lien valid for ten
days, can be extended).
[192] 11 U.S.C. § 545.
[193] Fla. Stat. Ann. § 651.071; N.C. Gen. Stat. Ann. § 58-64-60; Or. Rev. Stat. Ann. § 101.065.
See also N.H. Rev. Stat. Ann. § 420-D:16 ("... in the event of liquidation, all continuing
care agreements with a provider shall be deemed preferred claims against the assets of
the provider").
[194] Minn. Stat. Ann. § 80D.08. But the provision in the same law that allows residents to seek
appointment of a trustee in a bankruptcy case suffers from the same basic invalidity as
the Arkansas provision discussed above. Minn. Stat. Ann. § 80D.11(1).
[195] N.J. Stat. Ann. § 52:27D-346; N.Y. Pub. Health Law § 4617.
[196] Minn. Stat. Ann. § 80D.11.

other creditors.[197] In others – New York, for example – the receiver is vaguely told to "operate the community in such a manner as intended to assure safety and adequate care for such residents."[198]

In Florida, a court recently refused to appoint a receiver simply because the community's bank foreclosed on its mortgage, as the mortgage agreement itself provided that the lender would respect the rights of residents.[199] Thus, the special protections of these sorts of statutes are perhaps subject to some degree of pre-emption by contract, which suggests a weaker insolvency regime than most that aim to protect favored claimants.

Cemeteries, apartment complexes, and small utility companies round out this part of our journey. Cemeteries that are at or near capacity essentially cease to take in new funds, and draw on their endowments, in perpetuity, to keep the facilities in good repair. If the endowment should run short, the cemetery could become insolvent.

On the other hand, the endowment itself is typically protected from creditors, so there is no real need for the cemetery to file for bankruptcy. If the managers are looting the endowment, the attorney general's normal power over trusts would seem to be sufficient. But that involves the heroic assumption that the state attorney general is actually actively policing trusts and non-profits. There is the real chance that these cemeteries could end up in some sort of netherworld, which seems to have motivated a handful of states to draft special insolvency statutes – invariably involving a receivership, triggered by some regulator of burial grounds.[200] The frequent "pre-sale" of cemetery plots and related services also injects these cases with a consumer protection

---

[197] For example, in New Hampshire the receiver can use the proceeds of the liquidation to pay for residents' entry into new facilities. N.H. Rev. Stat. Ann. § 420-D:16. This would undoubtedly prompt an involuntary bankruptcy petition if there were substantial general unsecured creditors, who might lose their recovery as a result.

[198] N.Y. Pub. Health Law § 4617.

[199] *Devonshire At PGA Nat., LLC* v. *State ex rel. Dep't of Fin. Servs. of State of Florida*, 103 So. 3d 1060 (Fla. Dist. Ct. App. 2013).

[200] Fla. Stat. Ann. § 497.160; La. Stat. Ann. § 8:69.2; Tenn. Code Ann. § 46-1-312; Va. Code Ann. § 54.1-2313.1. See also 18 Va. Admin. Code 47-20-260.

element, if it turns out that the plot in question has been sold multiple times or the funds for the future funeral have been redirected.[201]

Indeed, within or without states with such specialized laws there is a long history of cemetery receivership law that undoubtedly escapes the attention of most bankruptcy attorneys.[202] The bulk of the "law" in this area seems to develop without engendering reported decisions, or academic commentary, and it's only apparent from a review of newspaper accounts of the surprising number of receiverships.

Another group of statutes provides for special receiverships for small utility companies.[203] Under the Illinois version, the receiver acts under the oversight of the court, as with most receiverships, and is compensated from the assets of the company. The receiver is instructed to "operate the public utility or telecommunications carrier to preserve its assets and to serve the best interests of its customers."[204] Rather than directly provide for a sale, the statute seems to assume that either the receivership will be returned to its owner or liquidated. The latter could presumably follow the sale of the company. In Virginia, such a receivership can be initiated by two-thirds of the customers of the utility, or the Board of Health, in addition to the more common initiation by the regulator of the company.

At this point the specialized state insolvency law begins to fragment, reflecting perhaps the focused interests of the various state legislatures. A handful of states have special receivership provisions for financially distressed condominiums. In Illinois, the distress must be severe (e.g., half the units are unoccupied), and proceedings are commenced by the

---

[201] E.g., *State ex rel. Johnson* v. *Mount Olivet Cemetery Co.*, 834 S.W.2d 306, 307 (Tenn. Ct. App. 1992) (receivership commenced in 1980). Oregon has a special receivership just for such pre-sale companies. Or. Rev. Stat. Ann. § 97.942.

[202] E.g., *Moist* v. *Belk*, 380 F.2d 721, 722 (6th Cir. 1967); *Cedar Bluff Cemetery Ass'n* v. *Zuck*, 120 N.E.2d 875, 880 (Ill. App. Ct. 1954); *People's Cemetery Ass'n* v. *Oakland Cemetery Co.*, 60 S.W. 679, 679 (Tex. Civ. App. 1901), writ refused.

[203] 220 Ill. Comp. Stat. Ann. 5/4-501; N.H. Rev. Stat. Ann. § 374:47-a; Va. Code Ann. § 56-265.13:6.1; Va. Code Ann. § 32.1-174.3. See also Ohio Rev. Code Ann. § 4928.2310 (providing that certain regulatory orders remain in force "notwithstanding any bankruptcy, reorganization, or other insolvency proceedings with respect to the electric distribution utility or any affiliate").

[204] See Illinois Bell Tel. Co. (SBC Illinois) & Madison River Commc'ns LLC, 2004 WL 2939427 (Sept. 8, 2004).

municipal government.[205] The court is given the power to reclassify the property, removing its condominium status. In Florida, the receivership provisions are closely tied to the authority of the State's Division of Florida Condominiums, Timeshares, and Mobile Homes.[206]

New Jersey's Multifamily Housing Preservation and Receivership Act is both more elaborate and sweeps more broadly, covering

> any building or structure and the land appurtenant thereto in which at least half of the net square footage of the building is used for residential purposes; and shall not include any one to four unit residential building in which the owner occupies one of the units as his or her principal residence.[207]

The statute is accompanied by a series of codified "legislative findings" that suggest that the aim was substandard housing, particularly that occupied by the poor.[208]

Perhaps on the other end of the economic spectrum – although still within the realm of receiverships – is Virginia's special receivership provisions for distressed "common interest community managers."[209] Common interest communities are essentially real estate developments with a mix of residential and recreational facilities – think pools, tennis courts, and golf courses – supported by assessments on the owners.[210] Receivership applications can be filed under seal, and a "Common Interest Community Management Recovery Fund" pays the receiver's expenses if the estate's assets are insufficient.

Then there is Nevada's rather skeletal statute providing for receivers to be appointed for insolvent time shares.[211] Enacted in 1987, it is the companion to an even more unique statutory provision providing for the appointment of receivers to oversee insolvent campgrounds that was enacted the same year.[212] Neither has apparently ever been

---

[205] 765 Ill. Comp. Stat. Ann. 605/14.5.

[206] Fla. Stat. Ann. § 718.501.

[207] N.J. Stat. Ann. § 2A:42-116.

[208] Id. § 2A:42-115; see also id., § 2A:42-117.

[209] Va. Code Ann. § 54.1-2353. See also Nev. Rev. Stat. Ann. § 116.790. Cf. Conn. Gen. Stat. Ann. § 47-258. ("In any action by the association to collect assessments or to foreclose a lien for unpaid assessments, the court may appoint a receiver of the unit owner ...")

[210] Va. Code Ann. § 55-528.

[211] Nev. Rev. Stat. Ann. § 119A.665.

[212] Ibid., § 119B.385.

the subject of written commentary, and the legislative history seems to be non-existent.

In general, the purpose of many of these statutes is unclear, at least as a matter of policy. For example, the latter two Nevada statutes provide nothing that is not already present in the general law of receiverships. And while some of the specialized state statutes are slightly unique in allowing a regulator or other party to commence proceedings, such a narrow aim could be achieved by more targeted means.

Perhaps these are best explained by politics, rather than policy. A politician desiring to make a statement about a particular problem could do worse than advancing a specialized receivership statute. And nearly any industry could be the subject of such a provision.

And then we come to the state "bankruptcy" laws. At one point, most states had statutes like these. For example, California's Insolvency Act of 1895 replaced the earlier Acts of 1880 and 1852.[213] The 1895 law expressly applied to corporations, and offered debtors a full discharge.

As one expert commentator has noted:

> With the growing tendency of American business to expand across state lines, the state bankruptcy acts were unsatisfactory, but their operation in many instances was more nearly approximate to Federal bankruptcy administration than many people realize. The state by making rights on contracts subject to state discharge provisions in insolvency could discharge debtors from most of their obligations. It could coerce releases from other creditors by preferring creditors who granted general releases. Furthermore, so far as corporate debtors were concerned, discharge was usually of no significance, for the corporation was customarily extinguished after the liquidation of its assets.
>
> State insolvency statutes in numerous instances created a state bankruptcy system.[214]

Many states still have these sorts of statutes "on the books." In some cases, the statutes are so old that it is not clear they were ever intended

---

[213] See Wilbur Fisk Henning, *Insolvency and Assignment Laws of California Annotated* (1895).

[214] John Hanna, Contemporary Utility of General Assignments, 35 *Va. L. Rev.* 539, 541 (1949).

to apply to corporations, even if the laws are not entirely pre-empted by the federal Bankruptcy Code.[215] And when a law like Delaware's dating from 1853 provides that

> [w]hoever is imprisoned for debt ... may obtain discharge from such imprisonment upon petition to the Superior Court of the county wherein he or she is imprisoned, and compliance with the provisions of this subchapter[216]

application to any sort of business debtor beyond a sole proprietorship, or perhaps a general partnership, would be strained. And the discharge only protects the debtor's personal freedom – any debt not fully paid in the proceeding can be collected from the debtor's future property.[217] Pennsylvania's version, dating from 1836, is limited to those debtors imprisoned for debts of less than $15 and who have been confined for more than thirty days.[218]

In a few states, seemingly useful statutes are actually still in force, although it may be difficult to convince the courts to apply them in the face of the Bankruptcy Code. New Hampshire's statute is of particular interest, inasmuch as it expressly applies to corporate debtors.[219]

The process is essentially an assignment for the benefit of creditors, wrapped with a discharge and other bankruptcy-like statutory provisions. The creditors pick the assignee by a vote of two-thirds of the creditors (in both amount and number), at a meeting of creditors.[220] At the commencement of a case, a "messenger" takes control of the

---

[215] See *Goldstein v. Columbia Diamond Ring Co.*, 323 N.E.2d 344, 349 (Mass. 1975). ("On the passage by the Congress of the Bankruptcy Act of July 1, 1898, which, as amended, is now Title 11 of the United States Code, the operation of our State insolvency statute, now G.L. c. 216, was suspended and continues to be suspended.") The Massachusetts insolvency statute was ultimately repealed in 1978, just in time for the new Bankruptcy Code.

[216] Del. Code Ann. tit. 10, § 7301. Similar statutes in other states include N.Y. Debt. & Cred. Law § 120; N.C. Gen. Stat. Ann. § 23-30.1.

[217] Del. Code Ann. tit. 10, § 7341.

[218] 39 Pa. Stat. Ann. § 325. See also N.H. Rev. Stat. Ann. § 568:43; 10 R.I. Gen. Laws § 13-10; Vt. Stat. Ann. tit. 12, § 3689.

[219] N.H. Rev. Stat. Ann. § 568:49. See also N.H. Rev. Stat. Ann. § 568:46. ("A partner, whenever his copartners will not join with him in a voluntary assignment, may file a petition in form and substance like a creditor's petition in the county where any of the partners resides, praying that the firm be adjudged insolvent, and all subsequent proceedings shall be the same as those in cases involving creditors' petitions.")

[220] N.H. Rev. Stat. Ann. § 568:23.

debtor's property, and even liquidates perishable property, turning all proceeds and property over to the assignee once appointed.

As outlined in the statute, the process really zips along: the debtor files full schedules within ten days of case commencement, a bar date is set for two months out, and assets or proceeds are to be distributed to creditors within eight months.[221]

Under the law, involuntary petitions are only permissible for debtors ineligible for bankruptcy under federal law.[222] The filing of a partnership pulls in the individual partners[223] – an approach somewhat inconsistent with the "modern" view of partnerships as legal entities, albeit in a statute that long predates the modern view – provided that the individual partners are residents of New Hampshire.[224]

While this might be a useful tool for reorganizing a small business, there is the obvious question of whether it complies with the federal Constitution. As the core of the statute has been in place since the 1860s, and the discharge provisions since the 1880s, the Contracts Clause would not seem to be a big concern, provided the court did not attempt to expand its jurisdiction beyond New Hampshire with regard to absent creditors.[225]

The New Hampshire Supreme Court did find that the State statute was suspended by the 1898 Bankruptcy Act, but that decision seems to have been based in the specific wording of the federal statute, which has since been repealed.[226] In a somewhat more recent opinion, that same court held that an individual debtor eligible to file under then chapter XIII of the federal Bankruptcy Act could not file under the New Hampshire statute, but it gave no explanation for its holding.[227]

The key problem for the law would be the discharge provision. Discharge provisions are clear sources of trouble for state insolvency laws – indeed, this is the only clear rule in the Supreme Court's

---

[221] Id. § 568:33.

[222] Id. § 568:43.

[223] Id. § 568:47. ("The insolvency of a partnership shall render each partner insolvent within the meaning of this chapter, and his property not exempt from attachment, books and papers shall pass to the messenger and assignee appointed in the partnership proceedings; but the assignee shall be nominated by the partnership creditors.")

[224] *Smith* v. *Hammond*, 44 A. 519, 520 (N.H. 1895).

[225] Howland's Appeal, 35 A. 943, 944 (N.H. 1893).

[226] *E. C. Wescott Co.* v. *Berry*, 45 A. 352, 353 (N.H. 1898).

[227] Appeal of Shamma, 369 A.2d 191, 192 (N.H. 1977).

bankruptcy-pre-emption jurisprudence. Presumably the discharge could be struck, while the remaining law remained in force.[228] A corporate debtor would not notice the difference, and could still benefit from what would amount to a formalized, "fast track" assignment process.

We might also question if the specific discharge in this statute is really problematic. The discharge in the statute is only granted upon the debtor's petition, and only operates in cases where creditors either receive more than a 50 percent recovery on their claims or vote, by a two-thirds supermajority, to grant a discharge.[229] The law contains the kind of protections against fraudulent discharges that we are accustomed to in federal bankruptcy law.[230] In short, we might wonder whether, notwithstanding some broad pronouncements in the case law, this is really a situation where federal law should prevail, so long as we continue to say that state insolvency laws are not pre-empted in full. [231]

Similarly, section 31 of Pennsylvania's Insolvency Act provides:

> Any creditor of an alleged insolvent may, in the court of common pleas of the county where the alleged insolvent resides or his principal place of business is situate [*sic*], by petition, under oath, aver that such person, persons, firm, limited partnership, joint stock company or corporation is insolvent, has not made an assignment for the benefit of his, their or its creditors, is resident or is carrying on business in said county; and:
>
> (1) has called a meeting of his creditors for the purpose of compounding with them, or has exhibited a statement showing his inability to meet his liabilities, or has otherwise acknowledged his insolvency; or

---

[228] In re Tarnowski, 210 N.W. 836, 838 (Wis. 1926).

[229] N.H. Rev. Stat. Ann. § 568:40.

[230] E.g., Id. § 568:51. ("If a debtor, or any officer of a corporation against which a petition in insolvency is pending, shall wilfully omit to file a list or schedule as ordered, or shall wilfully and fraudulently give false information or neglect to give true information to the assignee in relation to the estate or the claims of creditors, or to do any act or to furnish or discover any evidence in his power or knowledge material to the just settlement of the estate, he shall be guilty of a misdemeanor.")

[231] But see *Boese* v. *King*, 108 U.S. 379, 385 (1883). ("Undoubtedly the local [New Jersey] statute was, from the date of the passage of the [1867] bankrupt act, inoperative in so far as it provided for the discharge of the debtor from future liability to creditors who came in under the assignment and participated in the distribution of the proceeds of the assigned property.")

(2) has absconded or is about to abscond, with intent to defraud
     any creditor, or to defeat or delay the remedy of any creditor,
     or avoid being arrested or served with legal process, or con-
     ceals himself within or remains out of the Commonwealth,
     with like intent; or

(3) secretes or is about to secrete any part of his estate or effects,
     with intent to defraud his creditors, or to defeat or delay their
     demands, or any of them; or

(4) has assigned, removed or disposed of, or is about to assign,
     remove or dispose of, any part of his property, with intent to
     defraud, defeat or delay his creditors, or any of them; or

(5) has actually been imprisoned for more than thirty days, in
     a civil action, or, being arrested therefore, has escaped from
     custody; or

(6) has refused or neglected to comply with any order, judgment
     or decree for the payment of money, and in execution there-
     fore has been returned unsatisfied; or

(7) has suffered or permitted any attachment or sequestration to
     remain against any of his property, without attempting to dis-
     solve by rule taken for that purpose, or upon entering security
     for a period of thirty days, or having taken a rule to dissolve
     which has been discharged by the court, has not entered secu-
     rity within twenty days thereafter; or

(8) has made any pledge, assignment, transfer, conveyance or
     encumbrance of the whole or a large part of his stock in trade
     or property, without being able to meet his liabilities and with-
     out the consent of his creditors, either in payment of or as
     security for a debt then existing, or with the intent to prefer
     one creditor to another, or out of his usual course of business,
     or for the benefit of himself or his family.

A petitioning creditor must file a petition alleging one of the eight
items on the list, plus that the debtor is insolvent. Insolvency is defined
when the debtor's property "shall not in a fair valuation be sufficient in
amount to pay [its] debts." If the creditor carries its burden, a receiver
is appointed to take charge of the debtor's business.[232] The discharge
under this act is geared toward individuals, and is only applicable to
those creditors who voluntarily participate in any event, and thus is

---

[232] 39 Pa. Stat. Ann. § 71.

not apt to pre-emption concerns associated with New Hampshire's statute.[233]

Public sales of the debtor's property can be made free and clear of liens,[234] but otherwise it is not clear that the Insolvency Act provides much more than a standard assignment might. But at least into the 1980s there is some evidence that the Pennsylvania statute was still in use.[235]

State law, despite the apparent inability to grant a discharge, does offer some useful tools for resolving a failed or troubled business. There are real questions about the trade-offs inherent in these tools – less formality and less transparency – which we will return to later in this book. But first we return to the state and federal law we previously pushed to one side: the law covering the failure of financial institutions.

---

[233] Ibid., § 100.

[234] Ibid., § 77.

[235] In re Paolino, 49 B.R. 834, 835 (Bankr. E.D. Pa. 1985) ("... the state court ordered that the equity action proceed under Pennsylvania's Insolvency and Assignment Statute. Seven months later an involuntary petition was filed under chapter 11 of the Bankruptcy Code ... by four of the debtors' unsecured creditors, to whom is owed in excess of $5,000.00 of undisputed debts").

4 FINANCIAL INSTITUTIONS UNDER FEDERAL LAW

Time to tackle financial institution insolvency laws. As before, we start with the federal.

Financial institutions are arguably different from regular firms on several dimensions. Financial institutions often have liabilities that are either payable on demand, or after a very short term. Bank deposits are the classic example. But even whole life insurance policies are in some sense demand deposits, in that their cash value can be demanded with little or no notice to the insurance company. And most financial institutions take the funds raised from their short-term debt and invest them in long-term assets, like loans. "[W]hen short-term debt funds longer-term liabilities, a defining characteristic of banks and much of the shadow banking system, the institutions that result are inherently fragile."[1]

Many financial institutions are highly leveraged, with capital (or equity) typically comprising only a small fraction of total liabilities. This increases the risk of "runs," even in solvent financial institutions, because a small decrease in assets can put the balance sheet out of whack. Finally, financial institutions are subject to supervision, regulation, and examination in ways that traditional firms are not.

Reorganizations, at least reorganizations of the kind studied in this book, are also rare with regard to financial institutions. The following

---

[1] Kathryn Judge, The Money Problem: Rethinking Financial Regulation, 130 *Harv. L. Rev.* 1148, 1150 (2017) (book review).

explanation of banks applies in general terms to the whole of financial institutions:

> Many jurisdictions (including the United States) have traditional reorganization proceedings on their books, but few employ them. Banks are commonly reorganized, but without a moratorium and generally with close supervisory involvement. There is a good reason for this. For industrial firms, a moratorium on payments buys time, allowing insolvent firms to conduct business without the harassment of creditors. However, banks are in the business of effecting timely payments. A stay on payments is a stay on their core business. In a less competitive world of small semi-monopolistic banks with unsophisticated customers, the stay was not necessarily fatal. But in advanced economies, even unsophisticated customers have choices, and sophisticated customers will start a run on the bank at the first rumor of trouble. Bank "conservatorships" worked well in the Great Depression. However, we no longer live in that world, and therefore seldom see traditional reorganizations applied to banks.[2]

Of course, it is easy to overstate the differences between financial institutions and real economy firms, and banking, insurance, securities, or commodities law experts have some incentive to do so because it emphasizes the "specialness" of their profession. Bankruptcy or insolvency law experts, conversely, have similar incentives to overstate the general applicability of their specialized knowledge.

Since the advent of national bank charters during the Civil War, federal law has included special provisions for appointment by the Comptroller of the Currency of receivers for these banks.[3] The National Bank Act of 1864 gave the Comptroller the exclusive authority to close a bank, and to appoint a receiver to manage its affairs.[4] The receiver served as the Comptroller's agent, and the courts

---

[2] Thomas C. Baxter, Jr., et al., Two Cheers for Territoriality: An Essay on International Bank Insolvency Law, 78 *Am. Bankr. L.J.* 57, 70–1 (2004).

[3] *Kennedy* v. *Gibson*, 75 U.S. 498, 503 (1869); Robert R. Bliss & George G. Kaufman, U.S. Corporate and Bank Insolvency Regimes: A Comparison and Evaluation, 2 *Va. L. & Bus. Rev.* 143, 150 (2007).

[4] Garrard Glenn, The Law Governing Liquidation § 269 (1935). To quote John Hanna, "[t]his is one of the best law books in the English language." Glenn: The Law Governing Liquidation, 35 *Colum. L. Rev.* 317 (1935).

were called upon to approve the receiver's decisions only in limited
instances.[5]

Before the New Deal, the Comptroller and its appointed receiver
also enforced the personal liability of shareholders – which was capped
at the bank's full par value.[6] In short, shareholders could be compelled
to pay for their shares twice.[7]

At the outer limits of our inquiry are the provisions for the insolvency
of a local Federal Reserve Bank. These too start with the proposition
that the member banks in the Reserve Bank have double liability should
the Reserve Bank find itself short of funds.[8] That is, if we go through the
looking glass and the Federal Reserve Bank of New York somehow gets
into trouble, the banks of Manhattan will be "on the hook" to bail it out.

In the early days, nominally solvent banks also engaged in what
amounted to assignments for the benefit of creditors.[9] These assignments were typically combined with the voluntary liquidation of the
assigning bank, under provisions that are still in force.

Indeed, under current law, a national bank's shareholders, by
a two-thirds vote, can trigger the winding up of the institution.[10] A
notice of intent to liquidate must be sent to the Comptroller.[11] Under
the Comptroller's regulations, the bank must send periodic progress
reports during the process.[12]

The old receivership provisions are also still "on the books," for use
in the event that an uninsured national bank might fail.[13] These days,
the most likely candidate would be one of the handful of nationally

---

[5] *Hulse* v. *Argetsinger*, 18 F.2d 944, 945–6 (2d Cir. 1927).

[6] *Bushnell* v. *Leland*, 164 U.S. 684, 684 (1897). Shareholders in banks that were open could
be assessed, and sometimes these assessments would, in total, exceed the liability limits of
the shares upon closure. Helen A. Garten, A Political Analysis of Bank Failure Resolution,
74 *B.U. L. Rev.* 429, 434 (1994).

[7] The states had varying rules; Colorado had triple liability and California had unlimited
liability. Arizona became the last state to repeal shareholder liability in the 1950s. The
FDIC Act includes a provision stating that upon paying for insured deposits of a failed
member bank, the FDIC waives all claims on shareholders if such claims arise from state
laws.

[8] 12 U.S.C. § 502.

[9] *O'Conner* v. *Watson*, 81 F.2d 833, 835 (5th Cir. 1936).

[10] 12 U.S.C. § 181.

[11] 12 U.S.C. § 182.

[12] 12 C.F.R. § 5.48(e)(2), (3).

[13] 12 U.S.C. § 192.

chartered trust companies.[14] Many are part of gigantic financial conglomerates – Goldman Sachs Trust Company, N.A. and State Street Bank and Trust Company, N.A. provide representative examples – and it is hard to imagine these companies failing separate from their parents. Such a catastrophe would likely invoke Dodd-Frank's orderly liquidation authority, which we will consider momentarily. But other companies – including relatively well-known entities like Brown Brothers Harriman Trust Company, N.A. and The Northern Trust Company of New York, N.A. – might actually trigger use of the old receivership provisions, if their larger corporate groups were to experience financial distress.

And in recent months the Comptroller has published new, proposed rules on what such a receivership might look like – although the rules themselves are quite vacuous.[15] The Comptroller has been promoting the use of national charters by online lending companies.[16] Apparently all the well-developed case law regarding national bank receivers is too bothersome to learn again.[17] This is an extraordinary approach in what is still alleged to be a common law country.

Beyond the basic receivership provisions, the Comptroller has several additional avenues for appointing receivers of the banks it oversees:

- if one of the statutory grounds for appointment of the Federal Deposit Insurance Corporation as receiver for a federally insured depository institution exists,
- if the bank's board of directors consists of fewer than five members,
- if any bank fails to pay up its capital stock, by assessing shareholders, and refuses to go into liquidation,
- whenever the Comptroller is satisfied, as specified in various other statutes, that a national banking association is in default, and

---

[14] Many more trust companies are state chartered, and thus subject to resolution by state banking authorities.

[15] 81 Federal Register 92,594, 92,545 (2016) (noting the current existence of only 52 uninsured national banks, all of which are national trust banks).

[16] On April 26, 2017, the Conference of State Bank Supervisors sued the Office of the Comptroller of the Currency in federal court, alleging that the OCC's plan to charter fintech companies as special purpose national banks is unlawful because the process the OCC used to develop the plan was procedurally defective and because issuing such charters would exceed the OCC's authority. On April 30, 2018, the district court dismissed the suit as premature - the rules are not yet final.

[17] 3 Clark on Receivers ch. XXVIII (3d ed. 1959) collects most of it.

- if any national bank "located in Alaska or in a dependency or insu-
lar possession," which is not a member of the Federal Reserve
System, fails to keep on hand cash equal to at least 15 percent of
its aggregate deposits.[18]

The first is, of course, where most of the action is these days, and likely
has been since the creation of the FDIC. The last is likely an amusing
relic – unless you are the president of an Alaskan bank.[19]

Unlike the receiverships we have seen up to this point, federal
receiverships involving the Comptroller, or the FDIC, are not judicial proceedings.[20] Similar in nature is the Federal Credit Union Act
of 1934, which instructs the National Credit Union Administration
Board to close insolvent federal credit unions, with the board itself
acting as liquidating agent.[21]

Operating somewhat near the fringe of our inquiry, the federal Farm Credit System is sensibly supervised by the Farm Credit
Administration Board, in turn, perhaps inevitably established by the
Farm Credit Act. A variety of federally chartered specialized financial
institutions are members of the Farm Credit System.[22] If one of these
institutions gets into trouble, the Board can appoint a receiver, namely
the Farm Credit System Insurance Corporation.[23]

Congress has adopted the administrative receivership model for
most federal financial institutions chartered under Title 12 of the
U.S. Code.[24] In general, all these systems use the ancient language of
receivership in connection with a highly administrative or bureaucratic
process.[25]

---

[18] In order, these topics can be found in 12 U.S.C. § 191(a)(1); 12 U.S.C. § 191(a)(2); 12
U.S.C. § 55; 12 U.S.C. § 192.; 12 U.S.C. § 143. See also 12 U.S.C. §§ 144, 1821(c)(5).

[19] This only applies to those national banks not members of the Federal Reserve System,
which in turn is limited to territorial national banks that have the option of not being
member banks. See 12 U.S.C. § 466.

[20] *Hulse* v. *Argetsinger*, 18 F.2d 944, 945–6 (2d Cir. 1927) (national bank receiver is not subject to a court's supervision, except as the National Bank Act prescribes).

[21] 12 U.S.C. § 1787. See *Nat'l Credit Union Admin. Bd.* v. *RBS Sec., Inc.*, 833 F.3d 1125,
1129 (9th Cir. 2016); *Nat'l Credit Union Admin. Bd.* v. *Nomura Home Equity Loan*, Inc.,
764 F.3d 1199, 1203 (10th Cir. 2014).

[22] 12 U.S.C. § 2002.

[23] 12 C.F.R. § 627.2720(b). See also 12 U.S.C. § 2183(b).

[24] E.g., 12 U.S.C. § 1464(d)(11) (federal thrift receivers).

[25] *Steele* v. *Randall*, 19 F.2d 40, 42 (8th Cir. 1927); Richard M. Hynes & Steven D. Walt,
Why Banks Are Not Allowed in Bankruptcy, 67 *Wash. & Lee L. Rev.* 985, 989 (2010).

Whenever the Comptroller of the Currency appoints a receiver for an insured national bank, the Comptroller must appoint the Federal Deposit Insurance Corporation receiver.[26] As the exclusive statutory receiver of any insolvent insured national bank, the FDIC cannot be removed as receiver and the courts have no ability to interfere with the process.[27] Likewise, even under the old rules, and those still applicable to uninsured national banks, the Comptroller has the ability to appoint the receiver without ever going to court.[28]

The cold reality of bank insolvency in the age before the FDIC is plainly set out in the books of that era:

> The relationship between the bank and the depositor is that of debtor and creditor, and, in the absence of a statute creating it, the depositor is not entitled to a preference upon the insolvency of the bank, but must share pro rata with the general creditors of the bank.[29]

Indeed, in the years before the Federal Reserve took over the creation of paper money,[30] depositors were also subordinate to holders of the bank's demand notes.[31]

The situation was even bleaker than that for the depositors, as national bank receiverships also followed the "chancery rule" regarding secured claims.[32] Under that rule, a secured creditor could submit a claim for the entire balance due and participate in the general

---

[26] 12 U.S.C. § 1821(c)(2)(A)(ii).

[27] 12 U.S.C. § 1821(j).

[28] Hirsch Braver, *Liquidation of Financial Institutions: A Treatise on the Law of Voluntary and Involuntary Liquidation of Banks, Trust Companies, and Building and Loan Associations* §1015 at p. 1182 (1936).

[29] Id. at § 501.

[30] Adam J. Levitin, Hydraulic Regulation: Regulating Credit Markets Upstream, 26 *Yale J. on Reg.* 143, 174–5 (2009) (footnotes omitted):

> Prior to the Civil War, most paper currency was in the form of individual banks' notes, which cleared at a discount from face value. The NBA of 1863 allowed the creation of national banks, which were authorized to issue national bank notes, backed by U.S. government securities deposited with the Treasury Department. Shortly after the promulgation of the NBA, Congress moved to suppress state bank notes by taxing them out of existence. With the 1913 creation of the Federal Reserve, which issues the United States currency in the form of uniform par-clearing notes, national bank notes declined in importance, and they were phased out in 1935.

[31] Garrard Glenn, The Law Governing Liquidation § 272 (1935). ("The proceeds of liquidation go first to retire the bank's circulating currency notes, and then to the payment of depositors and other creditors.")

[32] *Merrill v. Nat'l Bank of Jacksonville*, 173 U.S. 131, 138–9 (1899).

unsecured creditor pool on that basis. This contrasts with the so-called bankruptcy rule – currently enshrined in section 506 of the Bankruptcy Code – that a secured creditor's unsecured claim is defined by the difference between the total due and the value of the collateral.[33]

In a typical modern bank insolvency case, the FDIC automatically takes all the rights in the bank.[34] The FDIC as receiver also has the ability to "transfer any asset or liability of the institution in default … without any approval, assignment, or consent with respect to such transfer," and to otherwise act in "the best interests of the [failed] depository institution, its depositors, or the [FDIC]."[35]

The FDIC operates under a duty to resolve the financially distressed bank in a manner that minimizes the cost to the FDIC's deposit insurance fund.[36] At the same time, depositors in the debtor-bank enjoy a statutory preference over all other creditors which also tends to reduce the strain on the deposit insurance fund.[37] The net effect is that general unsecured creditors, including deposits only payable abroad and shareholders, recover very little in FDIC receiverships.

The FDIC normally tries to sell a distressed bank to another. Thus, in 2008, Chase acquired Washington Mutual, pushing the New York bank into previously unoccupied Western territory.[38] The transfer is typically done through a "purchase and assumption" agreement, an example of which is seen below.[39]

---

[33] Frederic William Maitland, *Equity – Also the Forms of Action at Common Law – Two Courses of Lectures* 194–5 (1929).

[34] Subject to a small exception, in favor of Federal Reserve Banks and federal home loan banks, found in 12 U.S.C. § 1821(e)(14).

[35] 12 U.S.C. § 1821(d)(2).

[36] 12 U.S.C. § 1823(c)(4)(A)(ii). See Robert R. Bliss & George G. Kaufman, U.S. Corporate and Bank Insolvency Regimes: A Comparison and Evaluation, 2 *Va. L. & Bus. Rev.* 144, 161–2 (2007).

[37] The preference is of comparatively recent vintage; for a sizable part of the FDIC's history (that is, from 1935 to 1993), all depositors had the same liquidation priority as general creditors. That had implications for the FDIC when it became subrogated to the rights of insured depositors.

[38] In re Washington Mut. Inc., 461 B.R. 200, 211 (Bankr. D. Del. 2011).

[39] The history of FDIC's development of the purchase and assumption (P&A) approach is well told in Phoebe Clarke, *The History of The Purchase and Assumption Transaction, 1933–1966* (unpublished Federal Reserve Bank of New York manuscript). Importantly, the foregoing shows that the P&A approach developed independent of bankruptcy practices of the time.

PURCHASE AND ASSUMPTION AGREEMENT

WHOLE BANK

ALL DEPOSITS

AMONG

FEDERAL DEPOSIT INSURANCE CORPORATION,
RECEIVER OF SEAWAY BANK AND TRUST COMPANY,
CHICAGO, IL

FEDERAL DEPOSIT INSURANCE CORPORATION

AND

STATE BANK OF TEXAS,
DALLAS, TX

DATED AS OF

JANUARY 27, 2017

It is the basic model of FDIC receivership that 2010's Dodd-Frank Act, and its title II which creates the "Orderly Liquidation Authority," attempts to extend to Chase, Bank of America, Goldman Sachs, and other similar institutions, in the event they should be the defaulters, rather than the acquirers, in the next financial crisis.[40] This Orderly Liquidation Authority or OLA operates to supplant the Bankruptcy Code only if regulators choose to invoke it.[41]

The law – which is in some peril given the results of the 2016 presidential election – extends the FDIC's reach to include the holding company and unregulated subsidiaries, which previously would have failed under the normal Bankruptcy Code provisions. And the FDIC can also grab the assets of a failed broker-dealer.

One proposed use of OLA turns on the so-called single-point-of-entry (SPOE) strategy. The SPOE strategy envisions that a resolution under title II would occur only at the top-tier holding company, avoiding to the greatest extent possible the need for the initiation of insolvency proceedings at the level of the operating subsidiaries. If it works as planned, this approach minimizes the complexities and conflicts that would invariably arise if multiple resolution proceedings in the United States and foreign jurisdictions had to be commenced at the level of the operating subsidiaries.[42]

It is also designed to reduce the risk of runs on the operating subsidiaries by their depositors and other short-term creditors, like swaps and other derivatives counterparties. The SPOE approach instead envisions that these creditors would be spared and all losses incurred at the level of the operating subsidiaries would be absorbed by holders of the top-tier holding company's long-term debt. Whether SPOE will work as designed, particularly in a 2008-style scenario of widespread financial panic, is the subject of a good deal of debate.[43]

Outside of OLA, holding companies, even bank holding companies regulated by the Federal Reserve, are just like any other corporation, and they generally file bankruptcy the same way. Thus, a bank might be taken over by the FDIC and its holding company will then file a chapter 11 petition. The only potential exception comes in the case of

---

[40] Title II of the Act is codified at 12 U.S.C. §§ 5381 to 5394.

[41] 12 U.S.C. §§ 5382(c)(2), 5388.

[42] See Stephen J. Lubben & Sarah Pei Woo, Reconceptualizing Lehman, 49 *Tex. Int'l L.J.* 297, 299 (2014).

[43] See generally Stephen J. Lubben & Arthur E. Wilmarth Jr., Too Big and Unable to Fail, *Fla. L. Rev.* 69, 1205 (2017).

mutual thrift holding companies – that is, a mutual company that owns a savings and loan or thrift.[44]

In that limited case, special receivership provisions might apply, although the provisions in question have almost no content. Instead, the statute simply provides that "a trustee shall be appointed receiver of such mutual holding company."[45] Your elementary school teacher would say "by whom?" but there is no prohibition against congressional use of the passive voice.

Normally broker-dealers are handled under SIPA – the Securities Investor Protection Act – and the FDIC has nothing to do with them. Before the New Deal, stockbroker bankruptcies were handled like any other business (usually partnership) bankruptcy under the Bankruptcy Act, subject to a few additional rules developed to address things like margin purchases and cases where a stock certificate was actually in the customer's own name.[46]

In 1938, Congress enacted section 60(e) of the Bankruptcy Act to partially address the situation – the section provided for separate treatment of customers, as compared with general creditors.[47] This was an early glimmer of the fundamental difference between financial institutions and "normal" companies, perhaps.

Then the stock market experienced a tremendous post-war run, and by the late 1960s, trading volume was at an all-time high. But the industry was still operating in paper. Tremendous amounts of paper – stock certificates and related forms – were moving about lower Manhattan each day. The eventual "paperwork crisis" – perhaps the most boring crisis ever – caused the failure of several brokerage

---

[44] There are three major types of depository institutions in the United States: commercial banks, thrifts (which include savings and loan associations and savings banks), and credit unions. A thrift or savings and loan is a financial institution formed primarily to accept consumer deposits and make home mortgages. Credit unions are member-owned financial cooperatives.

[45] 12 U.S.C. § 1467a(o)(9).

[46] E.g., *Denton v. Gurnett & Co.*, 69 F.2d 750, 752 (1st Cir. 1934); In re Slattery & Co., 294 F. 624, 625 (2d Cir. 1923).

[47] Leon R. Yankwich, Preferences under Section 60 of the Bankruptcy Act, 3 *Hastings L.J.* 93, 106–7 (1952). Commodity brokers, discussed below, were never subject to section 60(e) of the Bankruptcy Act.

houses, who had lost track of customer's securities.[48] The crisis was further compounded when the American economy slowed, and trading volumes dropped in the Nixon years, cutting revenues at brokerage houses and causing further failures.

Two responses were adopted. First, the United States adopted a convoluted system of "beneficial" and "record" ownership, to immobilize most share certificates and thus routinize the paperwork. One wonders if the problem might have been more sensibly addressed if a few more years had passed, and computers allowed to develop more fully.

More relevant to our discussion is SIPA, which was also passed at this time. SIPA created SIPC – the Securities Investor Protection Corporation – a quasi-private company that oversees an insurance fund for customers. Although SIPC is an independent body, the SEC has oversight power over its bylaws and rules and may compel SIPC to promulgate regulations to effectuate the purposes of SIPA.[49]

The insurance in this case, unlike the more familiar FDIC deposit insurance, only protects against securities or cash missing at the point of insolvency – there is no guarantee of value. Indeed, the obligation here is to return the precise securities that the customer had before the broker failed – in cases where the broker has sold worthless or even bogus securities, those are precisely what the customer will get back. The insurance recovery is in kind, rather than in coin of the realm.

Most registered brokers and dealers are required to belong to SIPC,[50] and assessments against members are authorized by the law to maintain the insurance fund.[51] The law provides that the SIPC or the SEC may file an application for a protective decree with the U.S. district court if the SIPC determines that any member has failed or is in danger of failing to meet obligations to customers and meets one of four worrisome conditions.[52] Upon filing, the case is quickly referred to the bankruptcy court.[53]

---

[48] Wyatt Wells, Certificates and Computers: The Remaking of Wall Street, 1967 to 1971, 74 *Busn. Hist. Rev.* 193 (2000).

[49] 15 U.S.C. § 78ccc(e).

[50] 15 U.S.C. § 78o(b).

[51] 15 U.S.C. §§ 78ddd(a), (c), (d).

[52] 15 U.S.C. §§ 78eee(a)(3)(A), (b)(1); 78ggg(b). The institution of a case under SIPA brings a pending bankruptcy case to a halt. Irrespective of the automatic stay, SIPC may file an application for a protective decree under SIPA. 11 U.S.C. § 742.

[53] 15 U.S.C. § 78eee(b)(4).

The powers of the trustee in a SIPA case are essentially the same as those vested in a chapter 7 trustee appointed under the Bankruptcy Code, but the SIPA trustee operates with somewhat less court oversight.[54]

The goal is to return customer securities as soon as possible; often this is done by transferring customer accounts to a new brokerage firm.[55] When done, this provides customers with a priority claim in the SIPA proceedings, as customer property is quickly taken out of the overall estate.[56]

However, if the failed broker does not have sufficient assets to cover all customer positions, SIPC will make advances to customers, and become subrogated to the customers' rights in the SIPA proceeding, up to the insurance limits.[57] To the extent customer property and the SIPC advances are not sufficient to pay or satisfy in full the net equity claims of customers, customers are entitled to participate in the estate as unsecured creditors.[58]

Thus, like in the case of a depository bank, there is the creation of a special class of elite creditors, customers, who take ahead of normal creditors. And in both cases the decision to create such an elite is clearly designed to foster confidence in a particular industry, operating in a particular way.[59] But broker-dealer insolvencies are somewhat more like traditional insolvencies in that they involve the court in the process.

While commodities brokers appear at least superficially similar to stockbrokers, their insolvency cases are handled under a very dissimilar regime. First, the SIPC insurance fund may not be used to compensate commodities customers – parties with whom or for whom a commodity broker enters into commodity contracts.

This is true even where a commodity broker is liquidated under SIPA, which ensues with some frequency. As it happens, many of

---

[54] 15 U.S.C. § 78fff-1(a); see also 15 U.S.C. § 78fff-1(b)(2).

[55] 15 U.S.C. § 78fff-2(f).

[56] See 15 U.S.C. § 78fff-1(b) (SIPA trustee is to return actual securities to customers to the maximum extent possible).

[57] At present, $500,000 overall, with a sub-limit of $250,000 for cash. 15 U.S.C. § 78fff-3(a). Note that these amounts are only needed to fill the gap between what customer is owed and what the debtor-broker is actually holding on the date of insolvency.

[58] 15 U.S.C. § 78fff-2(c)(1).

[59] Onnig H. Dombalagian, Substance and Semblance in Investor Protection, 40 *J. Corp. L.* 599, 619 (2015).

the larger commodity brokers – or futures commission merchants (FCMs), as the Commodity Futures Trading Commission likes to call them – are also registered stockbrokers.

SIPA protects "customers" of registered broker-dealers who have entrusted those brokers with cash or "securities" in the ordinary course of business for the purpose of trading and investing. A SIPA customer is defined as "any person ... who has a claim on account of securities received, acquired, or held" by the debtor-broker.[60] Not every relationship with a failed broker-dealer is a customer relationship; for example, sometimes the unpaid party might be instead deemed a creditor or other investor in the debtor.[61]

Securities are limited to those investments registered with the SEC under the Securities Act of 1933.[62] Exclusions include not only commodities, but also many limited partnership interests, and many other unregistered pooled investments.[63]

Only those with "customer" status – which requires not only being a customer, but being a customer with regard to a security – are paid from the special SIPC-guarantee fund; others have no claim to the fund, and must wait to be paid from the general pool arising from the liquidation of the insolvent stockbroker's estate.

For "pure" commodities brokers, not subject to liquidation under SIPA, one option upon failure is a receivership, instituted by the CFTC.[64] Often these are used when fraud or other regulatory concerns are coupled with insolvency, as the CFTC has statutory authority to seek "equitable remedies" when there is a violation of federal law.[65]

For example, in *CFTC* v. *Lake Shore Asset Management*,[66] the CFTC moved to appoint a receiver to administer the assets of Lake

---

[60] 15 U.S.C. § 78lll(2).

[61] In re Hanover Square Securities, 55 B.R. 235, 238–9 (Bankr. S.D. N.Y. 1985).

[62] 15 U.S.C. § 78lll(14).

[63] In re Primeline Sec. Corp., 295 F.3d 1100, 1109 (10th Cir. 2002).

[64] Michael S. Sackheim, Judicial Equitable Enforcement of the Federal Commodities Laws, 32 *Am. U. L. Rev.* 945, 960 (1983).

[65] 7 U.S.C. § 13a-1(d)(3). Subpart (a) contains an oblique reference to the ability to commence a receivership. See *Commodity Futures Trading Comm'n* v. *Co Petro Mktg. Grp.*, Inc., 680 F.2d 573, 583 (9th Cir. 1982). ("We have little difficulty in finding that [7 U.S.C. § 13a-1] is broad enough to authorize the appointment of a receiver, an order requiring that the receiver have access to the firm's books and records, and an order for an accounting.")

[66] 646 F.3d 401 (7th Cir. 2011).

Shore Asset Management after suing it for fraud and violation of sundry sections of the Commodity Exchange Act. After assembling the assets, the receiver proposed a plan of distribution of the assets.

A CFTC receivership is still just an equity receivership, in the historical railroad tradition we saw in Chapter 3.[67] As such, the receiver gets most of her power from the appointment order, and acts under the supervision of the appointing court.

The SEC also uses receiverships in similar circumstances.[68] As with the commodities laws, neither the Securities Act of 1933 nor the Securities Exchange Act of 1934 expressly authorize the SEC to request the appointment of a receiver, yet courts have long concluded that the SEC has the power and authority to make such a request.[69] I have included an example on the next two pages.

In other related areas of securities law, the power of the SEC to control the insolvency process is more firmly rooted in statute. For example, with regard to unregistered mutual funds, the SEC can petition a court to appoint "a trustee, who with the approval of the court shall have power to dispose of any or all of [fund] assets, subject to such terms and conditions as the court may prescribe."[70] But even here, the fine details – or really, most of the details – are apt to be filled in by reference to general receivership law.

The Second Circuit has, on occasion, objected to the use of SEC receiverships as a kind of bankruptcy substitute, which operates "without the aid of either the experience of a bankruptcy judge or the guidance of the bankruptcy code."[71] This is entirely consistent with

---

[67] See *Commodity Futures Trading Comm'n* v. *Comvest Trading Corp.*, 481 F. Supp. 438, 440 (D. Mass. 1979). ("The CFTC is also correct that although the Commodity Exchange Act, as amended, does not specifically provide for the appointment of receivers, a federal district court, sitting in equity, has broad discretion to fashion appropriate relief to enforce the requirements of remedial statutes such as this act.")

[68] www.sec.gov/divisions/enforce/receiverships.htm.

[69] E.g., *Los Angeles Trust Deed & Mortg. Exch.* v. *Sec. & Exch. Comm'n*, 285 F.2d 162, 181 (9th Cir. 1960).

[70] 15 U.S.C.A. § 80a-41(d).

[71] *S.E.C.* v. *Am. Bd. of Trade, Inc.*, 830 F.2d 431, 438 (2d Cir. 1987) (instructing "that in actions of the present kind brought in the future by the SEC, we expect counsel for the agency, as an officer of the court and as part of his or her individual professional responsibility, to bring our views, as stated in this and other decisions, to the attention of the district court before the court embarks on a liquidation through an equity receivership").

UNITED STATES DISTRICT COURT
SOUTHERN DISTRICT OF FLORIDA

CASE NO. 16-CV-21301-GAYLES

SECURITIES AND EXCHANGE COMMISSION,

Plaintiff,

v.

ARIEL QUIROS,
WILLIAM STENGER,
JAY PEAK, INC.,
Q RESORTS, INC.,   UNDER SEAL
JAY PEAK HOTEL SUITES L.P.,
JAY PEAK HOTEL SUITES PHASE II L.P.,
JAY PEAK MANAGEMENT, INC.,
JAY PEAK PENTHOUSE SUITES L.P.,
JAY PEAK GP SERVICES, INC.,
JAY PEAK GOLF AND MOUNTAIN SUITES L.P.,
JAY PEAK GP SERVICES GOLF, INC.,
JAY PEAK LODGE AND TOWNHOUSES L.P.,
JAY PEAK GP SERVICES LODGE, INC.,
JAY PEAK HOTEL SUITES STATESIDE L.P.,
JAY PEAK GP SERVICES STATESIDE, INC.,
JAY PEAK BIOMEDICAL RESEARCH PARK L.P.,
AnC BIO VERMONT GP SERVICES, LLC,

Defendants, and

JAY CONSTRUCTION MANAGEMENT, INC.,
GSI OF DADE COUNTY, INC.,
NORTH EAST CONTRACT SERVICES, INC.,
Q BURKE MOUNTAIN RESORT, LLC,

Relief Defendants.
_____/

ORDER GRANTING PLAINTIFF SECURITIES AND
EXCHANGE COMMISSION'S MOTION FOR APPOINTMENT OF RECEIVER

WHEREAS Plaintiff Securities and Exchange Commission has filed a motion for the

appointment of a Receiver over Defendants Jay Peak, Inc., Q Resorts, Inc., Jay Peak Hotel Suites

L.P. ("Suites Phase I"), Jay Peak Hotel Suites Phase II L.P. ("Hotel Phase II"), Jay Peak

Management, Inc. ("Jay Peak Management"), Jay Peak Penthouse Suites L.P. ("Penthouse Phase

older Second Circuit case law that disapproved of the continued use
of equity receiverships after the codification of corporate bankruptcy
during the New Deal.

Despite this, the Second Circuit has never reversed a district court
decision approving a receiver's liquidation plan, perhaps because by

III"), Jay Peak GP Services, Inc. ("Jay Peak GP Services"), Jay Peak Golf and Mountain Suites L.P. ("Golf and Mountain Phase IV"), Jay Peak GP Services Golf, Inc. ("Jay Peak GP Services Golf), Jay Peak Lodge and Townhouses L.P. ("Lodge and Townhouses Phase V"), Jay Peak GP Services Lodge, Inc. ("Jay Peak GP Services Lodge"), Jay Peak Hotel Suites Stateside, L.P. ("Stateside Phase VI"), Jay Peak GP Services Stateside, Inc. ("Jay Peak GP Services") , Jay Peak Biomedical Research Park L.P. ("Biomedical Phase VII"), and AnC Bio Vermont GP Services, LLC ("AnC Bio Vermont GP Services") (collectively "Corporate Defendants") and Relief Defendants Jay Construction Management, Inc. ("JCM"), GSI of Dade County, Inc. ("GSI"), North East Contract Services, Inc. ("Northeast"), and Q Burke Mountain Resort, LLC ("Q Burke") (collectively, "Relief Defendants") with full and exclusive power, duty and authority to: administer and manage the business affairs, funds, assets, causes in action and any other property of the Corporate Defendants; marshal and safeguard all of their assets; and take whatever actions are necessary for the protection of the investors;

WHEREAS, the Commission has made a sufficient and proper showing in support of the relief requested;

WHEREAS, the Commission has submitted the credentials of a candidate to be appointed as Receiver of all of the assets, properties, books and records, and other items of the Corporate Defendants and Relief Defendants, including any properties, assets and other items held in their names or their principals' names, and the Commission has advised the Court that this candidate is prepared to assume this responsibility if so ordered by the Court;

IT IS THEREFORE ORDERED, ADJUDGED, AND DECREED that Michael Goldberg is hereby appointed the Receiver over Corporate Defendants and Relief Defendants, their subsidiaries, successors and assigns, and is hereby authorized, empowered, and directed to:

the time the matter reaches the Court of Appeals, the receiver has invested so much time and money in the process that it would be uneconomical to send the case to bankruptcy court. The SEC and the District Courts could, however, pay a bit more attention to the presumably binding decisions of the Court of Appeals.

But the district courts and the SEC continue to use receiverships to liquidate brokers involved in fraud, and the appellate court, as noted, has limited ability to police the issue.[72] Indeed, in fraud cases, a receivership can offer some obvious advantages over bankruptcy, because receivers are not subject to the in *pari delicto* defense – which provides that wrongdoers ought to bear the consequences of their wrongdoing without legal recourse against each other – as courts consider the receiver to be sufficiently removed from the bad actor, whereas bankruptcy trustees are not.[73] Whether this distinction makes any sense is another question entirely. And there is the ever-present question of "cost," which is apparent in bankruptcy, and allegedly lower in receiverships.[74]

Indeed, in many SEC and CFTC receiverships, the courts completely bar resort to the bankruptcy system. For example, the very same Second Circuit that was so hostile to the overuse of SEC receiverships in the foregoing paragraphs, held in *SEC v. Byers* that district courts had the "authority and discretion" to enter an anti-bankruptcy injunction "as part of their broad equitable powers in the context of an SEC receivership."[75] That is, once an SEC or CFTC receiverships is up and running, it may preclude the bankruptcy option, which we have seen is usually a looming threat in most other federal and state receiverships.

These regulatory receiverships also might be the only insolvency proceedings that can defeat an OLA proceeding under Dodd-Frank. Normally, the appointment of the FDIC as receiver under OLA preempts a pending insolvency proceeding: for example, bankruptcy and SIPA stockbroker cases "shall be dismissed" upon commencement of an OLA proceeding.[76] The assets vested in a trustee or receiver likewise are to be handed back to the defaulting bank immediately, but the statute neglects to mention federal court receiverships:

> Effective as of the date of appointment of the [FDIC] as receiver, the assets of a covered financial company shall, to the extent they

---

[72] *S.E.C.* v. *Malek*, 397 F. App'x 711, 714 (2d Cir. 2010). See American Board of Trade, 830 F.2d at 437 (observing, "we have never vacated or modified a receivership order on the ground that a district court improperly attempted to effect a liquidation").

[73] *Jones* v. *Wells Fargo Bank*, N.A., 666 F.3d 955, 965 (5th Cir. 2012). Of course, whether the defense should be applied to bankruptcy trustees is open to debate.

[74] Cf. In re W. End Fin. Advisors, LLC, No. 11-11152 SMB, 2012 WL 2590613 (Bankr. S.D.N.Y. July 3, 2012).

[75] *S.E.C.* v. *Byers*, 609 F.3d 87, 91 (2d Cir. 2010).

[76] 12 U.S.C. § 5388(a).

have vested in any entity other than the covered financial company as a result of any case or proceeding commenced with respect to the covered financial company under the Bankruptcy Code, [SIPA], or any similar provision of State liquidation or insolvency law applicable to the covered financial company, revest in the covered financial company.[77]

Thus, one could imagine a future Lehman taken over by the SEC in a receivership, where the receiver refuses to give way to the FDIC. Arguably this is a drafting error, but given the current state of Congress, and the broader politics of touching anything in Dodd-Frank, it might remain in the statute for the foreseeable future.

The regulatory preference for receiverships over bankruptcy cases is not without its drawbacks. In the litigation arising out of the Ponzi scheme masterminded by Allen Stanford, the United Kingdom Court of Appeal refused to recognize and aid a SEC receivership,[78] while indicating that the result might have been different if the case had been brought under American bankruptcy law.[79] The Court of Appeal found that the receivership was not a foreign proceeding that could be recognized under the United Kingdom version of the Model Law on Cross-Border Insolvency promulgated by the United Nations Commission on International Trade Law (UNCITRAL) in 1997,[80] because the receiver's powers derived, not from a law relating to insolvency or adjustment of debt, but from the order appointing him:

> The fact that the court may subsequently make orders which bring into force a process which can be recognized as an insolvency proceeding is immaterial unless and until it is done. The principles of the common law and equity do not "relate to insolvency" unless and until they are activated for that purpose.

---

[77] 12 U.S.C. § 5388(b).

[78] www.stanfordfinancialreceivership.com.

[79] In the Matter of Stanford International Bank LTD, [2010] EWCA Civ. 137, available at https://goo.gl/UimgzR. In another part of the opinion, however, the court did rule that American proceedings were in general unlikely to be recognized in the face of a competing proceeding filed in the bank's jurisdiction of incorporation (Antigua). The American court had criticized the Antiguan proceedings, suggesting that the liquidators appointed therein appeared to be mostly interested in collecting fees for themselves.

[80] The same model law was enacted as chapter 15 to the Bankruptcy Code in the United States. Generally, a chapter 15 case is ancillary to a primary proceeding brought in another country, typically the debtor's home country.

To date, American courts have been somewhat hesitant to extend the notion of regulatory receiverships as a replacement for chapters 7 and 11 to federal receiverships more generally.[81] And federal courts – including federal bankruptcy courts – remain certain of their ability to overcome a state court receivership, even when filed by officers or directors acting contrary to state court orders.[82]

What then does the Bankruptcy Code offer with regard to stockbrokers or commodities brokers? Section 109(d) of the Code stipulates that both types of brokers may be debtors only in a chapter 7 liquidation – forcing brokers to enter bankruptcy, if at all, under the special provisions in that chapter that address stock and commodities brokers, and precluding them from reorganizing under chapter 11.[83]

The stockbroker provisions of chapter 7 are rarely used.[84] Most stockbrokers are members of SIPC,[85] and thus fail under SIPA, and section 742 of the Code gives such SIPA proceedings primacy over the Code.[86] The legislative history makes plain that the intended coverage of the Bankruptcy Code's stockbroker liquidation subchapter is intrastate broker-dealers, and little more.[87]

But a debtor also might be a stockbroker for purposes of the Code, even when they are not a stockbroker under other laws. For example,

---

[81] *Gilchrist* v. *Gen. Elec. Capital Corp.*, 262 F.3d 295, 302–4 (4th Cir. 2001).

[82] In re Orchards Vill. Investments, LLC, 405 B.R. 341, 347 (Bankr. D. Or. 2009). See also In re Monroe Heights Dev. Corp., Inc., No. 17-10176-TPA, 2017 WL 3701857, at *17 (Bankr. W.D. Pa. Aug. 22, 2017). ("[I]f it ever becomes apparent that the state court proceeding resulted in an improper impediment to a corporate debtor's access to the bankruptcy system due to the appointment of a receiver that is not carrying out its duties in a disinterested manner, then the need to assure federal supremacy in the area of bankruptcy must overcome the initial deferral to the action of the state court, allowing those formerly in control of the debtor to file bankruptcy on its behalf.")

[83] Although there may be some attempts to slip into chapter 11, not unlike the attempts to evade the special railroad provisions of chapter 11 that we discussed in Chapter 3.

[84] Subchapter III (§§ 741 through 753) of chapter 7 of the Code.

[85] All securities brokers or dealers registered with the SEC under the 1934 Act are members of SIPC, except those engaged exclusively in the distribution of variable annuities or shares of open-end investment funds or are in the business of insurance or furnishing investment advice to limited classes of customers.

[86] Cf. *Sec. Inv'r Prot. Corp.* v. *Stratton Oakmont, Inc.*, 229 B.R. 273, 275 (Bankr. S.D.N.Y.), aff'd sub nom. *Arford* v. *Miller*, 239 B.R. 698 (S.D.N.Y. 1999), aff'd sub nom. In re Stratton Oakmont, 210 F.3d 420 (2d Cir. 2000) (attempted chapter 11 bankruptcy filing by broker superseded by SIPA proceeding).

[87] H.R. Rep. No. 595, 95th Cong., 1st Sess. 1, 267–8, reprinted in 1978 in U.S.C.C.A.N. at 5963, 6224–6.

a company that pretends to be a SIPC member, but is not, might be liquidated under subchapter III of chapter 7.[88]

Both SIPA and chapter 7 share a common belief that stockbrokers must be liquidated, in all cases. But from there they proceed upon distinctive paths. Most importantly, in a proceeding under the Bankruptcy Code the trustee is charged with reducing all securities (other than those in a specific customer's name) to cash, while under SIPA the trustee is to meet claims to "the maximum extent possible" by the return of securities. But a chapter 7 stockbroker proceeding is also a bit unlike "normal" chapter 7 as well, because under both the Code and SIPA, persons determined to be "customers" of the debtor are treated as preferred creditors.

The chapter 7 provisions for commodity brokers are like those for stockbrokers in their favoring of liquidation. The title of the subchapter is a bit misleading, because a close look at the definition of "commodity broker" reveals that it covers all sorts of brokers and clearing organizations[89] for a broad array of derivatives, not just those involving corn, wheat, or frozen orange juice concentrate.

Once one realizes that all sorts of swaps dealers and clearinghouses for the same could end up in a special subchapter IV chapter 7, a slow feeling of unease is a natural reaction.[90] The provisions of subchapter IV are skeletal, and they are supplemented, and in some cases superseded, by CFTC rules.[91]

These rules – gracelessly called the "Part 190 Rules" – are rather joyless things to read, and they notably have nothing to say about the possible liquidation of a clearinghouse under chapter 7. The basic aim, as with stockbrokers, is to provide customers with preferential

---

[88] In re Baker & Getty Fin. Servs., Inc., 106 F.3d 1255, 1260 (6th Cir. 1997).

[89] Section 101(6) of the Bankruptcy Code defines "commodity broker" to mean a "futures commission merchant [i.e., the CFTC term for commodity broker], foreign futures commission merchant, [or] clearing organization ... as defined in section 761 of this title, with respect to which there is a customer, as defined in section 761 of this title."

[90] For more on the issue of clearinghouses, see Stephen J. Lubben, Central Counterparties and Orderly Liquidation Authority, 36.9 *Futures & Derivatives L. Rep.* 1 (Oct. 2016), and Stephen J. Lubben, Always Crashing In The Same Car – Clearinghouse Rescue After Dodd-Frank, 3 *J. Fin. Reg.* 133 (2017).

[91] 17 C.F.R. § 190.01 et seq. 7 U.S.C. § 24 provides the statutory basis for these rules. The statute provides a broad grant of power to the CFTC, prefaced with the words "notwithstanding title 11 ..."

treatment over general creditors. And the definition of "customer property" contained in the Part 190 Rules is broader in several significant respects than the definition contained in section 761(10) of the Code.[92]

On the other hand, the CFTC's bankruptcy regulations define "commodity broker" more narrowly than the Bankruptcy Code. Specifically, the CFTC has defined "commodity broker" to include "any person who is registered or required to register as a futures commission merchant under the [commodities statute] ... with respect to which there is a customer."[93] FCMs that are not registered – for example, because they only engage in proprietary trading[94] – are not treated as "commodity brokers" for purposes of the rule, even though they would fit within the definition in the Code.

What happens if such an entity tries to file a chapter 7 petition is a bit unclear.[95] If the more restrictive definition found in the CFTC regulations were to be applied by the bankruptcy courts, would this be a regular chapter 7 case, outside of subchapter IV? Or if the court applied the Code definitions, maybe we would have a subchapter IV chapter 7 case, but with no CFTC rules? Probably the easier solution is for the bankruptcy court to simply ignore the CFTC's definition, since they have the ability to supplement the Bankruptcy Code on the treatment of customer property, and not rewrite its provisions generally.

Subchapter IV seems to provide many avenues for disaster, or at the very least befuddlement.

And then there is subchapter V of chapter 7 of the Bankruptcy Code.[96] Banks are normally entirely outside of the Bankruptcy Code, but under subchapter V certain "clearing banks" are permitted to seek relief under chapter 7, under heavily controlled circumstances. These clearing banks are defined as state and federally chartered banks that operate "system[s] utilized by more than two participants in which the bilateral credit exposures of participants arising from the transactions cleared are effectively eliminated and replaced by a system of guarantees,

[92] One court has found the rules too broad. In re Griffin Trading Co., 245 B.R. 291 (Bankr. N.D. Ill. 2000), vacated as moot, 270 B.R. 882 (N.D. Ill. 2001).

[93] 17 C.F.R. § 190.01(g).

[94] 17 C.F.R. § 3.10(c).

[95] Under section 109 of the Bankruptcy Code, they would still be excluded from chapter 11.

[96] 11 U.S.C. §§ 781–784.

insurance, or mutualized risk of loss." Fine use of the English language there.

It actually gets more confusing, because the definition just quoted was repealed in 2010 by the Dodd-Frank Act.[97] It is still referred to in the Bankruptcy Code, however.[98]

Section 109 of the Bankruptcy Code itself provides that

> a person may be a debtor under chapter 7 of this title only if such person is not ...
>
> [a domestic depository institution], except that an uninsured State member bank, or a corporation organized under section 25A of the Federal Reserve Act, which operates, or operates as, a multilateral clearing organization pursuant to section 409 of the Federal Deposit Insurance Corporation Improvement Act of 1991 may be a debtor if a petition is filed at the direction of the Board of Governors of the Federal Reserve System.

That is, we are dealing with an exception to the normal rule that most banks may not file under chapter 7. Unpacking section 109 a bit, we can see that these clearing banks come in two flavors, those who are uninsured state member banks, and those who are Edge Act companies (those companies organized under section 25A of the Federal Reserve Act). Not all Edge Act companies, or uninsured state member banks, may file under chapter 7, but only those who are also engaged in clearing.

The first type is a state-chartered bank, engaged in clearing, that has never become a member of the FDIC insurance scheme, yet is a member of their local Federal Reserve Bank.[99] Your garden-variety

---

[97] 12 U.S.C. §§ 4421, 4422. Repealed. Pub. L. 111-203, Title VII, § 740, July 21, 2010, 124 Stat. 1729.

[98] 11 U.S.C. § 109(b)(2), which provides that "an uninsured State member bank, or a corporation organized under section 25A of the Federal Reserve Act, which operates, or operates as, a multilateral clearing organization pursuant to section 409 of the Federal Deposit Insurance Corporation Improvement Act of 1991 may be a debtor" under subchapter V of chapter 7.

[99] Uninsured state member banks also may be subject to state law insolvency provisions. The Federal Reserve Act does not indicate that the Board's authority to appoint a conservator or receiver is exclusive of any state law proceedings so, in theory, the Depository Trust Company might also be subject to a New York State banking receivership. This might provide an incentive to use the Bankruptcy Code, which could clearly pre-empt an already under way state law receivership – provided the bankruptcy court does not abstain.

state chartered bank cannot become members of the Fed without deposit insurance.[100] But the Depository Trust Company (DTC), a subsidiary of The Depository Trust & Clearing Corporation, happens to be the one and only company that fits this category.

It is chartered under New York banking law, is a member of the local Federal Reserve Bank, and does not offer deposit insurance, as it does not take cash deposits. Instead, DTC is the central depository for most securities traded in the United States, including equities, corporate bonds, and municipal bonds, as well as commercial paper.

The other category of eligible clearing banks under subchapter V are those incorporated under the Edge Act – section 25A of the Federal Reserve Act.[101] These are federally chartered banks that engage in "international or foreign banking or other international or foreign financial operations." While there are several Edge Act companies, most are not engaged in clearing.[102] CLS Bank – a vital part of the $5 trillion-*a-day* global foreign exchange system – seems to be our prime (and perhaps only) candidate for inclusion here.[103]

So, we have a special subchapter of chapter 7 that applies to two entities. It has never been used.

And then we should also note that even if there was occasion for using the sub-chapter, the Federal Reserve Board has the ability to put these entities into a receivership "to the same extent and in the same manner as the Comptroller of the Currency may appoint a conservator or receiver for a national bank."[104] That would seem to suggest a Fed-appointed, rather than court-appointed, receiver. And indeed, the Fed has such power with regard to Edge Act corporations generally, not just those who engage in clearing.[105]

Why the Fed would want to use a chapter 7 procedure, when it has access to a receivership process that it controls, is a bit of a headscratcher. Presumably the receivership would be far more flexible than

---

[100] Some state chartered trust companies might fit this description, but they are not clearing banks.

[101] 12 U.S.C. § 611.

[102] In researching this book, I found twenty-one, including CLS Bank.

[103] www.cls-group.com.

[104] 12 U.S.C. §§ 339a; 624(a).

[105] 12 U.S.C. § 624. And the Fed can instruct the receiver or conservator to file a bankruptcy petition.

chapter 7 in any form, even if there is some suggestion that it should be invoked the ancient case law of the National Bank Act insolvency provisions, which mostly no longer apply to national banks, having been largely displaced by the FDIC.

Flexibility would seem to be the name of the game with regard to these two entities, which are structured differently than most other business. The potential for economic disruption due to delays or problems in liquidation or reorganization is extreme.

That leads us to the next riddle: while filing under chapter 7, and subchapter V, requires preapproval by the Fed, a filing under chapter 11 does not. That is, one of these special debtors can get into bankruptcy court if they want, it is just hard to get into chapter 7. But why would they want to get into chapter 7? There is a confusing twist here, as financial institutions are most often liquidated under insolvency law, but here the financial institutions in question will have a harder time achieving a straightforward liquidation under chapter 7.

Given even a brief bit of time to act, the federal government might also create a "one-off" bankruptcy system to deal with these specialized entities, putting yet another option on the table. We see an example of that in the Housing and Economic Recovery Act of 2008, which allowed the federal government to place Fannie Mae and Freddie Mac in a still ongoing conservatorship.[106]

That Act created a new regulator for the two companies, the Federal Housing Finance Agency, and this regulator has the power to put either entity into conservatorship or receivership. A receivership under the law, however, would involve the wind-down of the companies, so in the absence of political agreement about their future, and what a wind-down would look like, they remain in conservatorship.[107] Essentially the frozen relic of 2008, neither liquidated nor reorganized. Perhaps undead.

Returning to special sub-chapter V of chapter 7, if the provisions were ever to be used, which seems doubtful for the reasons noted, section 782 of the Code places the appointment of the initial trustee for

---

[106] Pub. L. No. 110-289, 122 Stat. 2654.
[107] *Perry Capital LLC* v. *Mnuchin*, No. 14-5243, 2017 WL 677589, at *3 (D.C. Cir. Feb. 21, 2017).

a clearing bank liquidation case in the hands of the Fed.[108] Subchapter V sets forth additional powers of a chapter 7 trustee in a clearing bank liquidation, including the ability to transfer the assets of the clearing bank to a "bridge bank" as the FDIC can do with regard to a failed insured bank or under Dodd-Frank's OLA.[109] These special powers – of both appointment and of the trustee – do give some indication of why the Fed might prefer chapter 7 and its sub-chapter V over a chapter 11 case of one of these special entities. But again, that presupposes the use of the Bankruptcy Code in the face of several other options.

On a somewhat less grand note are the federal receivership provisions overseen by the Small Business Administration (SBA). The Small Business Investment Act of 1958,[110] empowers the SBA to seek the appointment of a receiver for a Small Business Investment Company (SBIC) that has violated the Act and regulations.[111]

A SBIC is somewhat like a closed-end mutual fund, often structured as a limited partnership, licensed by the SBA and designed to provide equity capital and long-term financing to small businesses. SBICs may borrow from the Federal Small Business Administration on a long-term basis, and they receive favorable tax treatment under the Internal Revenue Code.

One commonly violated regulation, that can lead to the appointment of a receiver, involves capital requirements for the SBIC and the general obligation to pay the SBA what it is due.[112] The statute allows for the appointment of the SBA itself or someone else as receiver, and displaces the general, equitable requirements for appointment of a receiver. But the goal ultimately remains the same: gather the debtor's assets and repay creditors.

The SBICs were barred from the bankruptcy court in 1994, with the apparent goal of maintaining the SBA's priority rights in the debtor's estate. A similar amendment in 2000 barred bankruptcy filings

---

[108] Code § 782(a)(2) authorizes the Fed to "designate a successor trustee if required." Unlike § 782(a)(1), however, the language of § 782(a)(2) is not exclusive.

[109] 11 U.S.C. § 783.

[110] 15 U.S.C. §§ 681 et seq.

[111] 15 U.S.C. § 687c.

[112] *United States v. Audubon Capital SBIC, L.P.*, No. CIV.A. 13-589, 2013 WL 3155215, at *2 (E.D. La. June 19, 2013).

by New Markets Venture Capital companies, which were created that year by statute.[113]

These are companies designed to raise equity capital to support investment in low-income areas. As with SBICs, the SBA or someone else can be appointed receiver of these entities when they violate a relevant SBA regulation, which could include regulations related to solvency.[114] To date, there is no case law on this provision, but presumably it will be influenced by developments under the SBIC receivership provision.

So, what are we to make of the federal approach to financial institution insolvency? There is a general distrust of the Bankruptcy Code, reflecting the strong role of independent regulators of many of the potential debtors.

When the Bankruptcy Code is invoked, it is typically a partial, even convoluted embrace, such as with the liquidation of commodities brokers. Chapter 7 is the nominal frame for resolution, but the CFTC attempts to run the show despite the bankruptcy judge.

Financial institutions that are subject to an insurance scheme tend to avoid the bankruptcy system altogether, instead invoking a receivership process that has its roots in the bank receiverships of an earlier era. These days, the proceedings use the language of receiverships, but depart substantially from many other aspects of receivership law.

The key exception is broker-dealer insolvencies under SIPA, where the bankruptcy courts, and even parts of the Bankruptcy Code, are borrowed to fill out a system that has one foot in the banking receivership world. The trustee is in some sense subject to two masters: the court and SIPC, but SIPC controls the compensation of the trustee, a power normally entrusted to the bankruptcy court.

The overall theme, if there is one, is more than a bit vague. In the coming pages, I argue that exceptions to the normal bankruptcy rules of creditor equality can be justified by the societal need to protect certain vital financial transactions, but that the current scheme of financial institution insolvency overshoots what might be warranted by such considerations.

---

[113] New Markets Venture Capital Program Act of 2000, Pub. L. No. 106-554.
[114] 15 U.S.C. § 6891.

5   STATE FINANCIAL INSTITUTION INSOLVENCY LAW

State financial institution insolvency law sweeps more broadly than its federal counterpart, picking up a variety of institutions that fall below the gaze of federal regulators. But the law here is not all "small potatoes." Insurance companies, no matter what size, are regulated by the states, and thus their insolvencies are also a question of state law.[1] Some foreign banks have very significant state-licensed United States branches; these, too, are governed by state insolvency law. Uninsured banks are not unknown, and many of them have state charters.

As with state insolvency law generally, the state law regarding financial institutions must wrestle with the Contracts Clause.[2] In many cases, as we also saw before, the law we encounter in this chapter is also potentially subject to pre-emption by a federal bankruptcy filing. The latter issue turns on the scope of section 109 of the Bankruptcy Code, which prohibits many financial institutions from filing a case, or having a case filed against them.[3]

---

[1] E.g., Cal. Ins. Code, §§ 1064.1 to 1064.13.

[2] Bruce A. Markell, Changes in Attitudes, Changes in Platitudes: A Short Examination of Non-Uniform Approaches to Business Insolvency, 6 *Am. Bankr. Inst. L. Rev.* 35, 37 (1998). ("Hampered by the Contract Clause, insurance company regulation fails to achieve the national uniformity brought about by the Bankruptcy Code.")

[3] The relevant bit from 11 U.S.C. § 109(b):

> **(b)** A person may be a debtor under chapter 7 of this title only if such person is not –
>   **(1)** a railroad;
>   **(2)** a domestic insurance company, bank, savings bank, co-operative bank, savings and loan association, building and loan association, homestead association, a New Markets Venture Capital company as defined in section 351 of the Small Business Investment Act of 1958, a small business investment company licensed by the Small Business Administration under section 301 of the Small Business Investment Act

Many, but not all. Thus, the case law is replete with decisions on the vital question of whether some "bank-like" entity is actually a bank, or something else listed in section 109's now befuddling list of excluded entities, or rather something else that might slip into federal court.[4] But if the entity is on the list – that is, excluded from federal bankruptcy – the state procedure will operate without federal disruption.

Banks and insurance companies comprise the bulk of state chartered financial institutions. State chartered banks, which in theory could predate the creation of the federal government, were at one time frequently subject to state bank receiverships.[5]

In modern times, most state chartered banks are insured by the federal FDIC, and the FDIC is most often appointed receiver for the bank when it fails.[6] Thus, state bank receiverships are far less common than they used to be back in the Hoover administration. The same is true for credit unions, where the state regulators often appoint the National Credit Union Association as receiver for troubled state chartered credit unions.

of 1958, credit union, or industrial bank or similar institution which is an insured bank as defined in section 3(h) of the Federal Deposit Insurance Act, except that an uninsured State member bank, or a corporation organized under section 25A of the Federal Reserve Act, which operates, or operates as, a multilateral clearing organization pursuant to section 409 of the Federal Deposit Insurance Corporation Improvement Act of 1991 may be a debtor if a petition is filed at the direction of the Board of Governors of the Federal Reserve System; or

(3) (A) a foreign insurance company, engaged in such business in the United States; or

(B) a foreign bank, savings bank, cooperative bank, savings and loan association, building and loan association, or credit union, that has a branch or agency (as defined in section 1(b) of the International Banking Act of 1978) in the United States.

[4] E.g., In re Cash Currency Exchange, Inc., 762 F.2d 542, 548 (7th Cir.1985); In re First Assured Warranty Corp., 383 B.R. 502 (Bkrtcy. D. Colo., 2008) (holding that automobile warranty company who issued "vehicle service contracts" was not a "domestic insurance company" and could be subject to federal bankruptcy statutes).

[5] And sometimes there were efforts to put them into federal equity receiverships. *Commonwealth of Pennsylvania* v. *Williams*, 294 U.S. 176, 186 (1935). ("On the showing that their interests would be adequately protected by liquidation under the direction of the secretary of banking, the District Judge should have denied the application for the appointment of receivers, or, if he had already appointed them, should have discharged the receivers, and directed the surrender of the property in their possession to the secretary in order that the liquidation might proceed under the state statutes.")

[6] The FDIC is not, however, required to accept this appointment.

That has not always been the case, as some states have attempted throughout the years to run their own depository insurance schemes, covering various types of institutions.[7] As a general rule, these state-level insurance schemes have failed to achieve sufficient scale to become feasible in the long term.[8]

Other states allow private companies to operate depository insurance systems, often for credit unions and other smaller financial institutions. When they exist, the insurance company – be it public or private – typically is appointed receiver of the insured institution.[9]

Many state depository institution statutes have been modeled after the National Bank Act of 1864, itself drawing from earlier New York statutes, and provide for a technocratic form of receivership without court oversight.[10] Other states require the relevant regulatory authority to file suit for the appointment of a receiver, and the liquidation proceeds under court control,[11] at least when the FDIC is not involved.[12] The FDIC, acting under federal law, may always appoint itself as receiver of a state chartered, but federally insured, institution.[13]

Generally, as with federally chartered institutions, the state bank or other institution is closed and a receiver appointed if the bank is insolvent, in an unsafe and unsound condition, unable to pay a judgment, or unable to meet the withdrawal of a deposit when due.[14]

---

[7] FDIC, The FDIC's Supervision of Industrial Loan Companies: A Historical Perspective (Summer 2004), available at www.fdic.gov/regulations/examinations/supervisory/insights/sisum04/industrial_loans.html.

[8] See *Rhode Island Depositors Econ. Prot. Corp.* v. *Tasca*, 729 A.2d 707, 708 (R.I. 1999).

[9] *Hughes* v. *White*, 388 F. Supp. 2d 805, 818 (S.D. Ohio 2005). See Walace Hawkins, Guaranteed Deposits under Depositors' Guaranty Fund, 3 *Tex. L. Rev.* 152 (1925).

[10] E.g., 205 Ill. Comp. Stat. Ann. 5/58; Miss. Code. Ann. § 81-14-211; Nev. Rev. Stat. Ann. § 678.835; Tex. Fin. Code Ann. § 96.253. For more on the history of the National Bank Act, see Benjamin J. Klebaner, *Commercial Banking in the United States: A History* 53 (1974).

[11] E.g., Md. Code Ann., Fin. Inst. § 5-605; Mich. Comp. Laws Ann. § 487.12402 (banks); Mich. Comp. Laws Ann. § 487.3601 (thrifts); N.H. Rev. Stat. Ann. § 395:4; Vt. Stat. Ann. tit. 8, § 19301; Va. Code Ann. § 6.2-916. In Oklahoma, a hearing must be held before the state banking commission, rather than in a state court. Okla. Stat. tit. 6, § 1202. In Illinois, the court is notified after the fact in all cases where the FDIC is not appointed receiver. 205 Ill. Comp. Stat. Ann. 5/53.

[12] Once appointed receiver, the FDIC may not be subjected to the direction or supervision of any other federal or state agency in the exercise of its receivership powers. 12 U.S.C. § 1821(d).

[13] 12 U.S.C. § 1821(c)(8)(A).

[14] N.Y. Banking Law § 606; Or. Rev. Stat. Ann. § 706.600.

While the FDIC's domination of the bank receivership process is nearly complete at the federal level, there remains a real, if narrow, role for the state bank receiver.[15] For example, some states allow limited forms of uninsured banks. Connecticut law allows the organization of an uninsured bank that does not accept retail deposits – defined as deposits made by individuals who are not accredited investors under federal securities regulations.[16] Both Maine and Vermont allow for similar entities.[17]

State chartered trust companies also typically operate without FDIC insurance. Alaska, Nevada, Delaware, New Hampshire, South Dakota, and Wyoming are the leading jurisdictions for chartering these entities. In the table below, we see the trust companies chartered in New Hampshire, only about half of which actually have addresses in the state – and at least two of those are using the address of law firms in Concord, the state capital.

The federal International Banking Act (IBA) of 1978 amended the Federal Deposit Insurance Act and allowed the U.S. branches of foreign banks to apply for deposit insurance. A subsequent law then provided that deposits in any foreign bank branch established after December 19, 1991 are not in fact covered by U.S. deposit insurance. Such branches can be formed (and regulated) under either federal or state banking law, but only a narrow group – those formed between 1978 and late 1991 – might be federally insured. All indications are that the vast majority of these branches are both uninsured and chartered at the state level, often in New York.

All uninsured entities – be they branch or bank or trust company – fail outside the FDIC receivership process. Federal branches and federal entities will be subject to OCC receiverships, like those in the years before deposit insurance.[18] But the state licensees, of which there are more, will be subject to state banking receiverships.[19]

---

[15] Cf. Helen A. Garten, Devolution and Deregulation: The Paradox of Financial Reform, 14 *Yale L. & Pol'y Rev.* 65, 79 (1996).

[16] Conn. Gen. Stat. Ann. § 36a-70.

[17] Me. Rev. Stat. tit. 9-B, § 1231; Vt. Stat. Ann. tit. 8, § 12604.

[18] With the notable exception that modern "safe harbors" for derivatives contracts apply to these uninsured federal creatures. 12 U.S.C. § 4406a.

[19] Cal. Fin. Code § 609. In Nebraska, a majority of creditors can vote to appoint "liquidating trustees." Neb. Rev. St. § 8-197.

Trust Company	City	State
GLAS Trust Company LLC	London	
Fiduciary Trust Company of New Hampshire	Overland Park	KS
The 1911 Trust Company, LLC	Beverly	MA
Boston Partners Trust Company	Boston	MA
Cambridge Associates Fiduciary Trust, LLC	Boston	MA
Geode Capital Management Trust Company, LLC	Boston	MA
John Hancock Trust Company LLC	Boston	MA
Loomis Sayles Trust Company, LLC	Boston	MA
Loring, Wolcott & Coolidge Trust, LLC	Boston	MA
MFS Heritage Trust Company	Boston	MA
Putnam Fiduciary Trust Company	Boston	MA
Mercer Trust Company	Norwood	MA
Family Capital Trust Company	Peabody	MA
Cambridge Trust Company of New Hampshire, Inc.	Concord	NH
Charter Trust Company	Concord	NH
Lincoln Financial Group Trust Company, Inc.	Concord	NH
MillRiver Trust Company	Concord	NH
Newport Trust Company	Concord	NH
Vantage Trust Company, LLC	Concord	NH
Perspecta Trust LLC	Hampton	NH
New Hampshire Trust Company, The	Keene	NH
Fiduciary Trust Company of New England LLC	Manchester	NH
Fidelity Institutional Asset Management Trust Company	Merrimack	NH
State Street Bank and Trust Company of New Hampshire	Nashua	NH
Exeter Trust Company	Portsmouth	NH
Deutsche AM Trust Company	Salem	NH
Hemenway Trust Company LLC	Salem	NH
AB Trust Company, LLC	New York	NY

Such a receivership is presently ongoing with regard to the New Hampshire chartered Noble Trust Company, which for two years starting in 2006 hid investment losses by paying old investors with new investors' money.[20] Interestingly, the state banking commissioner was appointed liquidator not only of the trust company itself, but also of the LLC that owned the trust company.[21] In July 2017, the court approved the first distribution of $2 million to holders of more than $16 million in allowed claims.

In the "good old days" before deposit insurance, or much of a social safety net whatsoever, many states followed the federal rule that depositors were simply unsecured creditors.[22] Only a couple of states enacted any sort of preference statute for depositors,[23] and that situation prevails in those states that have not updated their bank receivership laws since the New Deal.[24]

State bank receivers in this pre-FDIC era followed a variety of laws regarding the payment of secured claims. Some followed the chancery rule, discussed in Chapter 4 with regard to national banks, which gave the secured creditor a full claim in the unsecured creditors' "pot." Some states followed the bankruptcy rule, and limited the degree of secured creditor deficiency claims.[25] Other states followed the "Maryland rule," whereby the amount of the secured creditor's claim would be reset at each dividend payment, and any amounts actually realized on collateral deducted at that time.[26]

---

[20] https://archives.fbi.gov/archives/boston/press-releases/2009/bs102709.htm.

[21] Documents from the case can be found at: www.nh.gov/banking/noble-trust/.

[22] *Fulton* v. *Escanaba Paper Co.*, 193 N.E. 758, 762 (Ohio 1934); *Great Atl. & Pac. Tea Co.* v. *Hood*, 171 S.E. 344, 346 (N.C. 1933). In a rare reorganization of a large New York trust company in a state court receivership, depositors received 70 percent of their deposits back in certificates of deposit with drawn out maturities, and 30 percent in notes that were payable only if the reorganized entity generated sufficient earnings. John Hanna, The Knickerbocker Trust Company – A Study in Receivership, 5 *Temp. L.Q.* 319, 344 (1931).

[23] See *State* v. *First State Bank of All.*, 239 N.W. 646, 647 (Neb. 1931) (upholding such a statute).

[24] At least thirty states have a depositor preference statute, but that leaves many without one. See generally James A. Marino & Rosalind L. Bennett, The Consequences of National Depositor Preference, 12 *FDIC Banking Rev.* 19 (1999).

[25] Even when there was no federal bankruptcy law in force. *State* v. *Nebraska Sav. Bank*, 58 N.W. 976, 980 (Neb. 1894).

[26] Hirsch Braver, *Liquidation of Financial Institutions: A Treatise on the Law of Voluntary and Involuntary Liquidation of Banks, Trust Companies, and Building and Loan Associations* § 1134 (1936).

The degree to which state bank receivership law has been kept fresh, or allowed to wither, varies a good deal. New York, home to many foreign bank branches and several trust companies, has frequently updated its receivership provisions.[27] And its courts and regulators have fairly frequent and recent experience conducting bank liquidations.[28]

Of course, if one is apt to believe that some of the new revisions are simply reflections of the lobbying might of the financial industry, the retention of an old-fashioned bank receivership statute might not be entirely regrettable. For example, some commentators lament that California's provisions that address foreign branches[29] and the liquidation of uninsured banks generally – which are not particularly old, having been revised in 2011– do not contain "safe harbors," providing for special treatment of derivatives contracts.[30] New York's statutes, on the other hand, do provide such special treatment.[31] But the real utility of such provisions is subject to substantial debate, to enormously understate the issue.

Several states also have rules governing the reorganization of insolvent banks.[32] This is another area of the law that has wilted since the advent of the FDIC, but remains in force (in some states) for potential application to the rare uninsured entity, or the equally rare cases where the FDIC refuses to resolve an insured state-chartered bank.[33]

One of the last New York cases to address bank reorganizations in that state, describes a plan, which

> provided for the contribution by each then stockholder of the bank of $3 per share for each share owned by such stockholder, which would produce $225,000 to be added to the assets of the reorganized bank ... The plan was consented to by stockholders owning 51,721 shares, and stockholders owning 23,280 shares refused

---

[27] The process for liquidating banks in New York is governed by Article XIII of the New York Banking Law.

[28] E.g., In re Liquidation of Jugobanka, A.D., 995 N.Y.S.2d 906, 907 (N.Y. Sup. Ct. 2014).

[29] Cal. Fin. Code § 1831.

[30] Id. § 673.

[31] N.Y. Banking Law § 618-a.

[32] Banks and Banking – Insolvency – Authority to Order Reorganization, 39 *Harv. L. Rev.* 386, 387 (1926).

[33] See *Sueltz v. Bank of Hazelton*, 238 N.W. 649, 649 (N.D. 1931) ("... acting under the provisions of section 20, chapter 99, S.L. 1927, more than 80 percent of the deposit creditors entered into an agreement to reorganize and reopen the bank").

their approval of the plan and refused to sign the agreement which would require them to contribute $3 per share to the fund. The plan was approved by an order of the Supreme Court which was modified and affirmed by the Appellate Division, Second Department.[34]

In New Jersey, a bank reorganization plan can be proposed by the banking commissioner, the bank, three or more depositors or other creditors of the bank with claims of $10,000 or more, or a 10 percent shareholder.[35] If someone other than the commissioner proposes the plan, the plan is filed with the commissioner for review. That regulator will approve the plan if it finds it fair, equitable, and feasible; the proposed directors and officers are acceptable; and the interests of the public will be served by the plan.[36] The plan can also provide for the termination of executory contracts and leases.[37]

An action to approve a plan is filed before the Superior Court by either the commissioner or bank itself, if they are the proponents of the plan, or by other proponents after approval by the regulator.[38] The court reviews the plan, essentially under the same basic standards that the commissioner previously applied.[39]

The proponents of the plan then solicit the acceptance of creditors and stockholders adversely affected by the plan, which are filed with the court.[40] If two-thirds of the creditors or shareholders accept – or are deemed to have accepted, by failing to respond – the plan becomes binding on all.[41] Upon confirmation of the plan, all "property dealt

---

[34] *Nyen Holding Corp.* v. *Kahle*, 29 N.Y.S.2d 793, 795 (N.Y. Sup. Ct. 1941).

[35] In South Carolina, it must be 5 percent of depositors and shareholders who desire a plan, and the role of the banking regulator appears much less prominent. S.C. Code Ann. § 34-7-40. In Maryland, the standards for who can propose a plan are similar, save for that the depositors must total 25 percent of the outstanding deposits. Md. Code Ann., Fin. Inst. § 5-611.

[36] N.J. Stat. Ann. § 17:9A-158(B). In California, the regulator must find the plan "fair and equitable to all customers, creditors, and stockholders." Cal. Fin. Code § 650.

[37] N.J. Stat. Ann. § 17:9A-161(B).

[38] Id. § 17:9A-159. See also Id. § 17:9A-160.

[39] Id. § 17:9A-162. For confirmation of the plan by the court, see Id. § 17:9A-166.

[40] Id. § 17:9A-164.

[41] Id. § 17:9A-164(G); accord Cal. Fin. Code § 652; Md. Code Ann., Fin. Inst. § 5-612. See also N.J. Stat. Ann. § 17:9A-165. ("The court, upon such notice and hearing as it shall determine, shall, subject to confirmation of the plan, provide for any class of creditors which is adversely affected by and is not bound by the plan, adequate protection for the realization by the creditors of such class of the value of their claims against the property dealt with by the plan.")

with by the plan shall be free and clear of all claims and interests, except as provided in the plan or in such order as the court may make authorizing or directing the transfer of such property."[42]

New Jersey's bank reorganization statute was substantially revised in 1948, and hardly ever used since. The law in other states that have retained bank reorganization statutes is typically similar, if somewhat less developed. In New York, the standard for approval of the plan is somewhat higher – at least 80 percent of the bank's creditors who will not be satisfied in full under the plan and two-thirds of its shareholders must consent.[43] In California, the margin is 75 percent of creditors and two-thirds of shareholders.[44]

South Carolina potentially takes the thresholds a bit lower, requiring approval of two-thirds of those present at a meeting to consider the plan to approve, but providing that half of shareholders and creditors constitutes a quorum at such a meeting.[45] The state also provides that there shall be no right to appeal from an order confirming a bank reorganization plan.

Somewhat more vital and current is the state law addressing the failure of insurance companies. Insurance has always been the domain of the states: first by tradition, and then by virtue of the curious McCarran Ferguson Act.[46]

That Act allows each state to regulate insurance companies within their boundaries and removes any assumption of federal pre-emption – including that which would normally arise under the Commerce Clause. The law can be seen as a kind of opposite of the more typical federal statute; in the area of insurance, Congress has affirmatively given away its power to the states.[47]

---

[42] N.J. Stat. Ann. § 17:9A-171.

[43] N.Y. Banking Law § 610.

[44] Cal. Fin. Code § 648; accord 205 Ill. Comp. Stat. Ann. 5/55.

[45] S.C. Code Ann. § 34-7-60.

[46] 15 U.S.C. § 1012. The Act was a response to the Supreme Court's holding in *United States v. S.-E. Underwriters Ass'n*, 322 U.S. 533 (1944), which reversed dubious nineteenth century precedent that insurance did not involve "commerce." *Barnett Bank of Marion Cty., N.A. v. Nelson*, 517 U.S. 25, 40 (1996).

[47] *Ruthardt v. United States*, 164 F. Supp. 2d 232, 238 (D. Mass. 2001), aff'd, 303 F.3d 375 (1st Cir. 2002); William Goddard, In Between the Trenches: The Jurisdictional Conflict Between A Bankruptcy Court and A State Insurance Receivership Court, 9 *Conn. Ins. L.J.* 567, 573 (2003).

Thus, the states have always had to deal with financial distress in insurance companies.[48] Model laws of various vintages, put forward by the National Association of Insurance Commissioners, provide the basis for many of the state laws. But New York, being New York, often drafts its own insurance laws. Nevertheless, the basic structure of insurance failure is fairly uniform across the states: the insurance regulator goes to court and gets a receiver appointed, often the regulator itself,[49] to take control of the insurance company.[50] An example is set forth on the upcoming pages.

Insurance receiverships, unlike bank receiverships, are typically focused on courts and judicial proceedings, rather than administrative action.[51] Which court is in charge varies by state. In Massachusetts, for example, only a justice of the Commonwealth's highest court may preside over insurer receiverships.[52] On the other hand, in many other states the general trial court judges preside over insurance receiverships.[53] The Michigan insurance receivership statute makes clear that the court hearing such proceedings is limited to the express terms of the statute, and has no authority to act under its general equitable authority.[54]

The company proceeds to wind up its business. In some cases the liquidation is preceded by a period of conservation.[55] The appointment of a conservator is also controlled by the state insurance regulator, although in California the FDIC can request a conservator as well.[56]

---

[48] In re Equity Funding Corp. of America, 396 F. Supp. 1266, 1275 (C.D. Cal. 1975). See also *Chicago Life Ins. Co.* v. *Needles*, 113 U.S. 574, 582 (1885).

[49] Iowa Code Ann. § 505.9. In New York, the regulator acting as receiver has a separate, dedicated staff, collectively known as the New York Liquidation Bureau. See also State ex rel. *ISC Financial Corp.* v. *Kinder*, 684 S.W.2d 910, 913 (Mo. Ct. App. W.D. 1985).

[50] Ala. Code § 27-34-50 (fraternal benefit societies); Del. Code Ann. tit. 18, § 5906; Haw. Rev. Stat. Ann. § 432:2-606 (fraternal benefit societies); Iowa Code Ann. § 508.22; Nev. Rev. Stat. Ann. § 696B.220; N.Y. Ins. Law § 7405; Utah Code Ann. § 31A-27a-401; W. Va. Code § 33-10-6.

[51] *Greenberger* v. *Pennsylvania Ins. Dep't*, 39 A.3d 625, 630 (Pa. Commw. Ct. 2012).

[52] Mass. Gen. Laws ch. 175, §§ 6, 180B, 180C.

[53] E.g., Cal. Insurance Law § 1011; Mich. Comp. Laws § 500.8104(3); 215 Ill. Comp. Stat. 5/188; N.Y. Insurance Law § 7417; Vt. Stat. Ann. tit. 8, § 7051.

[54] Mich. Comp. Laws Ann. § 500.8104.

[55] Mich. Comp. Laws Serv. § 500.8150.

[56] Cal. Ins. Code § 1011 (a).

1   KAMALA D. HARRIS
    Attorney General of the State of California
2   ANNE MICHELLE BURR
    Supervising Deputy Attorney General
3   MARGUERITE C. STRICKLIN (State Bar No. 103161)
    Deputy Attorney General
4   1515 Clay Street, 20ᵗʰ Floor
    Oakland, California 94612-0550
5   Telephone: (510) 622-2146
    Facsimile: (510) 622-2270
6   Email: Marguerite.Stricklin@doj.ca.gov

7   THOMAS J. WELSH (State Bar No. 142890)
    PATRICK B. BOCASH (State Bar No. 262763)
8   ORRICK, HERRINGTON & SUTCLIFFE LLP
    400 Capitol Mall, Suite 3000
9   Sacramento, California 95814-4497
    Telephone: (916) 447-9200
10 Facsimile: (916) 329-4900
    Email: tomwelsh@orrick.com
11   pbocash@orrick.com

12 Attorneys for Applicant Dave Jones,
    Insurance Commissioner of the State of California
13

ENDORSED
F I L E D
Superior Court of California
County of San Francisco

JUL 28 2016

CLERK OF THE COURT
By: _____ROSIE NOGUERA_____
                  Deputy Clerk

**EXEMPT from filing fees per Govt.
Code § 6103**

14

15   SUPERIOR COURT OF THE STATE OF CALIFORNIA

16   CITY AND COUNTY OF SAN FRANCISCO

17

18 DAVE JONES, INSURANCE
    COMMISSIONER OF THE STATE OF
19 CALIFORNIA,

20   Applicant,

21   v.

22 CASTLEPOINT NATIONAL INSURANCE
    COMPANY, and DOES 1-50, inclusive,
23

          Respondents.

Case No. CPF-16-515183

**ORDER APPOINTING INSURANCE
COMMISSIONER AS
CONSERVATOR AND RESTRAINING
ORDERS
~~(PROPOSED)~~**

Date: **July 28, 2016**
Time: **11:00 a.m.**
Dept: **302**
Judge: **Hon. Harold E. Kahn**

24

25

26

27

28

~~[PROPOSED]~~ ORDER APPOINTING INSURANCE COMMISSIONER AS CONSERVATOR

1   The Insurance Commissioner of the State of California (the "Commissioner") has filed his

2   verified Application in the above-captioned action, and has shown to the Court's satisfaction that

3   CastlePoint National Insurance Company ("CastlePoint")[1] is in such condition that its further

4   transaction of business will be hazardous to its policyholders, creditors, and the public, and good

5   cause appearing therefore;

6   WHEREFORE IT IS HEREBY ORDERED:

7   1.   The Commissioner is appointed as Conservator (hereinafter the "Conservator") of

8   CastlePoint and directed to conduct the business of CastlePoint or so much thereof as he deems

9   appropriate; and he is authorized, in his discretion, to pay or defer payment of some or all proper

10   claims, expenses, liabilities, and obligations of CastlePoint, in whole or in part, accruing prior or

11   subsequent to his appointment as Conservator.

12   2.   The Conservator is authorized to assume or reject, or to modify, any executory

13   contract, including without limitation, any lease, rental or utilization contract or agreement

14   (including any schedule to any such contract or agreement), and any license or other arrangement

15   for the use of computer software or business information systems, to which CastlePoint is a party

16   or as to which it agrees to accept an assignment of such contract; the Conservator is directed to

17   effect any such assumption or rejection or modification of any executory contract not later than

18   120 days after the date of the Order Appointing Insurance Commissioner As Conservator, unless

19   such date is extended by application to and further order of this Court; and all executory contracts

20   that are not expressly assumed by the Conservator shall be deemed rejected;

21   3.   The Conservator is authorized to take possession of all of the assets of CastlePoint,

22   including books, records and property, both real and personal, accounts, safe deposit boxes, rights

23   of action, and all such assets as may be in the name of CastlePoint, wheresoever situated;

---

[1]   For all purposes in this Order, the term "CastlePoint," wherever used and used in whatever
context or reference, shall mean and refer to CastlePoint National Insurance Company, as the
survivor by merger with, and shall be deemed to include all of the following predecessor entities:
the pre-merger CastlePoint National Insurance Company, Tower Insurance Company of New
York, Tower National Insurance Company, Hermitage Insurance Company, Kodiak Insurance
Company, CastlePoint Florida Insurance Company, North East Insurance Company,
Massachusetts Homeland Insurance Company, Preserver Insurance Company, York Insurance
Company of Maine, and CastlePoint Insurance Company.

- 1 -

Insurance receiverships are notable for their Dickensian length, and complexity. For example, one such liquidation was described thus:

> Home [Insurance Company], domiciled in New Hampshire, was declared insolvent on June 11, 2003, and is one of the largest property-casualty insurer insolvencies in United States history. The Company and its predecessors began operations in 1853. The Court entered the operative Order of Liquidation on June 13, 2003. The Liquidator has created a stand-alone liquidation operation which presently consists of 46 full and part time employees with offices in New York City (Home's former corporate headquarters) and Manchester, New Hampshire. From the start in 2003, the Liquidator has been engaged in marshalling assets, principally reinsurance, and determining claims.

The paragraph comes from the liquidator's sixty-second report, from September 2016. Your author worked on the chapter 11 case of this insurance company's parent holding company. That case commenced in 1998 and was done by mid 1999.[57]

State guaranty funds, set up and paid for by solvent insurance companies operating within the jurisdiction, pay covered policyholder claims, up to certain limits, which are often quite low.[58] And the laws of every state include provisions that require the receiver to pay policyholder claims in full before other unsecured creditors' claims.[59] Claims are filed with and accepted or rejected by the receiver.[60]

---

[57] In re Home Holdings Inc., Docket No. 98-bk-40319 (Bankr. S.D.N.Y. Jan 15, 1998).

[58] E.g., Ala. Code § 27-44-8; Cal. Ins. Code § 1063.2; Mass. Gen. Laws Ann. ch. 175D, § 5; Ky. Rev. Stat. § 304.36-020; 27 R.I. Gen. Laws Ann. § 27-34.3-8; Wyo. Stat. Ann. § 26-42-106. See also *de la Fuente* v. *Florida Ins. Guar. Ass'n*, 202 So. 3d 396, 401 (Fla. 2016). In New York, there are three distinct, statutory security funds, known as the Property/Casualty Insurance Security Fund, the Public Motor Vehicle Security Fund and the Workers' Compensation Security Fund. In addition, life insurance policy holders are protected by the Life Insurance Company Guaranty Corporation of New York, created under Article 77 of the State's insurance law. See also *Kentucky Ins. Guar. Ass'n* v. *Nat. Res. & Envtl. Prot. Cabinet*, 885 S.W.2d 315, 316 (Ky. Ct. App. 1994).

[59] E.g., Ariz. Rev. Stat. § 20-629; Colo. Rev. Stat. § 10-3-541; Kan. Stat. Ann. § 40-3641; N.Y. Ins. Law § 7434; N.D. Cent. Code § 26.1-06.1-41. Unlike in proceedings under the Bankruptcy Code, in insurance receiverships contingent claims are often disallowed. Ala. Code § 27-32-30; N.Y. Ins. Law § 7433(c).

[60] *Garamendi* v. *Golden Eagle Ins. Co.*, 27 Cal. Rptr. 3d 239, 248 (Ct. App. 2005) (contrasting bankruptcy and insurance insolvency).

An injunction protects the receivership estate from independent creditor action.[61] In some states the injunction is statutory and, like the bankruptcy automatic stay, goes into effect upon appointment of the receiver.[62]

A "domiciliary receiver" is commenced by the insurance commissioner[63] in the state of incorporation, while ancillary receiverships are commenced in other states where the company operates.[64] In this basic setup, the insurance receiverships mimic the structure of the old railroad receiverships of the nineteenth century, although the ancillary receivers in the insurance context proceed with more independence from the primary receivership than their railroad counterparts ever did.[65]

Many states require insurers to provide some security to the state in the form of bonds, securities, or other collateral, to ensure the performance of their obligations. Most states treat these as trust funds for policyholders, or perhaps local creditors generally. But the IRS treats statutory deposits just like general assets and gets priority over local policyholders under federal law.

Moreover, the existence of these funds, sprinkled across the country, provides a serious impediment to any notion of treating policyholders equally throughout the United States. Instead, the local insurance commissioner typically has an ability to take the fund for the benefit of in-state creditors or policyholders before distributing the remainder to the central receivership estate.[66]

Indeed, the co-ordination of receiverships across state lines presents a particular challenge for insurance company insolvency law based, as

---

[61] Del. Code Ann. tit. 18, § 5904; N.Y. Ins. Law § 7419. In Matter of Liquidation of Freestone Ins. Co., 143 A.3d 1234, 1240 (Del. Ch. 2016).

[62] Haw. Rev. Stat. Ann. § 431:15-313.

[63] E.g., Cal. Insurance Law § 1011; Mich. Comp. Laws § 500.8104(3); 215 Ill. Comp. Stat. 5/188; N.Y. Insurance Law § 7417; Vt. Stat. Ann. tit. 8, § 7051.

[64] Ariz. Rev. Stat. § 20-623; Kan. Stat. Ann. § 40-3651; Mass. Gen. Laws Ann. ch. 175, § 180F.

[65] E.g., 215 Ill. Comp. Stat. Ann. 5/221.8 ("The ancillary receiver of assets in this State of insurers domiciliary in reciprocal states and subject to delinquency proceedings therein shall, as soon as practicable, arrange the liquidation or other disposition of special deposit claims and secured claims proved in the ancillary proceedings in this State, and all remaining assets, after payment of expenses he shall promptly transfer to the domiciliary receiver.")

[66] Levin v. National Colonial Ins. Co., 806 N.E.2d 473 (N.Y. 2004).

it is, in the state judiciary.[67] In some early cases, the solution was to commence a federal equity receivership over the entire operation.

The Uniform Insurers Liquidation Act was approved by the National Conference of Commissioners on Uniform State Laws in 1939 to return the issue to the state level.[68] The Act is designed to cover disputes between an enacting state and a "reciprocal" state, which is defined in § 1 of the act as "any state other than this state in which in substance and effect the provisions of this act are in force." In states that have adopted the Act, insurance companies are liquidated under a single set of priorities, based on those in effect in the domiciliary state, as if the company comprised a single pool of assets.[69]

The Act provides that:

> During the pendency of delinquency proceedings in that or any reciprocal state no action or proceeding in the nature of an attachment, garnishment, or execution shall be commenced or maintained in the courts of this state against the delinquent insurer of its assets.

The provision is designed "to prevent attempts of local creditors to seize the assets within the state of a foreign insurer ... to the end that all creditors of the insurer would secure equal treatment."[70]

Despite adoption of the Act,.[71] disputes between ancillary and domiciliary receivers have not been entirely abolished.[72] If the domiciliary state is not a reciprocal state under the Uniform Act, the courts have allowed creditors to attach or garnish the assets located in other states, even if the other states have adopted the Act. And interstate tensions in general remain common in the insurance area.[73] In addition,

---

[67] See *Fuhrman v. United Am. Insurors*, 269 N.W.2d 842, 848 (Minn. 1978).

[68] *G. C. Murphy Co.* v. *Reserve Ins. Co.*, 429 N.E.2d 111, 114 (N.Y. 1981).

[69] *Home Ins. Co.* v. *Montgomery County Com'n*, 902 So. 2d 677, 678 (Ala. 2004); *Olivine Corp.* v. *United Capitol Ins. Co.*, 92 P.3d 273, 276 (Wash. App. 2004). See also *Levin* v. *Nat'l Colonial Ins. Co.*, 806 N.E.2d 473, 477 (N.Y. 2004).

[70] *Ace Grain Co* v. *Rhode Island Ins Co*, 107 F. Supp. 80, 82 (S.D.N.Y.), aff'd, 199 F.2d 758 (2d Cir. 1952).

[71] E.g., Cal. Insurance Law § 1011; Mich. Comp. Laws § 500.8104(3); 215 Ill. Comp. Stat. 5/188; N.Y. Insurance Law § 7417; Vt. Stat. Ann. tit. 8, § 7051.

[72] State, ex rel. *Driscoll* v. *Early Am. Ins. Co.*, 733 P.2d 919, 921 (Or. App. 1987); see also Stephen W. Schwab, et al., Cross-Border Insurance Insolvencies: The Search for a Forum Concursus, 12 *U. Pa. J. Int'l Bus. L.* 303, 317 (1991).

[73] *Koken* v. *Legion Ins. Co.*, 941 A.2d 60, 64 (Pa. Commw. Ct. 2007).

the federal policy of non-interference in insurance regulatory matters frequently collides with a party's assertion of federal claims in the federal courts.

Wisconsin subordinates claims on judgments to claims presented in the liquidation process itself, in an obvious attempt to preserve the domiciliary court's jurisdiction.[74] Whether such a move comports with the Constitution – in particular the Full Faith and Credit Clause – is doubtful.

After the receiver has marshaled assets and liquidated the estate's assets, the receiver will petition the court to approve a final distribution.[75] In more complicated estates, the liquidator may file and seek approval of a liquidation plan.

Many states have rehabilitation – that is, reorganization – provisions, in addition to their standard liquidation provisions.[76] One of the most notable in recent years has been the attempted rehabilitation of a long-term care insurance provider in Pennsylvania, which the state insurance regulators have been unsuccessfully attempting to convert to a liquidation for years.[77] By 2017 it appeared that this case was headed for a liquidation after all.

As one observer aptly reviewed the situation here:

Even when state commissioners put a company into rehabilitation, they often do so simply as an interim measure to give the commissioner's office a better opportunity to assess the status and prospects of a troubled insurer. Many of these proceedings end up in liquidation, and many others start there. It is principally with extremely large insurers that state commissioners effect a true rehabilitation.[78]

---

[74] Wis. Stat. Ann. § 645.68(6).

[75] Colo. Rev. Stat. § 10-3-533; 215 Ill. Comp. Stat. Ann. 5/210; Mich. Comp. Laws Serv. § 500.8144; N.D. Cent. Code § 26.1-06.1-43; Utah Code Ann. § 31A-27a-703.

[76] Tex. Ins. Code Ann. § 443.101. As to the powers and duties of the rehabilitator, see Tex. Ins. Code Ann. § 443.102.

[77] In re Penn Treaty Network Am. Ins. Co., 119 A.3d 313 (Pa. 2015). See also Matter of Rehab. of Indem. Ins. Corp., RRG, No. CIV.A. 8601-VCL, 2014 WL 1154057 (Del. Ch. Mar. 21, 2014) (insurance company that went from liquidation to rehabilitation, only to go back to liquidation).

[78] David A. Skeel, Jr., The Law and Finance of Bank and Insurance Insolvency Regulation, 76 *Tex. L. Rev.* 723, 733 (1998).

And even this may overstate the ability of regulators to reorganize an insurance company.

Like bank receiverships, insurance receiverships have at their heart the protection of a favored class. On the other hand, there are key differences between the two types of proceedings. For one, the court, although deferential in insurance receiverships, is more actively involved.[79] Even when the FDIC does not take the lead role in a bank receivership – which obviously changes the dynamic quite dramatically – a banking commissioner operates much more independence than an insurance commissioner. But in both cases, the regulators, and not creditors or other stakeholders, are at the core of the proceedings.[80]

After banks and insurance companies, where the law is fairly uniform among the states, state insolvency law branches off in a variety of unique ways.

A sizable number of states have special receivership provisions for what we might term as near bank entities: check cashing shops, money transfer businesses, currency exchanges, and other related businesses that sometimes cluster in a single storefront.

In many of these states, the law is based on the Uniform Money Services Act.[81] This law was put forward by the Uniform Law Commissioners in 2000, and has been adopted in Alaska, Washington, New Mexico, Texas, Iowa, Arkansas, and Vermont, moving west to east.[82]

The uniform law provides that money transmission, check cashing, and currency exchange businesses require a special license from the state. The uniform act contains optional provisions allowing regulators to place the business in a receivership in a variety of circumstances, including insolvency. The receivership provisions have been adopted in Alaska, Washington, Iowa, and Vermont.[83]

In addition, California, Michigan and Illinois regulate these businesses, although not through the uniform act. Their statutes also

---

[79] *Ito* v. *Inv'rs Equity Life Holding Co.*, 346 P.3d 118, 122 (Haw. 2015).

[80] *Taylor* v. *Ernst & Young, L.L.P.*, 958 N.E.2d 1203, 1213 (Ohio 2011).

[81] www.uniformlaws.org/shared/docs/money%20services/umsa_final04.pdf.

[82] And also Puerto Rico and the U.S. Virgin Islands.

[83] Alaska Stat. Ann. § 06.55.601; Iowa Code Ann. § 533C.701; Vt. Stat. Ann. tit. 8, § 2545; Wash. Rev. Code Ann. § 19.230.230.

contain regulatory receiverships for insolvent businesses.[84] The Illinois statute includes an elaborate outline of the priority of claims in such a receivership.

It is not clear that any of these provisions have ever been used. To the extent these businesses work as substitutes for banks for a sizable part of the population, the idea that they should fail under specialized procedures is entirely understandable. On the other hand, Congress has not acknowledged this, and the case law permits a bankruptcy filing to supplant such a receivership.[85] So, unlike most of the financial industry, here we see the federal-state layering that is typical with regard to business insolvency generally.

The number of insolvency tools can get complex if multiple state insolvency regimes are relevant in addition to the federal Bankruptcy Code. Consider Utah's regulation of escrow agents: one provision of the statute contemplates at least three distinct avenues of resolution, six if we count the three varieties offered under one option:

> If the commissioner takes possession of the business and property of the escrow agent in accordance with Title 7, Chapter 2, Possession of Depository Institution by Commissioner, *or* if the escrow agent files or is involuntarily placed into bankruptcy, *or* if a *receiver, conservator, or liquidator* is appointed to administer the affairs of the escrow agent ...[86]

At least two other states – Arizona and Washington – also regulate escrow agents and provide for special receivership proceedings.[87] But none contemplates all the permutations to the same degree as Utah.

New Jersey purports to regulate investment companies – and provides for receiverships of such companies, when the fund "shall become insolvent or shall suspend its ordinary business for want of funds to carry on the same."[88] The statute cryptically provides that the

---

[84] Cal. Fin. Code § 2149; Mich. Comp. Laws Ann. § 487.1041; 205 Ill. Comp. Stat. Ann. 405/15.1B. And Florida's Consumer Finance Act has a receivership provision that might be relevant here as well. Fla. Stat. Ann. § 516.23.

[85] Something recognized by the Vermont legislature. Vt. Stat. Ann. tit. 8, § 2555.

[86] Utah Code Ann. § 7-22-109 (emphasis added).

[87] Ariz. Rev. Stat. Ann. § 6-833; Wash. Rev. Code Ann. § 18.44.470.

[88] N.J. Stat. Ann. § 17:16A-19.

"court may proceed in the action in a summary manner or otherwise."
The receiver shall have the

> power to sue for, collect, receive and take into his possession all
> the goods and chattels, rights, and credits, moneys and effects,
> lands and tenement, books, papers, choses in action, bills, notes
> and property of every description belonging to such company, and
> sell and convey and assign the same, and hold and dispose of the
> proceeds thereof under the directions of the court.

Subject to the potential power of the court to act in a summary
fashion – which sounds rather thrilling, while also a bit disquieting[89] –
this appears to be a garden variety receivership instituted by the financial
institution's regulators.

The statute was passed in late 1938,[90] and in 1940 the federal
government regulated investment companies.[91] Hence, the statute
seems to have been something of a dead letter almost from inception –
unknown even to leading New Jersey securities attorneys whom I
consulted.

Of a similar nature is California's receivership provisions for securities depositors.[92] Not only is it doubtful that such a depository would
be subject to state regulation, but The Depository Trust Company is
the primary, indeed only, commercial U.S. securities depository currently in operation.[93] As previously noted, it is subject to regulation by

---

[89] Sadly, it appears that this is just New Jersey's old-fashioned way of referring to orders to
show cause, likely a relic of chancery practice (or possibly prerogative writ practice) which
the state formally abolished in the late 1940s. N.J. Court Rules, R. 4:67-2 ("If the action is
brought in a summary manner pursuant to R. 4:67-1(a), the complaint, verified by affida-
vit made pursuant to R. 1:6-6, may be presented to the court ex parte ...").

[90] 1938 laws, chapter 322, §§1 through 20 (17:16A-1 through 17:16A-20).

[91] Investment Company Act of 1940, codified at 15 U.S.C. §§ 80a-1 to 80a-64.

[92] Cal. Fin. Code §§ 30200, 30215. See also Cal. Fin. Code § 30004. ("'Securities depository' means any person or group of persons who acts as the custodian of securities in
accordance with a system for the central handling of securities whereby all securities of a
particular class or series of any issues deposited within the system are treated as fungible
and may be transferred or pledged by bookkeeping entries effected by that person without
physical delivery of such securities.")

[93] Federal Reserve Banks act as depositories for certain securities, like those issued by the
U.S. Government or certain governmental agencies. Strictly speaking, the local Federal
Reserve Banks are privately owned, but they are arguably not commercial.

New York banking regulators and the Federal Reserve, so is exempt from regulation by California.[94]

A handful of oddball financial institutions round out our tour of state law in this area. On the very fringes of our survey, but too interesting to omit, are Colorado's provisions that allow the state commissioner of financial services to institute proceedings against an insolvent "cannabis credit co-op." Under the law, the commissioner can be appointed liquidating agent, just as with any other financial institution.[95] Indeed, the Marijuana Financial Services Co-operatives Act is just another part of that state's title 11, the Financial Institutions Code.[96] The law was passed with legislative findings that marijuana businesses' "lack of access to financial services harms the public interest."

Far more pedestrian is Maine's regulation of payroll processors,[97] yet the law's insolvency provisions are comparatively elaborate. The law provides for voluntary and involuntary liquidation of regulated payroll processors. If the Superintendent of Consumer Credit Protection within the Maine Department of Professional and Financial Regulation determines the business is insolvent, "the administrator may appoint a receiver who shall proceed to close the payroll processor."[98]

The receiver is appointed without court involvement, and "has the power and authority provided in this chapter and such other powers and authority as may be expressed in the order of the administrator." Needless to say, that might be quite broad. The statute itself grants the receiver comprehensive powers – including the authority to "borrow money and issue evidence of indebtedness therefor" – and the regulator's order apparently could take such powers even further.

Presumably, the order could also attempt to prohibit federal bankruptcy filings by the payroll company, and its creditors, as well. State

---

[94] Cal. Fin. Code § 30005.
[95] Colo. Rev. Stat. Ann. § 11-33-122.
[96] Id. § 11-33-101.
[97] Me. Rev. Stat. tit. 10, § 1495. ("'Payroll processing services' means preparing and issuing payroll checks; preparing and filing state or federal income withholding tax reports or unemployment insurance contribution reports; or collecting, holding and turning over to the State Tax Assessor or to federal tax authorities income withholding taxes pursuant to Title 36, chapter 827 or federal law or unemployment insurance contributions pursuant to Title 26, chapter 13, subchapter 7 or federal law.")
[98] Me. Rev. Stat. tit. 10, § 1495-I.

courts and regulators have not been particularly successful in this regard, but there is no discernible reason why the federal courts should permit such moves by the federal financial regulators, while disdaining their state counterparts. Of course, it may simply be that a court is overawed by the regulatory complexity and responsibility faced by the CFTC or FDIC, while Maine's regulator of payroll processors garners no such respect.

Washington and Alaska provide our last two specialized statutes, and they are somewhat related. In the far north, Alaska has specialized firms called "BIDCOs."[99] These are firms that provide financial and management assistance for other businesses in the state. In 2015, they reportedly provided about $50 million of financing to Alaskan businesses, about $15 million of which was related to air passenger services.[100]

The BIDCOs are subject to minimum capital and licensing requirements.[101] And if the BIDCO becomes insolvent, Alaska's Division of Banking and Securities can petition for the appointment of a receiver.[102] The only guidance given to the receiver under the statute is that they "shall liquidate the property and business of the licensee."

Back in the lower 48, Michigan's BIDCO statute likewise provides that

> the commissioner may bring an action in the name of the people of this state in a circuit court to enjoin the violation or to enforce compliance with this act. Upon a proper showing, a restraining order, preliminary or permanent injunction, or writ of mandamus shall be granted, and a receiver or a conservator may be appointed for the defendant or the defendant's assets. The court shall not require the commissioner to post a bond in an action brought under this act.[103]

Washington State also has "industrial development corporations," which serve a similar function, even if they lack the catchy acronym.[104]

---

[99] Business Industrial Development Corporation.
[100] https://goo.gl/LchhNj.
[101] Alaska Stat. Ann. § 10.13.020.
[102] Id. § 10.13.820. See also Id. § 10.13.810.
[103] Mich. Comp. Laws Ann. § 487.1701. See also Del. Code Ann. tit. 5, § 3354; Idaho Code Ann. § 26-2728; Mont. Code Ann. § 32-11-413.
[104] Wash. Rev. Code Ann. § 31.24.005.

If a Washington industrial development corporation becomes insolvent, it is subject to resolution under the general bank receivership provisions in the state.[105]

Overall, the law of financial institutions at both the state and federal level has some notable similarities. Depending on the type of financial institution, we see varying degrees of distrust of courts. As with most financial institutions – or specialized insolvency regimes generally – one key unifying feature is the desire to protect a particular class of creditors from the effects of insolvency. This favored class typically drives the move away from general business insolvency law to some specialized provision, which is perceived as providing greater protection.

The success of this strategy depends in part on the scope of the federal Bankruptcy Code, and Congress' exercise of its constitutional powers under the Bankruptcy Clause more generally. Beyond these practical considerations, there is the question of what makes good policy. This is the focus of the remainder of the book.

---

[105] Id. § 31.24.200. The statute cites to the old version of the bank receivership provisions, which have since been recodified in chapter 30a.44.

6 LOOKING FOR PATTERNS

In the past five chapters, we have seen American business insolvency law in all its richness and variation. It is something of a mess. This chapter attempts to make some sense of it as a whole. How successfully the various laws achieve their goals, and whether there might be better ways to achieve such ends, or to organize a sensible business insolvency system, are items left for the final chapter.

To begin, we might note that American business insolvency law is comprised of both general rules – the Bankruptcy Code, equity receiverships – and rules of extreme specialization – such as receiverships of grain silos. Many of the latter, however, are so lacking in detail that if they were ever used, they would likely draw on their more general counterparts for substance.

For example, in the BIDCO receiverships discussed in the previous chapter, Delaware's statute simply provides that on finding that the BIDCO is insolvent:

> the Court of Chancery shall have the power to appoint a receiver to take charge of, settle and wind up the affairs of a licensee under the direction of the Court, to enjoin such licensee from doing business or to make such other order or decree as the circumstances shall warrant and the Court shall deem proper.[1]

This is essentially a wide-open grant of equitable power to the court, and ultimately the receiver, to do what it thinks is right to liquidate the insolvent company. In exercising this power, the court would

---

[1] Del. Code Ann. tit. 5, § 3354.

undoubtedly draw on its experience with receiverships generally, and perhaps even the experience of federal bankruptcy courts.

The point being, that while the law on the books suggests an extremely fragmented insolvency system, the law as actually practised is probably not quite so balkanized. Some of these insolvency systems are essentially just markers, thrown down by politicians to show that they are "doing something" about an issue, by creating an insolvency system that addresses that issue.

As the continued existence of laws releasing debtors from prison – and Pennsylvania's multiple assignment for the benefit of creditors statutes – also suggest, we are also not a country that frequently engages in statutory housekeeping. Other insolvency laws reflect the different constituencies and political actors that might support issues, each with little understanding of the other. Thus, the state legislator who supports a special insolvency regime for grain silos might have no idea that her colleague has also built a similar system within the law about escrow agents. Each bill is enacted on a stand-alone basis, with little thought about how the two seemingly distinct issues might intersect.

There is no Mycroft Holmes overseeing the entirety of American business insolvency law. As a result, there is a notable degree of fragmentation. In the foregoing chapters, I implicitly organized the material by dividing the financial institution laws from the others, and separating the federal and state laws.

In retrospect, was the first division warranted? That is, does business insolvency law naturally divide on the financial institution and real economy company line?

In some respects, the division makes sense, but it is probably overstated. Insured depository banks are clearly different from "normal" debtors. After all, the government backstops a key part of their balance sheet.[2] Any business that had such governmental backing would necessarily operate in a way that is different from other, privately financed, debtors.

---

[2] Strictly speaking, FDIC insurance is not provided by the government, in the sense that industry insurance premiums provide the insurance fund at least in the first instance. However, there is a governmental credit line that backstops the insurance fund, and thus confirms that the government is ultimately responsible.

We have encountered three major industries that operate with customer-creditor claim insurance: banks and related depositary institutions, insurance companies, and broker-dealers. But only the first integrates the claim insurance with the regulator. In the case of insurance companies and broker-dealers, the insurance function is distinct from the regulatory function, and largely overseen by non-profit, industry funded entities.[3]

Thus, while there is a tendency to refer to SIPC insurance as being "like" FDIC insurance, for example, there may be reasons to consider FDIC insurance as distinct from the others. The FDIC covers money, near money, and related instruments of depositors whose characteristics are understood and the value of which is relatively easy to determine. Market value issues are not a problem, and the insurance coverage is straightforward and comparatively easy to understand.

In short, FDIC provides blanket protection to bank depositors. In contrast, SIPC does not bail out investors when the value of their stocks, bonds and other investments fall for any reason, including fraud. In part, this is a result of the different nature of the financial institutions they protect, but it also means that the FDIC represents a more direct claim on the government purse, in a way that SIPC does not. The same basic point holds for insurance company claims, which are not supported by either the federal or state governments.

Financial institutions that are "too big to fail" are also different from debtors generally, because when they do fail they present systemic complications. This issue again is prone to overstatement: the failure of any large business always has ripple effects. But there is undoubtedly a group of firms – those designated for extra regulation by FSOC provides a good proxy[4] – whose failure will damage the economy beyond

---

[3] See *Sec. Inv'r Prot. Corp.* v. *BDO Seidman, LLP*, 222 F.3d 63, 66–7 (2d Cir. 2000).

[4] The "Financial Stability Oversight Counsel." Under Section 113 of Dodd-Frank, FSOC is authorized to determine that a non-bank financial company's financial distress, if it were to occur, could pose a threat to U.S. financial stability. Such "designated" companies will be subject to consolidated supervision by the Federal Reserve and enhanced prudential standards. The largest bank holding companies are also subject to such extra oversight. The Dodd-Frank Act established FSOC – whose members include the heads of Treasury, the Fed, the Securities and Exchange Commission and other agencies – to stamp out threats before they cause the level of carnage experienced in the 2008 financial crisis.

the debtor-firm and its immediate contractual counterparties.[5] Many of these largest financial institutions also present a kind of group risk that is distinct from the failure of any individual member of the group.[6]

In both situations, societal interests overtake basic debtor-creditor concerns. Indeed, in an ideal world, creditors of these sorts of institutions should demand higher returns from the firm's, in the expectation that their recoveries would be subordinated to the policy of protecting society at large. That the opposite is actually true, suggests the work still to be done in ending the public subsidies to large financial firms.

But what about insolvency? Given the different aims of resolving financial distress in insured and extremely large financial institutions, does it make sense to separate those firms from the rest of the universe of potential debtors?

The key advantage that regulators are said to offer, over bankruptcy or other insolvency specialist judges, is expertise. That is, the Fed and the FDIC have a much deeper understanding of financial institutions than any bankruptcy judge could ever have, because they also have a regulatory role.[7] The degree of the advantage probably turns on the financial institution in question: no doubt the FDIC is institutionally strong on depository banks, and perhaps less versed in broker-dealers, although perhaps still more knowledgeable than many judges.

The question is whether the judges' better understanding of insolvency outweighs these advantages, and whether the judges could be informed as to the regulatory concerns, although I largely leave such "reform" proposals for the next chapter. The expertise argument is also less compelling in some aspects of financial institution insolvency where the process unfolds before a non-specialist trial court judge. Insurance insolvency is the obvious example. Although insurance insolvency proceedings are sometimes presided over by experienced state court judges, they are not presided over by jurists who specialize in insolvency, or often even business law.

---

[5] See Peter Conti-Brown, Elective Shareholder Liability, 64 *Stan. L. Rev.* 409, 412 (2012); Adam J. Levitin, In Defense of Bailouts, 99 *Geo. L.J.* 435, 483 (2011).

[6] Kathryn Judge, Interbank Discipline, 60 *UCLA L. Rev.* 1262, 1267 (2013).

[7] See *Board of Governors of the Federal Reserve System of the U.S.* v. *MCorp Financial, Inc.*, 502 U.S. 32, 37–42 (1991).

In short, while American insolvency law is largely separated in one respect by a line drawn around financial institutions, that separation is rarely fully considered. Beyond the specific cases of government-insured balance sheets and systemic risk, it is not clear that "financial institutions" are not simply firms for insolvency purposes.

One common argument is that financial institutions hold other people's "stuff." That is a fine argument for extra regulation, but does it matter for insolvency purposes? And why then do we treat pawn-shops as "normal" business debtors under the Bankruptcy Code?

The same basic point can be made with regard to the fragile capital structure of many financial institutions: yes, they are fragile, and that certainly justifies regulation, but does it matter at the point of insol-vency? While the frequent use of short-term debt – including deposits, repo, and derivatives – is a regulatory concern, under most insolvency systems all debt is deemed to come due upon commencement of pro-ceedings. In other words, debt is debt for bankruptcy purposes. As such, it is not clear that the capital structure alone justifies distinct treatment.

Perhaps the best justification for separate treatment of financial institutions is that the very products the debtor "sells" make up a goodly portion of its assets and liabilities.[8] Thus, while Bogartco may be a leading manufacturer of trench coats and fedoras, those prod-ucts do not appear on the balance sheet with the same significance that Bank of America's loans and savings accounts do. And a financial institution's products are more apt to be destroyed by the insolvency process, in a way that will destroy the bank's going-concern value.

Real economy debtors face a related problem, but it is smaller in scope. When the debtor shingle manufacturer is dependent on asphalt deliveries by railroad, the normal solution in chapter 11 is to exempt the railroad from the bankruptcy process. This is done by paying the railroad in full under the "necessity of payment doctrine" or related concepts, even if other unsecured creditors will receive only pennies

---

[8] See Joseph H. Sommer, Why Bail-In? And How!, 20 *FRBNY Econ. Pol. Rev.* 207 (December 2014).

on the dollar.[9] But in the case of a depository bank, for example, this model becomes unworkable because every depositor is in some sense a "critical trade creditor."

All the laws we have seen in the preceding chapters serve to mitigate the effects of financial failure. Most aim to operate through orderly and centralized liquidation or through similar reorganization or rehabilitation, giving creditors of equal priority ratable and equitable distributions. But many of the laws relating to financial institutions actually depart from this goal by design.

For example, both commodity broker bankruptcy cases under chapter 7 and SIPA liquidations aim to protect a specific pool of money – so-called "customer property," the very term seeks to define away the insolvency issue – from the general insolvency process. Modern bank receiverships of all stripes aim to provide full recovery, or as close thereto as possible, to depositors as opposed to all other unsecured creditors of the bank.

Insurance receiverships likewise aim to pay policyholders, one set of contractual counterparties, before other counterparties. SBA receiverships simply keep the borrower out of bankruptcy and in the SBA's control to facilitate the SBA's ability to recoup its losses from a favored position of control over the insolvency process.

Thus, the financial institution distinction actually obscures understanding in this regard; the presence or absence of a financial institution is itself unimportant. A more meaningful way to distinguish among the various insolvency laws is to sort between those who favor creditor equality, and those that promote one, favored class of creditors over others.

To be sure, all insolvency systems contain at least small deviations from "pure" creditor equality. Employees are a frequent beneficiary.

---

[9] The necessity of payment doctrine was first enunciated in *Miltenberger* v. *Logansport Railway Co.*, 106 U.S. 286, 310–12 (1882). See also Alan N. Resnick, The Future of the Doctrine of Necessity and Critical-Vendor Payments in Chapter 11 Cases, 47 *B.C. L. Rev.* 183, 188 (2005). ("Whereas the six months rule directly changes the priority of claims by paying ordinary course claims incurred within the six months prior to a railroad reorganization before secured claims, the doctrine of necessity permits payment of prebankruptcy unsecured claims only when such payment is needed so that trade vendors or other creditors will not refuse to supply critical goods and services after the debtor files for bankruptcy protection.")

In Oklahoma, there is a general priority statute for employees in receiverships and assignments,[10] and California, which otherwise has a common-law assignment system, has an express priority for employees in assignments,[11] to take but two examples.[12]

Another common case of priority deviation involves the jurisdiction itself. For example, in Tennessee laws provide that when liquidating insolvent state banks, "the return of all state deposits, including funds held in trust by state officials, shall be preferred in payment."[13]

These sorts of preferences do eat away at the general rule of creditor equality and, in extreme cases, could flip the system over to one which favors an identifiable class of creditors. For example, the present "safe harbors" for derivatives in the Bankruptcy Code render the Code unusable to those financial institutions that could file a petition.[14] Thus it was widely reported that the AIG parent company was kept out of bankruptcy in 2008 because of the safe harbors.[15] Moreover, they make chapter 11 extremely difficult for those real economy debtors that use derivatives as part of their business model – transportation companies with fuel hedges provide one common example.

It is important to recognize that even under a general rule of creditor equality, exceptions to the "rule" are rife.[16] But special priorities do not, in the main, undermine the overall design of the particular insolvency system.

The law of business failure in the United States, taken as a whole, can thus be viewed as one where the default position is creditor equality.[17] But for various policy reasons, the legitimacy of which we will measure in the next chapter, a decision is sometimes made – note the

---

[10] Okla. Stat. tit. 40, § 3-303.

[11] Cal. Civ. Proc. Code § 1204.

[12] Other examples include Kan. Stat. Ann. § 44-312 and 28 R.I. Gen. Laws § 14-6.1.

[13] Tenn. Code Ann. § 9-4-401.

[14] See Stephen J. Lubben, Failure of the Clearinghouse: Dodd-Frank's Fatal Flaw?, 10 *Va. L. & Bus. Rev.* 127, 152 (2015).

[15] Michael Simkovic, Secret Liens and the Financial Crisis of 2008, 83 *Am. Bankr. L.J.* 253, 287 (2009).

[16] Jay Lawrence Westbrook, The Control of Wealth in Bankruptcy, 82 *Tex. L. Rev.* 795, 822 (2004).

[17] Jay Lawrence Westbrook, A Functional Analysis of Executory Contracts, 74 *Minn. L. Rev.* 227, 252 (1989). ("From the equality principle comes the rule of pro rata distribution to pre-petition unsecured creditors.")

intentional use of the passive voice – to move the resolution of financial distress onto a track that favors one group of creditors over others. A "policy decision" for these purposes can often be the simple result of bureaucratic inertia, or simple legislative deference to lobbyists, so we must consider the word "decision" to sweep broadly.

The majority of the law of failure operates under a rule of creditor equality, but a sizable minority of the law operates outside this rule.[18] This seems to be a first basis on which to sort insolvency processes within the United States. Thus, the Bankruptcy Code, equity receiverships, assignments for the benefit of creditors, and corporate dissolutions are all examples of what we might call the "First Rule," of creditor equality.[19] Those who prefer the language of long-dead civil-law empires, can equate the First Rule with the *pari passu* principle.[20]

But the First Rule has a notable exception, which we see in bank receiverships, commodity and stock brokerage failures, and insurance company receiverships. This exception – call it, the Policy Exception – abandons equality when policymakers decide that the insolvency process should instead be run for the benefit of a favored group of creditors. Both types of insolvency systems use the same basic language, but at heart they are quite different.

The Policy Exception has some congruence with the financial institutions category we used earlier, but the overlap is not complete. For example, we discussed several specialized receivership processes for financial institutions – BIDCOs and escrow agents, for example – that did not inherently involve special treatment for a targeted group of creditors. It is equally possible that we might find the Policy Exception operating outside of the financial industry, although it is clear that historically that has been where the Policy Exception most often has been thought justified.

---

[18] David Skeel explores the historical origins of the equality rule in a recent working paper. David A. Skeel, The Empty Idea of 'Equality of Creditors,' 166 *U. Pa. L. Rev.* 699 (2018).

[19] *Begier* v. *IRS*, 496 U.S. 53, 58 (1990): Equality of distribution among creditors is a central policy of the Bankruptcy Code. According to that policy, creditors of equal priority should receive pro rata shares of the debtor's property.

[20] Anthony Duggan, Proprietary Remedies in Insolvency: A Comparison of the Restatement (Third) of Restitution & Unjust Enrichment with English and Commonwealth Law, 68 *Wash. & Lee L. Rev.* 1229, 1244 (2011).

Grain elevator and nursing home receiverships provide examples of Policy Exception systems operating outside finance. In both cases, state policymakers have devised special receivership proceedings to protect specific constituencies. In the nursing home case patients, who in strict legal terms might be both creditors and customers, are clearly the prime focus.[21] Likewise, in grain elevator cases, the focus of the receivership is on the users of the elevator, rather than creditors as such. The Policy Exception is at work here, albeit in service of non-creditor constituencies. The focus of these receiverships nonetheless subordinates creditor equality to "something else."

This First Rule-Policy Exception dynamic thus offers a useful way for considering the law of failure. When we approach an insolvency system, an initial question can be: "Does this system operate under the First Rule, or is it an example of the Policy Exception?" If we decide that the system in question is an example of the First Rule, we can proceed to examine the various deviations from the Rule that we observe in the system – as noted earlier, some modicum of deviation is inevitable – to consider whether the exceptions are not so numerous that the system has some switched over to the kind of favoritism normally seen under the Policy Exception. Whether this is a sensible use of the Exception would then seem to be a useful question.

There are also questions of scope with regard to the Policy Exception. There seems to be little doubt that bank deposits, insurance contracts, and brokerage accounts are worthy of protection from the normal insolvency process. Both the going-concern value of the debtor company and the social utility of these financial instruments would be destroyed if exposed to the normal insolvency regimes. But can we say the same for everything that presently comes within the Policy Exception? And inclusion within the Exception is not without societal cost.[22]

Any approach to business reorganization in particular must strike a balance between the need to stabilize the financially distressed debtor,

---

[21] See Mass. Gen. Laws ch. 111, § 72M.
[22] See generally Stephen J. Lubben, Subsidizing Liquidity or Subsidizing Markets? Safe Harbors, Derivatives, and Finance, 91 *Am. Bankr. L.J.* 463 (2017).

and the desire and expectation that creditors' and stockholders' pre-existing legal rights will be honored to the greatest extent possible. This tension has long been recognized. For example, in *Brockett* v. *Winkle Terra Cotta Co.*, the court stated:

> Reorganization of distressed corporations is primarily and principally a business (economic) problem. It is a means whereby those variously interested financially in a distressed business seek, through continuance of that business as a going concern, to work out for themselves more than they could gain by sale of the assets or of the business to others. Reorganization is occasioned by the situation that the business cannot go on as it is. If it is to continue in control of all or of some of those financially interested in it, a readjustment is necessary. Such readjustment involves suspension or alteration of some or all existing legal interests in the business and property and may involve extinguishment of some interests. It is only because of such changes in legal rights that the matter of reorganization comes into courts.[23]

The First Rule is not some sort of commandment, or "fixed principle" to use an insolvency term encrusted with history,[24] but rather a starting point for analysis. Ideally, each move away from this core ideal will be done after thoughtful consideration of the reasons for making such a move. Again, that type of analysis will be more the focus in the next chapter, but for now it is simply important to understand the First Rule-Policy Exception dynamic as a useful descriptive tool.

Another way to consider American insolvency law is by jurisdiction or by moving from the general to the more specific. To a large degree, American business insolvency law is multi-layered, often to an extreme.

Financial institutions provide some of the most intense examples. Clearing banks, which were discussed in several chapters, might be resolved under state bank receiverships, federal banking receiverships, or chapters 7 or 11 of the Bankruptcy Code. In some cases the FDIC

---

[23] 81 F.2d 949, 953 (8th Cir. 1936).
[24] *Case* v. *Los Angeles Lumber Prod. Co.*, 308 U.S. 106, 116 (1939).

might become receiver of the institution under OLA. Or Congress might enact a new statute just for them, in certain circumstances.

A typical business corporation might reorganize through a sale under a state-law assignment or receivership, or under chapter 11 of the federal Bankruptcy Code. If it were instead to liquidate, dissolution proceedings, the same assignment or receivership, or chapter 7 beckon.

Structurally, it makes sense to distinguish between state and federal proceedings, because the state proceedings are often subject to preemption by the federal. This is true even for insurance companies, where the federal government has voluntarily given states primary authority, but could presumably rescind that deference at any time.

State insolvency procedures thus operate with a degree of uncertainty largely absent from the federal system. One of the few exceptions again comes from the financial sector, where a traditional bankruptcy proceeding can be supplanted by a Dodd-Frank OLA proceeding. But otherwise the federal bankruptcy courts are at the top of the business insolvency hierarchy, at least when we are considering First Rule systems.

The bankruptcy system, and the SIPA liquidation process for most broker-dealers, is also the only piece of the American business insolvency structure that is centered on specialist judges.[25] The remainder of the system utilizes either administrative processes, or the general court system, to co-ordinate resolution of financial distress.

Thus, while we might consider the law of failure as having both federal and state elements, it also makes sense to further arrange the law by the three basic models of proceedings. A fourth category of proceeding, which involves neither judicial nor administrative oversight, is also important here. For example, in many states an assignment for the benefit of creditors is almost entirely under the control of the assignee. We might call this last category the "professional control" model.

A simple taxonomy might start to look something like this:

---

[25] Jonathan C. Lipson, Against Regulatory Displacement: An Institutional Analysis of Financial Crises, 17 *U. Pa. J. Bus. L.* 673, 706 (2015).

	Specialist judge	Generalist judge	Administrative	Professional
Federal	Bankruptcy	General Receiverships	FDIC Receiverships	
	SIPA	SEC-CFTC Receiverships	OCC Receiverships	
		SBA Receiverships		
State	Insolvency Statutes	General Receiverships	Some Bank Receiverships	Some ABCs
		Agricultural Receiverships		Dissolution
		Insurance Receiverships		
		Some Bank Receiverships		

The inclusion of state insolvency statutes under the specialist judge category is highly debatable. For example, under the New Hampshire insolvency statute, insolvency cases are assigned to the probate courts.[26] Perhaps a century ago or more, they well might have had substantial experience with business insolvency cases. But since it is unclear that the state's insolvency statute is even viable at present – at best, it might be "on ice" for future use – to the extent the probate courts have much insolvency experience, it more likely comes from dealing with insolvent decedent estates.[27]

Likewise, although the Delaware chancery courts are vested with jurisdiction over insolvent corporations under that state's corporate receivership statute, they seem to have some reticence about using that power.[28] While the statute itself allows appointment of receivers "whenever a corporation shall be insolvent," recent case law suggests something more is required before the court will actually use the statute.[29] Despite the codification of receiverships in Delaware, they are still viewed by the

[26] N.H. Rev. Stat. Ann. § 568:1. See also N.H. Rev. Stat. Ann. § 568:49.
[27] N.H. Rev. Stat. Ann. § 554:19-b.
[28] Del. Code Ann. tit. 8, § 291.
[29] *Pope Investments LLC v. Benda Pharm., Inc.*, No. CIV.A. 5171-VCP, 2010 WL 5233015, at *6 (Del. Ch. Dec. 15, 2010).

judiciary as akin to an equitable remedy, available at the discretion of the court. In any event, the Delaware chancery judges, although they have clear business experience, are not truly insolvency experts.

Dissolution of the firm, which I described earlier as a kind of liquidation mechanism, is listed under the "professional" category. This is again something of an uneasy fit – the "professional" in this case is not always an insolvency professional.

The chart also makes clear how little American law uses the specialist model, and even the administrative model is limited to the more heavily regulated end of the financial institutions category. The bulk of the law of failure is focused around judicial proceedings with generalist judges – even if the greatest number of cases probably resides in bankruptcy courts.

This illuminates a singular emphasis on transparency in American insolvency law. An extreme example of this can be seen in Dodd-Frank's complex system of financial institution insolvency. Under the 2010 law, the preference remains that large financial institutions in financial distress file petitions in bankruptcy court. Only if doing so would constitute a risk to the system is OLA to be invoked.

While some doubt the wisdom of this first stage, and others view it as a bit of political theater to be dealt with before the "real" insolvency tool is invoked, if we take it at face value, it does signal a legislative preference for courts and judicial process over technocrats in the first instance.[30] Whether it makes sense to conduct "Policy Exception" cases – where the focus is priority of a favored class, rather than equality – in a judicial setting is something I consider in the final chapter.

One might also wonder if the court is really in control in financial institution cases. In many of the proposals for financial institution bankruptcy, the court's role is strictly confined.

In short, there are consequently two dimensions along which to consider the law of failure: The First Rule-Policy Exception dynamic, and the question of where administration is centered.

The federal-state question is also of relevance, because of the reality of the Supremacy Clause, which renders most state insolvency

---

[30] Stephen J. Lubben, Financial Institutions in Bankruptcy, 34 *Seattle U. L. Rev.* 1259, 1278 (2011).

proceedings somewhat fragile. In addition, as noted in earlier chapters, the states labor under the restrictions of the Contracts Clause. While the modern law of the Clause is somewhat uncertain, especially as applied to insolvency systems, there is at least an argument that the Clause presents an absolute prohibition on discharge of debts that predate the state law in question.[31] Further confusing the issue is the suggestion that the presence of a federal bankruptcy law precludes state-law discharges of any sort.

If this summary of the law is correct, states never can enact retroactive discharges and have been unable to enact discharges of any sort since at least 1898, when the Bankruptcy Act commenced a now continuous string of federal bankruptcy legislation. But as we also noted in earlier chapters, a discharge is of lesser importance when the debtor is a limited liability entity. While not all business debtors have limited liability – general partnerships, for example, do not – an ever-growing share of business debtors will. In such cases, an asset sale to a newly formed buyer can achieve essentially the same result.[32]

The real question then is one of successor liability in the buyer. For example, many state common-law successor liability doctrines are expressly targeted to corporate assets sales. The effect of these doctrines is to treat asset sales as if they were mergers. At the very least, this illustrates a complexity in state insolvency law that warrants classifying it as distinct from federal insolvency law.

In this next version of the taxonomy, I account for all three aspects of the law of failure by shading those procedures that involve the Policy Exception, while the others involve the First Rule.

The state bank receivers are equivocally shaded, because where they fall on the First Rule-Policy Exception turns on whether the state has enacted a depositor preference statute. In those states with a depositor preference – including Montana and Nebraska which have had such provisions since the early twentieth century – we see a pure form of the Policy Exception. A depositor preference in a system without deposit

---

[31] See generally James W. Ely, Jr., *The Contract Clause: A Constitutional History* (2016).

[32] Oscar Couwenberg & Stephen J. Lubben, Essential Corporate Bankruptcy, 16 *Eur. Bus. Org. R. Rev.* 39, 56 (2015).

	Specialist judge	Generalist judge	Administrative	Professional
Federal	Bankruptcy	General Receiverships	FDIC Receiverships	
	SIPA	SEC-CFTC Receiverships	OCC Receiverships	
		SBA Receiverships		
State	Insolvency Statutes	General Receiverships	Some Bank Receiverships	Some ABCs
		Agricultural Receiverships		Dissolution
		Insurance Receiverships		
		Some Bank Receiverships		

insurance represents a plain effort to favor one group of creditors, in place of the general equality of the First Rule.

The fact that the FDIC did not benefit from a depositor preference until 1993 – after a brief period in its early years with such a preference – does make it clear that the operation of the Policy Exception in insured bank receiverships is somewhat complex. Congress initially decided to prefer depositors by establishing insurance for these creditors, rather than through the insolvency process itself. Before the federal preference was established, the FDIC insurance fund's claim in the receivership, after paying off insured depositors, was subject to whatever the prevailing state law was in cases involving state-chartered banks. The Policy Exception was thus a step removed from the receivership.

The decision to adopt a federal depositor preference, which would apply in any receivership conducted by the FDIC, was largely motivated by reducing the cost of bank failure for the FDIC insurance fund. As such, the 1993 enactment was as much about transferring recoveries from creditors to the insurance fund as it was about the specific policy of preferring depositors. Thus, I focus on the adoption of FDIC insurance during the New Deal as the point at which Congress decided to follow a Policy Exception approach to bank insolvency, rather than the 1993 decision to adopt a depositor preference.

Another possible way of distinguishing among American business insolvency procedures turns on whether the debtor or third parties take the primary role in initiating the process, and the role the debtor-firm, or its managers, might have after the process has commenced.

As a general rule, only chapter 11 of the Bankruptcy Code allows for the full, debtor-in-possession model for which American bankruptcy law is so famous. Every other procedure within the American "law of failure" replaces the debtor's managerial authority with a receiver, assignee, trustee, or some similar figure.

In assignments for the benefit of creditors, the debtor plays a role in selecting the assignee, and thus this procedure might come closest to chapter 11 in terms of continued debtor control. The assignee operates under a duty to creditors, as does the DIP in chapter 11, and the selection of an entirely unacceptable assignee is bound to provoke an involuntary bankruptcy petition. Thus, on this dimension we might place chapter 11 at one pole, and all other procedures at the other, with assignments ranging a bit closer to chapter 11 than other procedures.

The question of initiation produces a wider variety of models. Bankruptcy can be either voluntary or involuntary. Assignments are always initiated by the debtor, who needs to voluntarily transfer the assets to the assignee.

General receiverships are formally involuntary, but historically equity receiverships were often "friendly," that is commenced by a creditor that was encouraged, if not selected, by the debtor.[33] One goal in enacting sections 77 and 77B – the first federal reorganization provisions – was to end the need for this co-ordination with creditors, which many found distasteful.[34]

Many of the financial institution receiverships operating under the Policy Exception are only invoked by regulators. Thus, the decision to favor a specific class of creditors is typically paired with a unique initiation process, controlled by neither debtor nor creditor.

---

[33] William O. Douglas & John H. Weir, Equity Receiverships in the United States District Court for Connecticut: 1920–1929, 4 *Conn. Bar J.* 1, 3 (1930). ("Nearly all these receiverships were of a friendly nature.")

[34] William O. Douglas, Improvement in Federal Procedure for Corporate Reorganizations, 24 *A.B.A. J.* 875 (1938).

But commencement by regulator is not confined to Policy Exception cases. Indeed, any of the specialized insolvency processes tend to give regulators at least the right to commence proceedings. In some cases this right is exclusive within the proceeding itself, subject to the ability of the debtor or creditors to institute overriding federal bankruptcy proceedings.

The reorganization or liquidation of a business is not a lawsuit in the ordinary sense of a procedure designed to settle issues between individual litigants, but a complex, collective proceeding that involves both mediation and corporate finance. The process is largely designed to meet the two distinct, and often contradictory, goals of insolvency law.

First, insolvency law seeks to preserve and maximize the value of the insolvent business. Second, the law aims to ensure a fair distribution of the assets among the claimants. But even stated with this degree of generality, both of these would-be goals are subject to some significant exceptions.

Under the Bankruptcy Code, the first half of the first goal is achieved through the automatic stay. But such a stay is not vital, particularly if the debtor is a limited liability entity.[35] Here, the transfer of the debtor's assets to a receiver, trustee, or assignee will achieve the same ends, because the debtor will be left with no ability to pay. That is why in Chapter 3 I included corporate dissolutions among the "law of failure," inasmuch as those procedures provide a common forum for creditors to assert claims against the debtor, one final time.

For the reasons discussed in Chapter 1, preservation of the debtor is often equated with maximization of the debtor's value. Of course, stasis does not necessarily maximize anything.

Indeed, a wealth of 1980s and 1990s bankruptcy scholarship is rooted in the certainty that fewer chapter 11 and more chapter 7, or even state law foreclosures, would better move assets to their "highest and best use." This scholarship tended to treat all assets – be they embroidery machines, bulldozers, trademarks, patents, or "big-box" stores – as fungible, almost like an indistinguishable stack of poker chips. No doubt some of this was the result of academics who spent,

---

[35] See generally Oscar Couwenberg & Stephen J. Lubben, Essential Corporate Bankruptcy, 16 *Eur. Bus. Org. L. Rev.* 39 (2015).

and probably still spend, more time with balance sheets than at the plant. On an accounting statement, one asset looks pretty much like another.

There was a certainty that the pain of liquidation was the "proper medicine" for what ailed bankrupt companies, not unlike the more recent debate between austerity and stimulus in the broader economy.[36] These scholars approached liquidation with a strange sort of enthusiasm, quite certain that advocating pain represented intellectual courage. The stinging that such an approach to business bankruptcy would engender was inevitably fobbed off on other areas of the law, which the insolvency scholar need not worry about.[37]

In those proceedings that I have classified under the heading of the Policy Exception, there is essentially no effort to maximize the value of the insolvent business. The focus is preservation of the business for the benefit of the preferred claimants – any maximization is purely incidental. Thus, it was asserted that the FDIC's goals in selling Washington Mutual were focused on quickly removing any potential risk to the deposit insurance fund – bondholders and other creditors be damned. In some sense, it could be argued that the value maximization happened at the point of adopting the Policy Exception, for example, a belief that excepting bank accounts from the insolvency process would be better for all – even bondholders – in the end.

With regard to the second basic goal of insolvency law – the fair distribution of the assets among claimants – the laws we surveyed in the prior chapters largely assume that distribution according to the dissolution scheme will inevitably achieve equality. While we might question the propriety of this assumption, for present purposes it is sufficient to observe that, with the possible exception of chapter 11, the dissolution of a business entity provides the basic model for payment of claimants in most insolvency proceedings.

---

[36] Cf. Lynn M. Lopucki, The Unsecured Creditor's Bargain, 80 *Va. L. Rev.* 1887, 1889 (1994).

[37] See Stephanie Ben-Ishai & Stephen J. Lubben, Involuntary Creditors and Corporate Bankruptcy, 45 *UBC Law Review* 253 (2012). ("[T]he issue of tort, environmental, and tax creditors is typically acknowledged and then swept to the side by observing, 'they should have a priority.' No effort is actually made to give them a priority ...")

Even in the case of Policy Exception proceedings, once the favored claimants are accounted for, distribution tends to follow the dissolution paradigm. Chapter 11, although allowing consensual deviations from the basic model, operates against a baseline of the dissolution rule. All claimants must get at least that much.[38]

This understanding of insolvency law provides the important insight that most of the action in insolvency law thus happens at the point of one particular goal: preservation and maximization of assets. And even there, we have already noted that much of the focus is on preservation.

In other words, much of American business insolvency law operates on a very narrow front, aiming to preserve the debtor's assets against unbridled creditor collection efforts. Indeed, much of the structure of business insolvency law seems designed to address a basic defect in general debtor-creditor law. This suggests a wide area of potential innovation, turning on approaches that do not mimic those of dissolution. Of course, any such innovations need to be balanced against their costs: the costs of switching, and the costs of litigation arising from complexity.

The end result is a series of ways to think about the "law of failure." In the next and final chapter, I turn to a brief consideration of how the extant law might be improved.

---

[38] 11 U.S.C. § 1129(a)(7).

7   AVENUES FOR REFORM

For nearly four decades, discussions of American business insolvency law have been in thrall to, and boxed in by, Thomas Jackson's creditor bargain conception.[1] This notion, that all bankruptcy or insolvency law should be tested by what the debtor and creditor would have negotiated before insolvency, both overly narrows the discussion and frustrates advancement.[2]

The diversity in business insolvency law that we have encountered in this book shows that societal responses to problems of insolvency are varied, and not easily measured by reference to a simple metric of bilateral negotiation. Indeed, by framing insolvency law as negotiation, the creditors' bargain approach begins with a stunted view of law, which necessarily alters the analysis.

Even if debtor and creditor decided that the best way to solve their disputes was to row over to Weehawken with pistols, society as a whole surely has some ability to say "no." Insolvency law is more than contract: it involves policy decisions that cannot be left to private

---

[1] E.g., Thomas H. Jackson, Bankruptcy, Non-Bankruptcy Entitlements, and the Creditors' Bargain, 91 *Yale L.J.* 857 (1982). The idea's modern influence can be seen in Mark J. Roe & Frederick Tung, Breaking Bankruptcy Priority: How Rent-Seeking Upends the Creditors' Bargain, 99 *Va. L. Rev.* 1235 (2013) and Anthony J. Casey, The Creditors' Bargain and Option-Preservation Priority in Chapter 11, 78 *U. Chi. L. Rev.* 759 (2011), to take but two prominent examples.

[2] Cf. Anthony J. Casey & Aziz Z. Huq, The Article III Problem in Bankruptcy, 82 *U. Chi. L. Rev.* 1155, 1209 (2015). ("The goal of bankruptcy law is to mimic the welfare-maximizing agreement that would have been reached by creditors if transaction costs had been low enough and the bargain had occurred. That hypothetical deal would maximize value – and hence minimize the destruction or distortion of state-created rights either prior to or during bankruptcy.")

bargaining alone. In the Jacksonian model, only the debtor and the creditor matter and we trust that they alone will reach the right decision.

The simplicity of the creditors' bargain model is undoubtedly key to its attraction.[3] But that same simplicity is also the source of its failure, in that the model does a poor job of describing both extant insolvency law and some ideal insolvency system. And by describing all insolvency in terms of what debtors and creditors might have agreed to, if they had been possessed with abundant foresight (or no foresight at all, in some conceptions), insolvency law is necessarily confined to a status little different from basic, bilateral debt collection law. At most, insolvency advances just a bit further – in the sense that it is collective – from this ancient root.

That ignores the potential for insolvency law by fiat. Certain policy options, whether wise or ill-considered, are simply beyond the pale in the creditors bargain framework. That itself represents an implicit policy choice imbedded in the creditors' bargain model.

There is also the entrenched assumption that state debtor-creditor (and property) law is the baseline against which all bankruptcy or insolvency law should be measured. There is nothing divine about debtor-creditor law, or which suggests that bankruptcy should bend to it, rather than vice versa.[4]

In the international sphere, the view I am espousing is sometimes termed "insolvency exceptionalism." In many countries – Germany offers a representative example – insolvency is a purely administrative matter. All substantive legal rules come from "normal" law.

The United Kingdom's Supreme Court has in recent years embraced this limited view of insolvency court jurisdiction. In the court's view, insolvency courts should have no broader jurisdiction than any other trial court. Indeed, in a recent speech before an insolvency convention in London, Lord Neuberger, then the chief judge on the court, argued that to hold otherwise would give undue incentives for the commencement of insolvency proceedings.[5]

---

[3] Jonathan C. Lipson, Bargaining Bankrupt: A Relational Theory of Contract in Bankruptcy, 6 *Harv. Bus. L. Rev.* 239, 266 (2016).

[4] Emily L. Sherwin, Constructive Trusts in Bankruptcy, 1989 *U. Ill. L. Rev.* 297, 362–4 (1989).

[5] www.supremecourt.uk/docs/speech-170619.pdf.

The notion of businesses filing bankruptcy cases simply to gain undue advantage in litigation is an old chestnut in the literature, with little basis in fact.[6] Yes, the occasional celebrity (broadly defined) will file a bankruptcy case to get out from under a burdensome contract, but in every such case the courts have exercised their discretion to stop the use of the insolvency system for such ends. There is no reason to undercut the utility of insolvency simply to thwart a problem that courts already address. And broad insolvency court jurisdiction, often combined with special "insolvency-only" policy choices, is frequently required to achieve that utility.

Needless to say, I do not propose to be bound by the creditor bargain framework in this chapter. But I also do not intend to spring a general theory of insolvency law upon the reader who has kindly stuck with me thus far.

I proceed with the knowledge that policymakers – both legislative and bureaucratic – have a wide array of permissible and plausible policy choices before them. Indeed, the history of bankruptcy law in this country is, at its core, the story of the move from a narrow bankruptcy law, that originally mimicked English approaches and applied only to merchants, to the wide-ranging law that now applies to wage earners, farmers, municipalities, territories, small and gigantic corporations alike.

I thus use this final chapter to consider a range of possible approaches to American insolvency law. That presupposes that the law should change, or could be improved, so I begin this chapter with a brief discussion of why that might be true.

Business insolvency law is always going to be a bit messy in a federal system, unless the federal government is willing to entirely pre-empt the field. For more than two centuries, Congress has shown no inclination to do so.

---

[6] See, e.g., Douglas G. Baird & Thomas H. Jackson, Corporate Reorganizations and the Treatment of Diverse Ownership Interests: A Comment on Adequate Protection of Secured Creditors in Bankruptcy, 51 *U. Chi. L. Rev.* 97, 101 (1984). More recent efforts to revive the argument include Casey & Huq, The Article III Problem in Bankruptcy, 1200, and G. Marcus Cole & Todd J. Zywicki, Anna Nicole Smith Goes Shopping: The New Forum-Shopping Problem in Bankruptcy, 2010 *Utah L. Rev.* 511, 521 (2010).

Thus, we will always have at least two layers of insolvency law. A further obstacle comes from the Supreme Court's strange hesitancy to police the line between the state and federal systems.[7] While often suggesting that the presence of a federal bankruptcy law suspends comparable state insolvency laws in their entirety, the Court has only actually held that the discharge provisions of such laws are forbidden.

Given the reality of a multi-layered insolvency system, some degree of forum shopping is also going to be inevitable. For debtors, their advisors, and stakeholders, the primary question will always be, "Can we better achieve our goals through an insolvency proceeding in this particular jurisdiction compared to some other jurisdiction?"

Nonetheless, there are reasons to believe that the American "law of failure" is in need of some sprucing up. For example, while it seems perfectly plausible that state law insolvency systems might be cheaper and more efficient than the federal bankruptcy system, our review of those state systems should raise some concerns.

In particular, how much of the apparent benefit of those systems is the result of the comparative lack of transparency in, for example, an assignment for the benefit of creditors as compared to a chapter 7 case? This might suggest that what is really going on is a transfer of value from creditors to the debtor – that is, the state system is not inherently "better" in general, but only better from the debtor's perspective.[8]

It seems reasonable to suggest that if a creditor's rights are to be altered by a process that carries the government's sanction, the process should be open to all affected by it. But such is not always the case under present law, as we have seen.

We might also consider the degree to which American business insolvency law is not just multi-layered, but simply duplicative. While it might be inevitable that two insolvency procedures will be available to all business debtors – one state and one federal – we have seen that in most cases a corporate debtor will have three or more options.

---

[7] Cf. John Hanna, Contemporary Utility of General Assignments, 35 *Va. L. Rev.* 539, 549 (1949). ("The [*International Shoe Co.* v.] *Pinkus* opinion scarcely left the bar in a state of luminous saturation.")

[8] See generally Andrew B. Dawson, Better Than Bankruptcy?, 69 *Rutgers U.L. Rev.* 137 (2016).

In nearly all cases a state receivership, a state assignment for the benefit of creditors, and a filing under the Bankruptcy Code are on the table. There is also the possibility of just walking out, turning off the lights, closing the door, and dropping the keys off with the landlord or the bank. As the late Vern Countryman once said, a certificate of incorporation is a bankruptcy discharge in advance.[9] If the debtor operates in a specialized industry, additional state or federal insolvency procedures become available. At some point the proliferation of procedures again raises concerns of opportunism and inefficiency.

As noted in the prior chapter, the aims of the wider business insolvency system are first to maximize the value of the debtor through collective proceedings that prevent a run on the debtor's assets and second to achieve equivalent treatment of similarly situated creditors, under a single law and a single, collective claims resolution process. We might refer to the first goal as the "Anti-Run Principle." And the second goal I have already referred to as the "First Rule" of business insolvency.

The First Rule and the Anti-Run Principle provide the foundation for the traditional insolvency system.[10] The second supports the first, in that equality is impossible without a prohibition on debtor runs.[11] As for the First Rule, the New York Court of Appeals summarized the ancient principles thus:

> The equitable doctrine that, as between creditors, equality is equity, admits, so far as we know, of no exception founded on the greater supposed sacredness of one debt, or that it arose out of a violation of duty, or that its loss involves greater apparent hardship in one case than another, unless it appears, in addition, that there is some specific recognized equity founded on some agreement, or the relation of the debt to the assigned property, which entitles the claimant, according to equitable principles, to preferential payment.[12]

---

[9] Bankruptcy Reform Amendments: A Legislative History of the Bankruptcy Amendments and Federal Judgeship Act of 1984, Public Law 98-353 at page 142 (1992). Assuming the owner does nothing to facilitate "piercing the corporate veil," of course.

[10] That is, the core that has not been overtaken by Policy Exception considerations.

[11] "An important purpose of bankruptcy law is to prevent individual creditors from starting a 'run' on the debtor by assuring that they will be treated equally if the debtor is precipitated into bankruptcy, rather than being given either preferential treatment for having jumped the gun or disadvantageous treatment for having hung back." In re Elcona Homes Corp., 863 F.2d 483, 484 (7th Cir. 1988).

[12] *Cavin v. Gleason*, 11 N.E. 504, 506 (N.Y. 1887).

The move from individual debtor-creditor collection to bankruptcy or other collective insolvency processes necessarily involves the embrace of the First Rule.[13] But as I argued at the outset of the chapter, the permissible policy goals extend far beyond. Policies designed to mitigate the effects of the debtor's failure are natural additions to these two basic points.

This might suggest that we should leave the extant insolvency system as it is. After all, the United States is a common law system, which will never have the supposed tidiness of the Napoleonic Code or any similar, modern-day equivalents. And it is undoubtedly true that coherence projects to have a tendency to make any legal field less nimble.

But a key problem with the proliferation of insolvency tools is that no single insolvency process – outside the core procedures, like the Bankruptcy Code – can generate enough use to provide useful information to potential debtors and their advisors. No attorney can fully advise their clients what a restructuring under Dodd-Frank's OLA or Nevada's campsite receivership provisions might look like, because there have never been any cases commenced under these laws. That is, the current state of affairs actually undermines the growth of the common law wisdom in the business insolvency area by splitting the action among myriad competing forums.

That the insolvency system would benefit from consolidation thus suggests that new policy goals are better preserved within an insolvency system that retains as many common elements as reasonably possible, while allowing specialized procedures to build off the common core. Rather than create a new insolvency regime for each new policy issue, legislators would be better advised to adapt the extant structure to new demands.

It is this conception of the need for reform that motivates the following discussion.

One reform we might consider has been hinted at several times already: complete federalization of business insolvency law. There are many practical reasons why this is unlikely to occur – the lobbying

---

[13] In re Forbes, 128 F. 137, 139 (D. Mass. 1904).

power of state insurance regulators provides one exemplar – yet we might consider, at least briefly, whether this might not be the best policy nonetheless.

To fully federalize the law of failure, Congress would not only have to expressly state that the Bankruptcy Code pre-empts all state law insolvency procedures, but also provide for those businesses that are outside the Bankruptcy Code's reach. Insurance companies and uninsured, state-chartered banks are the most obvious examples. Marijuana businesses might be another.[14]

While the Bankruptcy Code probably already comprises the biggest single part of the law of failure, such a move would produce some gains from further consolidating cases in the bankruptcy court system. And courts generally would no longer be faced with difficult questions of pre-emption: everything would be pre-empted.

The most obvious drawback comes from the perception that federal court is more expensive than state court. And while empirical evidence on this front is notably lacking, it seems plausible that a federal bankruptcy proceeding might be more expensive than a comparable state insolvency proceeding. But it also bears noting that there really are no comparable cases at present, since different debtors use different procedures. There is, however, a sizable body of evidence that chapter 11 costs exhibit economies of scale – that is, there is a fixed cost component that is more easily absorbed by a large debtor. A move to federalize insolvency law would thus have a concentrated effect on small business debtors.

The basic problem stems from the "one-size-fits-all" nature of chapter 11 in particular. Smaller debtors simply cannot support the extreme formality of a chapter 11 proceeding. Any attempt to federalize insolvency law would therefore require a move away from the general applicability of the current Code, back toward something more like the New Deal's Chandler Act, which included a distinct reorganization procedure for publicly traded companies.

---

[14] Broadly defined to include businesses that get revenues from marijuana businesses, such as landlords of such businesses. The U.S. Department of Justice has taken the position that business that rely on marijuana, even derivatively, may not file federal bankruptcy petitions.

What is required is a middle ground between formal bankruptcy, as it currently exists, and out-of-court workouts, which are simple creatures of contract law. The need would be greatest for smaller businesses, but even larger businesses that aim for a comparatively simple restructuring might benefit from such a provision. For example, a simple "off-the-rack" debt for equity swap need not invoke all of the trappings of a full chapter 11 case – committees, examiners, and whatnot.

In short, while the full federalization option might be ideal in an abstract policy sense, it would involve substantial changes to existing law. Even putting to one side the dysfunction of the present Congress, not to mention the Executive Branch's limited interest in policy these days, such a move would require overcoming the opposition of those invested in the *status quo*. Of course, the same could be said of any reform effort.

There is also the bigger question of whether full federalization is appropriate in our Constitutional system. Bankruptcy attorneys tend to think of their part of the federal system in isolation, indeed it is a frequent jest amongst the bankruptcy bar that a bankruptcy lawyer thinks the Code prevails over all other law.

Fully federalizing insolvency law would be one more step along the path toward greater federal powers that commenced with the Civil War, and accelerated during the New Deal and World War II. Outside the world of insolvency, that would not necessarily be viewed as a good thing. And while it is well beyond the scope of this little book to fully develop the concept of federalism, this concern bears mentioning even simply because it weighs on the probability of adopting such an approach to the law of failure.

As an alternative, one might consider that business insolvency law should be reorganized around two tiers: federal and state law. At both levels, business insolvency law would be consolidated, something that represents a greater challenge for most states, as compared with the federal government where the Bankruptcy Code already represents the core of federal insolvency law.

Washington State has already undertaken something like this by revising its receivership statutes in 2004, and again in 2011, to create a comprehensive system of insolvency that encompasses not only receiverships but assignments for the benefit of creditors.

The law enumerates in one location the various statutory grounds for appointment of a receiver previously scattered throughout the Revised Code of Washington,[15] with the significant exception of insurance company receiverships, which are still subject to special rules.[16]

There is no central authority to command all fifty states to reform their insolvency law. Even if it would appear to be both good policy, and in the self-interest of the states, we might doubt that all would do so.

Congress could facilitate the process by defining broad guidelines for state insolvency structures, thereby clarifying the confused state of pre-emption law in this area. State laws that met the guidelines would benefit from a kind of "safe harbor" against pre-emption – at least by the Bankruptcy Code, the Contracts Clause being outside Congress' jurisdiction, but perhaps of lesser concern in modern times.

How should insolvency law be organized within this broad, two-tier framework? Unsurprisingly, I would suggest commencing with the basic structure outlined in the prior chapter: namely, insolvency systems should presumptively follow the First Rule, unless policymakers consciously decide to invoke the Policy Exception.

This would avoid the propagation of insolvency systems, seen in early chapters, which inhabit the vague middle between these two approaches. For example, why have special receivership provisions for campsites or time shares if there is no intention to protect a special class of creditors from the normal operation of the First Rule? A carefully articulated reason for involving the Policy Exception – whatever we think of the merits of that argument – would at least ensure a kind of coherence to the creation of insolvency processes.

Of course, what I am proposing here is a set of best practices for insolvency legislation, something that is hard to enforce with respect to actual politicians. But we are engaged in an exercise of imagination as much as actual policymaking at this point: how could the "law of failure" be improved, in the abstract? Implementing those changes obviously presents its own challenges, and a careful reader might rightly wonder about a bankruptcy academic's ability to measure such political concerns.

---

[15] Wash. Rev. Code Ann. § 7.60.025.
[16] Ibid., § 7.60.300.

Once we envision our reform program in broad terms – with state and federal layers, and focused on reconsolidation around the First Rule – we might begin to think about specific topics within that law of failure that could benefit from repair. Consider, for example, the question of initiation of insolvency procedures.

In general, in business insolvency law, like bankruptcy under either chapter 7 or 11, the process can be initiated either by the debtor or by the debtor's creditors. Under the Bankruptcy Code, early filing is encouraged, and litigation regarding access to the process is discouraged. Thus, we do not spend a lot of time worrying about issues such as whether the debtor is insolvent.[17]

Many state proceedings are somewhat more complex. Assignments require a willing debtor to get under way, while receiverships often operate under the opposite rule. In the "good old days," equity receiverships could be initiated by joint debtor and creditor consent, and the Supreme Court approved this move, but in the New Deal these were maligned as "collusive," a taint that continues to this day.

Other specialized insolvency mechanisms are often triggered by either regulators, or members of a protected class. Either tends to confuse insolvency receiverships with regulatory receiverships, perhaps the natural result of our overuse of the term "receivership." The initiation question, however, is vastly different when placing an apartment building in a receivership for failing to follow sanitation laws from what it is when placing the same in a receivership for failing to pay creditors.

In the first case, regulators and tenants have an obvious interest in obtaining court oversight over the debtor's management. In the second, it is not clear that tenants – unless they have some special status, perhaps under a rent control regime or something of that sort – should have any sort of rights that creditors do not enjoy generally. This is particularly true if the landlord's default has not interfered with the tenant's ability to inhabit the apartment.

In the financial institution context, we often see insolvency proceedings that are initiated by regulators. This contrasts with general

---

[17] I appreciate that there may not be much practical difference between a formal insolvency requirement that is generously interpreted, and the American system of no insolvency requirement, with abusive filings instead policed by a rule of "good faith."

insolvency law, where either the debtor or its creditors controls the commencement of proceedings. Indeed, with regard to many types of financial institutions, regulators are the only parties that can commence proceedings.

Nonetheless, exclusive reliance on government initiation of bank insolvency proceedings has very real drawbacks. The most important drawback is regulators' natural tendency toward delay. Because regulators can suffer political embarrassment when institutions fail on their watch, they have strong incentives to postpone closing an ailing institution as long as possible.

On the other hand, the same basic incentives operate on many corporate boards. Lehman's haphazard descent into chapter 11 was largely the result of a board that refused to engage in any sort of bankruptcy planning, apparently fearing that doing so would remove pressure for a governmental bailout.

In sum, the question of initiation within the law of failure is one that cries out for careful reconsideration. In many cases, entire insolvency systems might be replaced with a simple provision recognizing a regulator's ability to commence insolvency proceedings in particular circumstances.

For example, the grain silo receivership laws might be better replaced with a provision giving agricultural regulators the ability to commence a federal bankruptcy proceeding, despite opposition from the silo's managers. This would avoid the current system of state receivership that then prompts a federal bankruptcy petition, and instead allow everyone to simply "cut to the chase."

A good rule of thumb might be that all insolvency systems should allow both the debtor and its creditors to initiate proceedings. Then, in special circumstances, regulators can also have powers to begin a case. For example, in the bank receivership process, current law only allows bank regulators or the FDIC to commence a receivership. Adding the ability of the bank itself or creditors to commence actions increases the chances of initiation at an appropriate time. Not only might the debtor or creditors commence such a case themselves, but their ability to do so might also further discourage regulatory delay.

To be sure, creditors in particular might commence cases for reasons that the regulators find problematic. And an ill-conceived insolvency filing against a financial institution might have implications for the broader financial system, as well as the debtor. There is substantial risk that a creditor-initiated proceeding would effectively kill the financial institution because of the complete loss of confidence in the institution. Indeed, while debtor and regulator initiation makes some sense with regard to banks, this might be a case where creditors should not have initiation rights, or at most very limited rights.

The Bankruptcy Code already partially addresses this concern by providing for sanctions in cases where involuntary bankruptcy petitions are commenced in bad faith. Even stronger disincentives may be warranted in the case of banks and other systemically important institutions, along with an ability to deal with such situations quickly should they arise nonetheless. The FDIC, in particular, would maintain even greater powers to police such activities since it acts as both "judge" and trustee in most bank receivership proceedings in this country.

Closely related to the commencement question is the issue of how proceedings should rank. Some of this is already addressed by the Supremacy Clause: federal law naturally overtakes state law. But what about federal receiverships as compared with federal bankruptcy cases? While the Second Circuit Court of Appeals has attempted to bring some order to this area, its efforts have largely failed, and Congressional action might provide a more lasting solution.

Other obvious points of focus for reform efforts are the related questions of creditor engagement and transparency. The problems here can be seen by considering a recent opinion from a bankruptcy court in New York.[18]

The debtor, incorporated in New York but operating out of an address in New Jersey, commenced an assignment for the benefit of creditors in the Union County Surrogate's Court in New Jersey. Creditors received notice of the assignment, but it appears they largely failed to participate.

The assignee proceeded to sell most of the debtor's assets to a newly formed corporation, backed by the old shareholders. The assignee negotiated only with this buyer, and did little to seek out other buyers. In addition, before the sale was approved by the New Jersey court, the

---

[18] In re Scandia Seafood (N.Y.), Inc., 2017 BL 160131 (Bankr. S.D.N.Y. May 12, 2017).

assignee essentially allowed the proposed buyers to take charge of the debtor's assets. This included all the debtor's inventory, while all debts were predictably left with the assignee. Creditors received notice of the sale, but again failed to appear.

Then the assignee sued under state law to recover preferential payments to creditors.[19] The creditors began to pay attention.

Among other things, they filed an involuntary bankruptcy petition against the debtor in New York. Since the preferences in question had happened more than ninety days before the bankruptcy filing, one beneficial effect of putting the debtor into bankruptcy, from the creditors' perspective, was that it would end the preference litigation. While New Jersey law allows an assignee to attack preferences that occurred within 120 days of an assignment, bankruptcy law only "claws back" preferential payments to creditors that happened within ninety days of bankruptcy.[20]

The assignee asked the bankruptcy court to dismiss the case, noting that the filing would have an obviously injurious effect on the estate. The assignee also suggested that the New Jersey case was so far along as to be essentially irreversible. Finally, the assignee suggested bad faith by the creditors, in that they only filed the bankruptcy case upon facing preference liability.

The court conceded that allowing the bankruptcy case to proceed would have some detrimental effects on the estate. Nonetheless, the court decided to let it progress:

> The continuation of the Chapter 7 case may have the effect of ending the chance to pursue preference actions under the New Jersey statute. But in my judgment, it is far more important, and potentially far more remunerative, to the estate and its creditors, for an independent fiduciary to review the pre-assignment dealings between the Assignee and the owners, to review the management agreement that was executed, and to review the sale that was made, so that those matters, if appropriate, may be subjected to challenge.[21]

The court likewise noted that "evidence that I have received suggests that there was an appalling lack of diligence in ensuring that the prior owners paid a fair price for keeping the business and its assets."

[19] N.J. Stat. Ann. § 2A:19-3.
[20] 11 U.S.C. § 547.
[21] In re Scandia Seafood (N.Y.), Inc., 2017 BL 160131, 10 (Bankr. S.D.N.Y. May 12, 2017).

So, we have a case where it is alleged that the creditors were largely apathetic, and the assignee was "in bed" with the debtor's shareholders. And if the assignee had been a bit more strategic, and not woken the creditors from their slumber, it seems plausible that the New Jersey process would have proceeded on its merry way, without interruption.

The case does not reflect well on the New Jersey assignment process, where the court apparently failed to ask anything about the assignee's marketing efforts, but I have no reason to believe that it is a widely atypical representation of what often happens in state insolvency proceedings nationwide. One possible exception might be California, where a handful of firms that act as assignees also play a prominent role in the broader insolvency practice, including bankruptcy. But even in California we might suspect that assignments are often conducted with varying degrees of competency.

Docket List		Docket:	R2849
Case Type: Superior Deed of Assignment		**IMO: Scandia Seafood (NY) Inc.**	

P	12/6/2016	Deed of Assignment for the Benefit of Creditors : Deed of Assignment for the Benefit of Creditors
	12/6/2016	Notice of Assignment
	12/6/2016	Petition for Appt of Appraiser/Acct/Auctioneer/General & Special Counsel
	12/6/2016	Application for Waiver of Assignee's Bond
	12/8/2016	Order for Appt of Appraiser/Acct/Auctioneer/General & Special Counsel
	12/8/2016	Order for Waiver of Bond
	12/29/2016	Notice of Motion : To Sell Assets and Approve Agreement
	12/29/2016	Certification in Support
	12/29/2016	Application in Support of Notice of Motion on Short Notice
	1/13/2017	Order to Sell Assets/Approve Mgmt Agreement
	3/13/2017	Proof of Publication

One key drawback of many of the state insolvency regimes is the placement of cases before generalist judges, who might well struggle to oversee sporadic insolvency cases in addition to typically heavy civil dockets. There is also the basic problem that it is essentially impossible for an outsider to learn much about this case, beyond what is reported on the federal bankruptcy court's docket.[22] As I write this, New Jersey's

---

[22] Searching on New Jersey's rather antiquated web page, using the case number on the documents filed in federal court, is an exercise in futility.

judiciary's web page flagrantly displays its 2012 copyright, although on using it, one wonders if it is not more than six years out of date.[23]

My attempts (through Seton Hall's librarians) to find documents about the aforementioned assignment were met with the following response from the Union County Surrogate's Court:

> Attached is our docket sheet for the Scandia Seafood Deed of Assignment. Anyone can come to our office to look at the file. We can send you copies of what you want for $3 a page.

Late in the second decade of the twenty-first century, the state judiciary is only hesitantly embracing the internet. The docket, in all its glory and limited detail, appears in full above.

What then might a reformed law of failure look like? It would begin with the foundation discussed earlier: Congressional approval of state insolvency laws.

That approval would ideally work hand in hand with state law. Indeed, this would seem to be an area calling out for a uniform law.

A uniform law of state business insolvency could standardize not only assignment and receivership practice across jurisdictions, but also consolidate the host of specialized state law we have seen in the earlier pages of this book. Such a uniform law might offer state legislatures a menu of insolvency choices, which could be enacted as desired. Chapters on receiverships and assignments would be standard, but for those states that want to experiment with a more formal state court insolvency procedure, such could be available as well.

Use of a uniform law would mean that case law could be developed at the state level in sufficient mass to support the statute. Moreover, if the uniform law was developed in conjunction with the federal statute authorizing such laws, debtor-firms would have more confidence that invoking the procedure would not result in expensive and complex pre-emption litigation.

Such a uniform law could not address all the transparency concerns with state insolvency laws – funding for state judicial web pages is still apt to be subject to larger forces – but it could at least provide some

---

[23] https://portal.njcourts.gov/webe6/ACMSPA/.

a more established structure for creditor participation and debtor disclosure in state proceedings. And a uniform law could provide states with a ready solution to an issue that many state legislators have limited interest in devoting substantial time to addressing.

At the same time, the Bankruptcy Code could be revised both for a modern era and to accommodate the broader American insolvency system. In 2014, the American Bankruptcy Institute came forth with a full-fledged plan to reform chapter 11, but what I have in mind is somewhat more modest.[24]

In addition to providing a framework for federal-state coexistence, the Bankruptcy Code should be revised to address the unanswered questions in the current Code. Are debtors allowed to pay pre-bankruptcy creditors to help keep the business running?[25] Is the "absolute priority rule" flexible or indeed "absolute"? Somewhat connected, can a small holdout group use the rules to torpedo a reorganization, or is there some "flex" in the Code, that can be overseen by bankruptcy judges?

Other items to address while engaged in this housekeeping exercise might include formalizing the norm that secured creditors pay for the cost of the bankruptcy case, in all respects, when using chapter 11 as a glorified foreclosure system. And there are good arguments for reversing the Supreme Court's decision in *Travelers Casualty & Surety Co. of America* v. *Pacific Gas & Elec. Co.*,[26] which allows some creditors to "gross up" their claims with additional charges, thereby undermining the basic collectivity that stands behind the Code.

And maybe it is time to give tort and other involuntary creditors a priority. Nearly all bankruptcy academics support such a move, yet Congress has never really embraced it.

With regard to small businesses, I would join the American Bankruptcy Institution in scrapping most of the 1994 and 2005 small business reforms – which mostly seem to be designed to discourage use of the Code by small businesses.

---

[24] https://goo.gl/dcS1BV.

[25] The U.S. Supreme Court recently suggested the answer is "yes." *Czyzewski* v. *Jevic Holding Corp.*, 137 S. Ct. 973, 985 (2017).

[26] 549 U.S. 443 (2007).

Instead, as I noted earlier, a short "chapter 10" might be in order, which allows debtors to effectuate a quick creditor haircut. An off-the-rack plan, which could be filed with the bankruptcy petition rejecting the contracts set forth on a schedule and reducing all unsecured claims by __ percent, would do the trick. Another standard plan might cancel all shares and distribute the same to the creditors.

If accepted by the requisite chapter 11 standard – majority in number and two-thirds in dollar amount – but without any classification, the plan would bind all.[27] No committees, and a pre-bankruptcy disclosure form would support creditor voting soon after commencement of the case.

Thus, a revised federal system would work hand in hand with a revamped state insolvency law system, that itself would be standardized around a uniform statute.

Any reform effort should also consider the Policy Exception, both in terms of its scope and the structure used for resolving the financial distress of debtor-firms that legitimately fall within the Exception.

On the question of scope, the most fundamental inquiry is whether a particular debtor would indeed be affirmatively harmed by application of the First Rule and normal insolvency procedures. The second, but closely related question, turns on a consideration of the costs of excepting the debtor from traditional debtor-creditor law.

Inclusion of depository banks and insurance companies in the Policy Exception is an easy call. The products they provide have clear utility, and application of the normal bankruptcy system would be problematic, even fatal. Imagine a chapter 11 case for a life insurance company. Existing policyholders would face the strong temptation of withdrawing cash balances (either directly or in the form of loans), while new policyholders would hesitate to sign up. Liquidity would quickly evaporate, and soon the company's ability to pay claims would come into question.

---

[27] The classification point is apt to be more complex than it appears at first blush. I have heard plenty of senior creditors complain that European restructuring proceedings often lump subordinated and senior debt holders together, allowing the sub debt to impose a plan on the senior creditors in a way that would not be possible with separate classification. The problem could just as easily run in the other direction too.

Stock and commodity brokers present a harder call, particularly with regard to their customer-facing operations. While banks and insurance companies create new products out of their customer's deposits, brokers are essentially engaged in safekeeping. While there is a clear case for pre-insolvency regulation to ensure good business practices, invoking the Policy Exception seems less warranted here, as long as the law makes clear that customer property is not the debtor's property. That the customer's property rights are in fact vague under UCC Article 8 and related laws does not itself justify invoking the Policy Exception.[28]

And then there is the case of derivatives and repurchase agreements (or "repos," in the argot), which before the financial crisis were taken outside the normal insolvency process without the consequent regulation that typically comes when the Policy Exception is invoked. Dodd-Frank at least partially tries to rectify that last point but, even if we accept that derivatives and repos might be greatly harmed by traditional bankruptcy procedures, we might wonder if they represent the kind of clearly beneficial financial product that would justify the use of the Exception.

Less controversially, one might wonder if the majestic scope of the present safe harbors provides a kind of Policy Exception that is unwarranted by the benefits that repos and derivatives do provide. Limits on upending settled trades are one thing, but a broad exemption from the automatic stay and the debtor's normal powers to assume and reject contracts might well be another.

Once we figure out what financial products or other businesses warrant inclusion within the Policy Exception, we should consider the variety of models used to address insolvency in this area. In particular, the move from the First Rule to the Policy Exception entails a rejection

---

[28] Under the confused security ownership system in the United States, most customers hold beneficial interests in securities. Beneficial interests in securities are interests in rights that a broker holds in bulk form, which in turn is an interest in a security registered in the name of a depository. Who has actual property rights, in the traditional sense, is more than a bit unclear. See James Steven Rogers, Policy Perspectives on Revised U.C.C. Article 8, 43 *UCLA L. Rev.* 1431, 1546 (1996). ("The term 'security entitlement' can then be used as a convenient shorthand for 'the package of rights that a person who holds a securities position through an intermediary has against that intermediary and the property held by that intermediary.'")

of creditor equality, in furtherance of prioritizing one class of special importance. Indeed, under the Policy Exception, it is all about the priorities – both ordinal and temporal – rather than equality.

While courts are natural features of an insolvency system under the First Rule, where a neutral party is often required to settle disputes about rank and entitlement, a Policy Exception case represents a pure exercise of legislative authority to provide priority to a protected group. It is not clear that it makes sense to put such cases before a judge, yet that is routinely the case in insurance receiverships, and is the preferred model for large global financial institutions under Dodd-Frank. Doing so may simply obscure what is actually going on in a Policy Exception case.

The American law of failure is the natural complement to our law of business creation. It has been relatively easy to form a business for nearly a century and a half, and the ability to straighten things out when that business goes awry is an equally important part of the entrepreneurial process.

That is, there is a great deal of value in maintaining the American law of failure's flexibility and even "optionality." At the same time, and without engaging in too much of the law professor's fantasy of some sort of perfect legal system, it does seem that the law of failure is in need of some attention.

Some of this is a legacy of Congress' historical reluctance to use its powers under the Bankruptcy Clause. Even in the first half of the twentieth century, state lawmakers could not be entirely sure that the federal law was here to stay. Only with the benefit of hindsight can we say that it was probably a fool's errand to update state "bankruptcy" procedures that are likely pre-empted by the Bankruptcy Code, and its predecessor the Bankruptcy Act.

But note the slight hesitancy even in that statement. We cannot be sure which state insolvency laws have been pre-empted, because the Supreme Court's case law in this area is notable mostly for its timidity. Such is the price of placing constitutional law experts in charge of insolvency law.

Part of my goal in writing this book is to get insolvency lawyers – both practitioners and academics – to think about business insolvency law as involving more than the Bankruptcy Code. What do we want the entire system to look like?

At present, discussions on this question focus almost exclusively on the Code. In the academic setting, we teach the Code because that's what most students will use, but as a question of policy, where do the state laws fit in? Financial institution insolvency is not the province of the bankruptcy professor, but rather the banking law professor. As a result, it becomes one of many regulatory questions in a course that is overstuffed following the financial crisis.

But just as it makes sense to consider business or financial law in general as a whole, insolvency law – the back end of the entrepreneurial equation – should be considered as a whole too. This book has attempted to start that conversation.

INDEX

185